T0330260

From Economic to Legal Competition

NEW HORIZONS IN LAW AND ECONOMICS

Series editors: Gerrit De Geest, *University of Ghent and University of Antwerp, Belgium and University of Utrecht, The Netherlands*; Roger Van den Bergh, *University of Rotterdam and University of Utrecht, The Netherlands*; and Paul Fenn, *University of Nottingham, UK*.

The application of economic ideas and theories to the law and the explanation of markets and public economics from a legal point of view is recognized as one of the most exciting developments in both economics and the law. This important series is designed to make a significant contribution to the development of law and economics.

The main emphasis is on the development and application of new ideas. The series provides a forum for original research in areas such as criminal law, civil law, labour law, corporate law, family law, regulation and privatization, tax, risk and insurance and competition law. International in its approach it includes some of the best theoretical ad empirical work from both well-established researchers and the new generation of scholars.

Titles in the series include:

Inflation and the Enforcement of Contracts
Shirley Renner

Law and Economics and the Labour Market
Edited by Gerrit De Geest, Jacques Siegers and Roger Van den Bergh

Economic Efficiency in Law and Economics
Richard O. Zerbe Jr.

The Economics of Harmonizing European Law
Edited by Alain Marciano and Jean-Michel Josselin

Post-Chicago Developments in Antitrust Law
Edited by Antonio Cucinotta, Robert Pardolesi and Roger Van den Bergh

From Economic to Legal Competition
New Perspectives on Law and Institutions in Europe
Edited by Alain Marciano and Jean-Michel Josselin

From Economic to Legal Competition

New Perspectives on Law and Institutions in Europe

Alain Marciano

Professor, University of Reims-Champagne Ardenne, OMI-EDJE, Institute of Public Economics and GREQAM-CNRS, France

and

Jean-Michel Josselin

Professor, University of Rennes 1 and CREREG-CNRS, France

NEW HORIZONS IN LAW AND ECONOMICS

Edward Elgar
Cheltenham, UK • Northampton, MA, USA

Published by
Edward Elgar Publishing Limited
Glensanda House
Montpellier Parade
Cheltenham
Glos GL50 1UA
UK

Edward Elgar Publishing, Inc.
136 West Street
Suite 202
Northampton
Massachusetts 01060
USA

A catalogue record for this book
is available from the British Library

Library of Congress Cataloguing in Publication Data

Marciano, Alain.
From economic to legal competition: new perspectives on law and institutions in Europe
/ Alain Marciano and Jean-Michel Josselin.
    p. cm.—(New horizons in law and economics)
Includes index.
    1. Legislation—Economic aspects. 2. Competition. 3. Legislation—Economic aspects—European Union countries. I. Josselin, Jean Michel. II. Title. III. Series.

K3316.M37 2003
343'.0721—dc22

2003046388

ISBN 1 84376 006 1

Typeset by Cambrian Typesetters, Frimley, Surrey
Printed and bound in Great Britain by MPG Books Ltd, Bodmin, Cornwall

Contents

Figures

Tables

Contributors

Jürgen G. Backhaus, University of Erfurt, Germany.

Didier Danet, National School of Public Health.

Sophie Delabruyère, University of Reims-Champagne Ardenne, OMI-EDJ, France, and Department of Economics, University of Turin, Italy.

Kristel de Smedt, Limburg University Centre and Metro Institute, University of Maastricht, Netherlands.

Michael Faure, Metro Institute, University of Maastricht, Netherlands.

Lars P. Feld, University of Marburg, SIAW and CESifo, Germany.

Reginald Hansen, independent researcher.

Jean-Michel Josselin, University of Rennes 1, CREREG-CNRS, France.

Alain Marciano, University of Reims-Champagne Ardenne, OMI-EDJE, Institute of Public Economics and GREQAM-CNRS.

Manuela Mühl, Limburg University Centre, Netherlands.

Yvon Rocaboy, University of Rennes 1, CREREG-CNRS, France.

Pierre Salmon, University of Burgundy, LATEC.

Dieter Schmidtchen, Center for the Study of Law and Economics, University of Saarlandes, CSLE, Germany.

Bernard Steunenberg, Department of Public Administration, Leiden University, Netherlands.

Lode Vereeck, Limburg University Centre and University of Maastricht, Netherlands.

Preface

This book evolved out of a conference organized in May 2001 in Marseilles, France, sponsored by the Institut d'Economie Publique under the auspices of the European Association of Law and Economics. Scholars invited to give papers were given carte blanche, but were asked to revise their contributions after the conference discussions. We present here a selection of them. They reflect the current research on the subject, unified by the same concern, namely the understanding of competition in the market for law, in the perspective of the European legal integration. They also show a diversity of opinions that we did not try to iron out.

We heartily thank Danièle Durieu and all the participants in the conference. The publishing process has been both friendly and efficient. We are very grateful for that.

1. Introduction: Co-ordinating demand and supply of law: Market forces or state control?

Jean-Michel Josselin and Alain Marciano

INTRODUCTION

The idea that competition plays an important role in the provision of law has gained an indisputable legitimacy among economists. It does not only convey the acknowledgement of the influence of rules and institutions on economic competition, but also that governments, when institutional competition is at stake, or legal producers, in the case of legal competition, are rivals and compete just like producers of goods and services compete in usual markets. In other words, if we admit that rules are goods that must be produced (and not simply discovered by judges), then their provision must be organized according to market mechanisms. Thus, legal competition, as a decentralized market process of provision of law in which legal clubs compete, can be contrasted with a monopolist and centralized lawmaking process, mainly backed up by the coercive power of the State. Even if the contrast between these two models is not so neat in reality, where practices mix with reasoned arguments, these approaches nonetheless constitute two theoretical references that allow us to understand and to model many important situations in which new institutions have to be elaborated. Besides the building of new legal systems in the former communist countries or the provision of law in cyberspace, the harmonization of law related to the European integration process is certainly one of the major issues to be discussed. This is the focus of the chapters presented in this volume.

The example of the European Union is all the more interesting in that it clearly illustrates the relationship between legal competition and the interrogations about future federalism: when several local (or national) jurisdictions are granted with the right to produce legal rules, it is indeed crucial to know if these clubs must be located on the same level – competition remains horizontal – or may be located on different levels – competition is both horizontal and vertical. Therefore, if competition in the legal market works without notable failures, then there is no necessity to assign legal responsibilities to the central governmental level and competition may remain horizontal. In this perspective, a confederation is the most appropriate constitutional framework. By contrast, when there exist limitations on market mechanisms or market failures, it becomes necessary to assign legal responsibilities to the central level and competition involves different institutional levels: a federation is the regime corresponding to such a situation. In other words, a confederation corresponds to a competitive system – perfect or not –, while federalism implies, besides competition, State intervention, some degree of centralization and procedures of harmonization.

With regard to the present situation in Europe, it may remain possible to choose between these two contrasted models: even if centralization has made its way through the process of integration, it still seems possible and it could be preferable to envisage a constitutional structure based on a decentralized and competitive provision of legal rules. Such is the argument put forward by the advocates of legal competition, by insisting upon the benefits that European citizens could draw from this competition. They stress that, by analogy to what happens in ordinary markets, competitive pressures on the market for rules should stimulate innovation and sophistication in legal rules and also motivate lawmakers 'to compare their own legal products with those available in competing jurisdictions' (Ogus, 1999, p. 409), 'to adapt their products' (ibid.) and to imitate the innovations made by the leading jurisdictions. As a consequence, legal competition ensures the elimination of inefficient rules, prevents, if not precludes, predatory behaviours and unjustified wealth transfers by the central level. It also guarantees the respect of individual preferences – since the problems are dealt with at the smallest (and supposedly most appropriate) institutional level. Therefore, undoubtedly, legal competition should define the organization of the future legal organization. In other words, decentralization should be the 'rule' (Van den Bergh, 2000) or 'the starting point' (Faure, 2000) and centralization the exception.

In counterpoint, usual criticisms against legal competition deal with its effects. The argument that benefits may not systematically outweigh costs is of course far from trivial, but it should come at a second stage. The first one should examine the reality of competitive pressures in the field of law. To put it differently, before enquiring into the efficiency of legal competition, one must make sure that such competition does or can exist. In this perspective, the major problems come from the possibility of arbitrage between the different legal regimes. Indeed, citizens must have the opportunity to compare and then to choose the legal system that is most appropriate to their needs and preferences. Legal arbitrage is then related to the existence of enough legal regimes to guarantee the effectiveness of competition and to make sure that individuals can find rules corresponding to their preferences. The more numerous legal clubs are, the easier arbitrage is and the more competitive is the market.

However, an elastic supply in legal clubs is not an easy condition to verify. Thus, an analysis of the merits and virtues of legal competition has primarily to concentrate on the conditions which permit legal arbitrage. It is only within this set of conditions that the positive or negative consequences of competition can be analysed. It may well be that, most of the time, legal arbitrage must then give way to the intervention of the state.

The chapters that constitute this volume are presented in the perspective of the debate over the merits of, and conditions for, a competitive provision of law, with a special focus on the European Union. These chapters contribute to an economic theory of legal competition in that they deal with three major aspects of the competitive provision of legal rules. The first section concerns the conditions under which citizens and firms arbitrate between the different legal orders. This section presents the problem of legal competition from the demand side of the market and in particular the chapters that analyse the conditions required for the respect of the sovereignty of the citizens. The second aspect concerns the answers and reactions by the producers of legal rules. Here, the problem is analysed from the supply side of the legal market: the second section presents the chapters relating to the consequences of the competitive pressures on the behaviour of the lawmakers. As to the third aspect, justifications must be given to the intervention of the state. The last section finally presents the chapters discussing the conditions under which it may efficiently control the process of law provision.

LEGAL ARBITRAGE AND THE CONDITIONS FOR AN EFFECTIVE COMPETITION IN THE PROVISION OF LAW

In order to make a difference between the situations in which arbitrage is possible or not, it is useful to refer to a criterion put forward by Ogus, who proposes 'to distinguish situations in which legal rules can be envisaged as a homogeneous product [. . .] from those in which it has heterogeneous qualities' (1999, p. 406). Now, if arbitrage, and thus competition, are difficult if not impossible in the case of heterogeneity between the different legal clubs, it does not imply that legal arbitrage is without any problem when legal products are homogeneous. On the contrary, information costs and in addition transaction costs raise difficulties.

Heterogeneous Legal Clubs and Asymmetries of Information: the Difficulty of Legal Arbitrage

The diversity of specialized legal clubs could be presented as a necessary condition for a genuine competition between legal clubs. By contrast, when a monopoly is granted with the responsibility to create legal rules, the absence of different sources for the law by definition prevents any arbitrage.[1] However, the existence of several, diverse and specialized legal clubs may prevent or discourage legal arbitrage. It happens, in particular, when diversity turns into heterogeneity. Arbitrage is then useless and competition does not make sense.

There are two possible situations in which legal rules have, or are perceived as having, heterogeneous qualities. First, when the differences between the competing legal cultures are too large to be bridgeable and, second, when there exists imperfect and asymmetric information. In these two cases, comparison is not a matter of the quantity of information that has to be gathered. It is rather a problem relating to the quality of information: individuals from parallel legal regimes cannot compare different rules because they are unable to assess the characteristics and performance of the norms used in the different systems. Individuals cannot understand the meaning of these rules, in particular their convention dimensions. Furthermore, they are unable to infer this meaning from the observation of the behaviour of others (Josselin and Marciano, 1995). In other words, they face the problem raised among others by Legrand (1997) when he argues that 'legal transplants' are impossible: a rule generated in one context cannot be generalized in order to be used in a different context. It is as if there was no competition between the different clubs.

Obviously, there are situations in which transplants are useless. For instance, as Benson rightly notes, there are certainly no reasons to transplant the rules used between diamond merchants into the group of oil traders (Benson, 2000). The transaction costs as well as the costs of adaptation that would result would obviously exceed all the benefits that such a transplant could create. Other instances can be quoted: ethnic or religious differences may act as barriers to a possible comparison of the rules used in different jurisdictions. On the other hand, in the perspective of the creation of a harmonized legal system, as in Europe, it may be necessary to avoid diversity degenerating into heterogeneity. A social contract would then be necessary in order to ensure the publicity of the law and the generalization of its meaning among its potential users.

Legal Arbitrage, Information Costs and Competition

Even if one assumes that individuals live in a world of homogeneous legal rules and that asymmetries of information do not prevent individuals from comparing them, legal arbitrage may nonetheless be difficult because of the existence of information costs. Different methods for lowering information

---

[1] Although competition may still exist inside a given system when the allocation of competences among the jurisdictions is not tightly established.

costs associated with alternative legal rules can then be envisaged. Standardization is one of the most frequently discussed solutions (see for instance Van den Bergh, 2000). The European law provides many illustrations of the willingness to create a 'level playing field'. Environmental law, as we will see latter, is one of these domains. Corporate law may also be cited as an other area in which standardization has an important role to play. Company laws in Europe are constructed to provide harmonization. The Treaty of Rome, with articles 54 and 58, acknowledges that federating nations requires the creation, not to say the construction, of a common market. The extent to which it can and should apply to law remains largely undetermined. The present book may contribute to a better understanding of this problem.

These instances of what has been called 'negative integration' illustrate the purpose that has been pursued by the European legislators, namely to remove *all* internal barriers to trade, thereby allowing the different legal producers to effectively and efficiently compete. However, standardization does not necessarily imply total and centralized harmonization of rules and may not be aimed at the suppression of legal competition. As, Van den Bergh puts it, 'competition and harmonization may be complements, rather than substitutes' (2000). Harmonization may provide a sound basis for further competition, which is all the more important since transaction costs often contribute to weaken the efficiency of market forces.

Legal Arbitrage, Transaction Costs and Competition

However important information costs can be, they are neither the sole nor the most decisive costs that affect legal arbitrage. Of equal importance is the second type of costs, namely the transaction costs related to the effective possibility given to the individuals to choose their preferred legal rules. Indeed, citizens dissatisfied with the law produced by 'their' local government must have the possibility to move into a different jurisdiction. Exit and inter-jurisdictional migration are thus important modes of legal arbitrage and therefore important causes for competitive pressures. It has frequently been argued that a major difference between institutional competition and ordinary market competition 'lies in the *territorial nature* of governments' (see Vanberg and Kerber, 1994). In this perspective, citizens have to change their residency in order to be relieved of the authority of a particular government, and the sunk costs resulting from exit may not be compensated by the benefits expected from a change of legal regime. It is most likely that 'people may stay even if the (legal) regime does not suit their need optimally [. . .] Thus, the legal regime may not be decisive [because] . . . job location and residence are that important in reality, there is often little left for people to choose' (Faure, 2000; see also Rose-Ackerman, 1992). Therefore, when considering legal competition, the individual elasticity of location relative to legal rules may be much closer to zero than for any other good. It happens that individuals are not necessarily interested – aside from the fact that individuals may not have the possibility to be mobile, as is stressed by many opponents to inter-jurisdictional competition – in arbitraging between different legal systems. Hence the reduction of competitive pressures or even the absence of competition, even if law is produced by decentralized legal clubs.

Now, one should not overemphasize the transaction costs resulting from the necessity to move from one jurisdiction to another and, thus, restrict attention to physical mobility as a source of competitive pressures on lawmakers. There indeed exist institutional procedures that can make competition effective even if physical mobility is impossible.

Legal arbitrage without physical mobility: functional legal arbitrage
First, some authors have proposed to envisage governments without territorial monopolies (Frey, 2001). The perspective of FOCJ or functional governance can be envisaged as a means to reduce the importance of the constraint of physical mobility and to restore institutional arbitrage (Frey and Eichenberger, 1995, 1996, 1997). Now, functional arbitrage is particularly well suited to legal competition which indeed does not necessarily imply physical mobility. Firms or citizens may change their residency or location but most of the time, legal competition is a-territorial and individuals or firms are authorized 'to select the jurisdiction whose principles are to apply to their transaction or business' (Ogus, 1999, p. 408). Of course, functional arbitrage is not likely to solve all the problems resulting from the costs of mobility and remains limited to the problems resulting from transaction costs. In the case of heterogeneous rules and asymmetric information, or when there exist high information costs, functional arbitrage faces the same difficulties as spatial arbitrage does. It nonetheless remains that functional legal arbitrage increases the domain of competition, by allowing individuals to refer to many different and parallel systems of law.

However, functional legal arbitrage may be at the origin of another type of difficulty. Indeed, when physical mobility is at stake, an individual who decides to move to another jurisdiction bears himself the costs of change. By contrast, functional arbitrage imposes costs even on immobile residents for it creates uncertainty and variability with regard to the legal framework that organizes individual behaviour and relationships with others. The role of uncertainty in the individual choice of a legal system and its influence on competition is at the core of Sophie Delabruyère's chapter. She analyses how and how far uncertainty reduces the scope of competition. More precisely, the chapter discusses two forms of uncertainty. First, uncertainty may stem from the fact that an individual ignores the rule that is likely to be used in a possible litigation. Then, should a dispute arise and anticipating a possible disagreement on the legal system with which they would settle the dispute, individuals are likely to prefer standardized norms. Second, uncertainty may be caused by the fact that, before being confronted with a legal problem, individuals ignore the existence and the nature of the problem and thus the legal solutions as well as their preferences with regard to these solutions. In this perspective, an individual may not be able to choose *ex ante* a legal system, impossible that it is to know what are the gains to be maximized. This calculus reduces the competitive pressures that exist on the legal producers. The latter may then be induced to propose general rules to nonetheless attract possible litigants. In both cases, Delabruyère argues that a constitutional framework would reduce these two sources of uncertainty, thereby permitting competition to develop. In other words, competition has to be 'organized'.

Collective legal arbitrage: The role of secession
When high transaction costs reduce individual mobility, limit the freedom to choose a legal system and therefore prevent legal arbitrage, one can envisage a collective solution under the form of a secession. Thus, as a source of competitive pressures, the right to secede is an important means to control governments. The argument has been developed particularly with regard to the making of the European Institutions. Bernholz (1991) argues that the right to secede should not be given to member-states but to any subgroup in the European Union that exceeds a certain number of members. Typically, the idea that regions could secede from their state or even the European Union fits into this framework. In this perspective, Drèze (1993) proposes a system allowing 'quasi-secession' (to borrow a word from Brosio and Revelli, 2000), in which some local jurisdictions could claim a direct constitutional link with the central government and the suppression of any link with a national government. In the case of Europe, Drèze then proposes to define a 'status of regions of Europe': regions could move from a national state to the European one: 'A geographical area, currently part of a member state of the European Community [. . .] could henceforth belong to the community directly without being any longer part of a member state' (1993, p. 265). In other words, some kind of secession could be authorized to take into account specific regional characteristics.

Part of the problem indeed consists in asking which are these areas that could be interested in such a status. Drèze envisages the case of Corsica or Vlanderen as regions that could claim it. A justification can be proposed on the argument that peripheral regions are characterized by preferences and costs of control that do not correspond to those of 'central' regions (Josselin and Marciano, 1998, 1999). That of course does not comprehend all the aspects of the problem. Will those regions really ask for such a status? Aren't there other types of regions that would consider quasi-secession? Furthermore, Brosio and Revelli envisage the possibility of 'opting out' for 'those regions where per capita income is above the national average of the member states in which they are located'. They thus 'consider a region belonging to a member state of a supranational political entity such as the European Union, [whose inhabitants] for ethnic, linguistic or geographic reasons, . . . cannot move from the region where they reside to any other region of the state [. . .] The residents in the region can decide by majority voting whether to opt out of the member state [. . .] or to be part of the member state and join its income redistribution system' (Brosio and Revelli, forthcoming 2003).

Interestingly, there is some ambiguity as to the ability of secession to restore legal arbitrage through 'vertical mobility'. It may increase competition between more independent regions (enhancing Tiebout properties of competitive governments). At the same time, the national levels would lose part of their prerogatives, which would be both an incentive and a distortion of the existing system of checks and balances.

Thus, legal arbitrage seems to function through physical or, more probably, non-physical forms of mobility. Nevertheless, it is crucial to design a kind of constitutional framework whose goal is to ensure or restore competition by allowing individuals to compare the different rules (by lowering the costs of information) as well as by permitting them to effectively choose between these rules. We must then assess the consequences of these individual or regional pressures. The next section thus analyses the reactions of the lawmakers to the behaviour of the consumers.

BEHAVIOUR OF THE LAWMAKERS AND THE CONSEQUENCES OF LEGAL COMPETITION

As was said above, competitive pressures are a major source of efficient legal change. Not only are lawmakers motivated to innovate but also these innovations are assumed to lead to 'new *superior* outcomes' (Vanberg and Kerber, 1994, p. 208; emphasis added). A positive interpretation of competition thus insists on the fact that 'Good rules may spread as one group emulates those rules that prove effective in another group' (Benson, 2000, p. 8). The analysis clearly rests on an evolutionist argument according to which efficient rules are selected. Now, the problem does not only lie in the difficulty to evaluate what a 'new *superior* outcome' means but also in the fact that doubts have frequently and repeatedly been cast upon the efficiency of evolutionary processes.

Indeed, many argue that competition could certainly degenerate into a destructive process, characterized by a prisoner's dilemma, whereby countries or local governments fail to enact or enforce efficient legislation. Lenient rules not only attract newcomers but also transfer the costs (at least a part of them) to the neighbouring jurisdictions. These strategic behaviours can myopically be seen as beneficial by some jurisdictions, but others will soon be lured into grabbing short term benefits. It is the famous race-to-the-bottom argument. This has been analysed with regard to some issues such as the gambling legislation in the USA, where it seems that competition has resulted in the promotion of more permissive legislation. The race-to-the-bottom argument has also been analysed in other domains, such as product liability (Faure, 2000) or environmental issues. In the present volume, Faure and De Smedt take the opportunity of discussing the *White paper on environmental liability* to restate the question. In analysing the fear that 'local governments . . . compete with lenient environmental legislation to attract industry' (Faure and De Smedt, this volume), they show that there are no reasons to be too pessimistic. Their chapter confirms the absence of 'evidence that, under competition, the feared race to the bottom is more than theoretical' (Scott, 2000, p. 204). Moreover, Faure and De Smedt note that the problem has rarely been raised by the European Institutions in terms of destructive competition but rather in the perspective of harmonizing the conditions of competition. However, they remark that, on the one hand, there is no direct and causal link between the existence of different rules and risks of race-to-the-bottom and, on the other hand, 'it is quite possible to create a common market without a total harmonization of all legal rules' (Faure and De Smedt, this volume).

There is a second aspect of destructive competition as the result of the behaviour of the lawmakers or, more precisely, as the consequence of the process of innovation. Indeed, if competition requires innovation, innovation in turn creates differences between the rules used in the different legal systems. Obviously, differences in legal rules are both the logical consequence and the fuel of competition. However, because of the fragmentation (even if temporary) of the economic space they generate, rules are as many non-border barriers to trade. Pierre Salmon stresses this point in his chapter (see also Salmon, 2000 and Breton and Salmon, 2001). These barriers to trade and to competition may be produced by the State but are also provided by non-state organizations. It is in particular the case of the German Book Traders association whose complex system of rules is examined by Jürgen Backhaus and Reginald Hansen in their chapter. They analyse the principle according to which the resale or end-sale price charged for new books is a fixed or list price. The end price system has been operated in the German language area for more than a century and, therefore, is defended on the basis of cultural diversity. On the other hand, the system has been challenged by the European Commission for being an obstacle to competition. Backhaus and Hansen analyse the economic argumentation presented by the Commission, namely that 'cultural diversity is best promoted or at least not harmed by fierce price competition'. They demonstrate that to forbid the discount of books by the booksellers can be criticized as an antitrust policy designed to protect interests of the producers but has above all to be defended for the cultural issues that are involved. Price competition and economic efficiency may indeed work at the expense of cultural diversity. Existing customary norms should then be protected in the name of Hayekian organizational efficiency.

When mobility is not possible (individuals may not wish to leave their original cultural area), it does not, however, mean that competition disappears since it does not necessarily require exit. Competition without exit – provided that citizens are capable to compare the results of the various jurisdictions – may work if citizens have the possibility to express their dissatisfaction and vote out the assumed inefficient legislators. Here direct competitive pressures are replaced by pressures resulting from comparison between lawmakers. The latter react to or, more precisely, anticipate the vote of the residents. Models of yardstick competition are based on this principle.

From the perspective of the behaviour of the lawmakers, legal competition cannot be considered as systematically negative. The so-called and so feared race-to-the-bottom can be considered as a myth rather than as a reality, at least whenever competition is organized (either in a spontaneous or intended way). The argument requires even more nuance when alternative forms of competition are considered. One of them is policy mimicking, whereby one jurisdiction is influenced by the actions of neighbouring jurisdictions. What Feld, Josselin and Rocaboy demonstrate in their chapter is the necessity to take strategic behaviours into account whenever competition among the few better describes the situation than a Tiebout setting. The application of a tax-mimicking model to the French regions shows that the devolution process engaged in this country brings about an overall convergence of rates at higher levels than before decentralization. This kind of spontaneous and strategic harmonization provides a significant lesson for the law market. If one cannot be certain that competition will lead to superior outcomes, on the other hand, there are no reasons to condemn legal competition *per se* for its expected negative and destructive results. At the same time, the Tiebout setting must not hide alternative forms of competition that may prove even more accurate. Any governmental intervention must take account of it when organizing the market for law.

STATE INTERVENTION

To prevent economic inefficiency and to help preserve organizational efficiency may be the task of governmental intervention. Static arguments rest on the public good nature of law as well as on the external effects it breeds. Further, the process itself of centralization is to be questioned. If legal competition must be organized, the dynamics of this organization must be assessed since it might in return threaten competition.

An Economic Account of State Intervention: Market Failures in the Provision of Law

It has frequently been argued that the model of pure legal competition, just like pure competition on ordinary markets, cannot comprehend all the aspects of the provision of law. In particular, there exist market failures that may be cured by the intervention of the State.

First, the nature of law is at stake. Legal competition works because legal rules are considered as club goods in a Tiebout setting. Now, law may also be viewed as a pure public good. The argument has been used by the advocates of a federal constitution during the constitutional debates that prepared the shift from a confederation to a federation in the USA at the end of the 18th century. In particular, the creation of the US Supreme Court of Justice has thus been justified: provision of law has to be federal rather than local '[t]o avoid the confusion which would unavoidably result from the contradictory decisions of a number of independent judicatories' (Federalist Paper 22, 1987, p. 182). Typically, the argument refers to the public good nature of the law. Beside law provision by the State and by Parliament, court decisions can also be considered as public goods. Indeed, as said by Cooter and Rubinfeld (1989, p. 1070), 'from a social point of view, trials are a mechanism of collective choice' for 'the production of justice has positive side effects which go beyond the private interests of the parties seeking to resolve their dispute' (Mühl and Vereeck, this volume; see also Vereeck and Mühl, 2000). Furthermore, as noted by Mühl and Vereeck, 'the use of information embodied in a verdict is non-rivalrous and the exclusion of future litigants from that information is undesirable' (this volume). The publicness of law may then imply production by states. In practice, the European states do subsidize court services. However, as a consequence of this subsidization, the demand for trials increases, creates court delays, thereby reducing the quality of the legal system. Thus, government intervention, due to the collective nature of the legal rules, creates inefficiencies in the legal market by increasing the delays required to render justice. The existence of these delays then implies the payment of judicial interests. If one moves to competition between different legal systems, hence between different judicial interest rates, the analysis made in this volume by Mühl and Vereeck advocates that one has to favour the harmonization of these rates among the members of the federation.

Second, the pure decentralization setting cannot comprehend spillovers.

Because of the transboundary nature of the corresponding externalities, environmental matters are one of the subjects in which a centralized provision of rules seems to be the most justified: 'This corresponds with the basic insight that if the problem to regulate crosses the borders of competence of the regulatory authority, the decision-making power should be shifted to a higher regulatory level, preferably to an authority which has jurisdiction over a territory large enough to adequately deal with the problem' (Faure and de Smedt, this volume). For instance, as Faure and de Smedt analyse it in their paper, it has been one of the justifications put forward by the promoters of the *White Paper on Environmental Liability*; thus, paragraph 6, dealing specifically with the subsidiarity issue, states that a directive would be necessary 'to avoid inadequate solutions to transfrontier damage'. Faure and de Smedt add that 'The Commission firmly states that national legislation cannot effectively cover transboundary environmental damage as various watercourses and protected habitats cross the borders of the Member States' (ibid.). However, one has to note that not all environmental problems have a transfrontier nature (Oates and Schwab, 1988). Furthermore, as Faure and de Smedt demonstrate 'some have warned that the argument that centralized powers are necessary to deal with transboundary problems should not be accepted too easily' (this volume; see also Van den Bergh, 1998).

These two sets of arguments cannot allow a definite and clear-cut conclusion about the standard public goods – externalities for the intervention of the State. One has to find other rationales to explain centralization in the provision of rules.

The Limitation of Legal Competition and the Dynamics of State Intervention

A first argument is that central legislators want to protect citizens. For instance, Faure and de Smedt argue that the willingness to guarantee the citizens a similar, or at least basic, environmental quality has to be viewed as an explanation for the centralized provision of environmental legislation. The argumentation rests on the assumed efficiency of the central government and, as a corollary, acknowledges the inefficiency of the decentralized provision of rules. It is another form of the race-to-the-bottom argument. Furthermore, it is assumed that the central government acts on behalf of the citizens. Then, it introduces an agency problem. Are the citizens, namely the political principals, certain that their political agents behave in conformity with their mandate? Such an argumentation opens an interesting path to understanding the process of centralization in the provision of law.

The phenomenon of a centralized (hence monopolized) system of lawmaking may be explained by an inefficient agency contract through which the principals are incapable of controlling the behaviour of their agents. The latter, taking advantage of their information and position, themselves increase their own prerogatives. As we have shown elsewhere, the agency relationship is reversed since the agents may behave as a principal (Josselin and Marciano, 2000). In these situations, the discretionary power of the agent is induced by the particular structure of the agency relationship; it is the reason why this kind of discretion has been labelled 'structure-induced discretion' (Steunenberg, 1996). The model can, in particular, be applied to the behaviour of the European Court of Justice (Josselin and Marciano, 2001) or may be extended so as to include the behaviour of other components of the European institutions such as the Brussels bureaucracy. Bureaucracy is indeed frequently pointed out as a source for centralization in international or supranational organizations (see in particular Vaubel and Willet, 1991; Frey, 1997; Vaubel, 1994, for an application to the European Union). The problem is that bureaucrats are unelected agents and therefore cannot be controlled like other politicians. With regard to the European decision-making process, three procedures exist that are assumed to allow the control of the European Commission: the advisory committee procedure, the management committee procedure and the regulatory committee procedure. In their chapter, Schmidtchen and Steunenberg evaluate these procedures as different ways to induce the compliance of the agent – the European Commission – with the preferences of the principal – the Council. They show that the most restrictive procedure is the regulatory committee procedure, through which 'the Commission may only implement a proposal when the committee presents a positive opinion; in case of a negative opinion, the Commission has to submit its proposal to the Council' (Schmidtchen and Steunenberg, this volume). Obviously, the complexity of intricate agency relationships pave the way for centralization. In other words, one may say that the very existence of Europe, as an institutional ambition, provides an explanation for centralization.

Such is the argument developed by Salmon. In his chapter, he considers the possibility of extending the seminal Niskanen model in order to give an account of the centralization of the European institutions. After having analysed the Niskanen model in the perspective of the European decision-making process, Salmon concludes that there is a 'limited' scope for bureaucratic expansionism *à la* Niskanen in the EU arrangements. The limitation comes from the fact this expansionism cannot be considered as out of the control of the European member-states. In other words, bureaucratic centralization could not have developed without the acquiescence of a majority of the member-states' governments. Salmon then offers a second level of explanation, which is that centralization in Europe results from the existence itself of a European project. In other words, it means that centralization could not have succeeded if the member-states had not behaved in a way favourable to centralization. The explanation thus provided is interesting for it contradicts the idea of the inefficiency of the agency contract that exists between the member-states and the European institutions. It is an explanation that allows us to consider that nations are conspiring against themselves (Salmon, 1995). Finally, Salmon adds a third level of explanation, the willingness of central institutions to centralize competences that belong to local governments to allow themselves more facility to 'implement [their] policy preferences' (this has been the attitude of Margaret Thatcher and of Ronald Reagan). It contradicts 'what is often taken as a natural congruence between the objective of free, unregulated markets, and that of political decentralization' (Salmon, this volume).

Does State Intervention Threaten Legal Competition?

In the preceding sections, we have insisted upon the importance of having the possibility to choose between legal producers. We have also stressed that at the same time State intervention, justified on economic or organizational grounds, was usually considered as unavoidable. These two results concur to raise the same question about the reality of competition between lawmakers when one of them is the State. The problems related to the intervention of the State are twofold. It can prevent horizontal and vertical competition. It means that, first, individuals cannot choose their preferred rules and, second, that private courts are not authorized to compete in all domains with public courts. The criticism that State intervention could be fatal to competition has especially been raised with regard to the French legal system. The criticism probably originates in the paradox that (apparently) inefficient, for being slow and expensive, public courts nevertheless dominate the legal system. The chapter by Didier Danet both refutes these criticisms and explains the domination of public courts. First, he notes that the French Civil Code (article 1134) authorizes individuals who are dissatisfied with the rules proposed by the legal codes to develop their own rules. A restriction nonetheless exists: one cannot create conventions which are likely to threaten public order and morality. However, Danet explains that courts are not prone to give an extensive interpretation of what public order means. Furthermore, public and private courts also compete with regard to the resolution of legal disputes since individuals can choose 'their' judge, as it is authorized by article 2059 of the Civil Code. It remains that, and this is the second part of Danet's chapter, one has to explain why private courts do not prevail in the French legal market. In contrast to what is usually put forward as a flaw in a centralized legal system, Danet provides examples showing that the explanation has to be found, first in the fact that private courts are not necessarily more efficient that public courts and, second, that the insecurity and high transaction costs 'inherent to the adoption of a "do-it-yourself" order' lead individuals to refer to the public rules and the public courts. Thus, what Danet teaches us in his chapter, is that pure competition creates costs that individuals and litigants do not necessarily want to bear. This argument is present in many of the chapters of this volume. It means that competition probably has to be carefully organized to function properly.

CONCLUSION: ECONOMIC COMPETITION AND LEGAL COMPETITION

The present book intends to demonstrate that legal competition is as important as standard economic competition in markets for private goods. Public intervention can both replace or promote market forces and the balance between the two is quite subtle. As to the markets for private goods, the European Union has already created an efficient institutional watchdog on competition. Should the same happen on the markets for law? Is the European Court of Justice entitled to take this role? Who will be the impartial spectator, spontaneously or rationally regulating the provision of law? We hope that this book will contribute to this debate.

REFERENCES

Benson, Bruce L. (2000), 'Jurisdictional choice in international trade: implications for Lex Cybernatoria', *Journal des Economistes et des Etudes Humaines*, **X** (1): 3–31.
Breton, Albert and Pierre Salmon (2001), 'External effects of domestic regulations: comparing internal and international barriers to trade', *International Review of Law and Economics*, **21**(2): (June), pp. 135–55.
Brosio, Giorgio and Federico Revelli (2000), 'Income distribution, social security and the demand for quasi-secession', in: V. Dardanoni, G. Sobbrio, *Istituzioni Politiche e Finanza Pubblica*, Milano: Angeli, 231–49.
Brosio, Giorgio and Federico Revelli (forthcoming 2003), 'The political economy of regional opting out: distributive implications of a prospective Europe of Regions', *Economics of Governance*.
Cooter, Robert and Daniel L. Rubinfeld (1989), 'Economic analysis of legal disputes and their resolution', *Journal of Economic Literature*, **27**: 1067–97.
Drèze, Jacques. (1993) 'Regions of Europe: a feasible status, to be discussed', *Economic Policy* **8**(17): 265–87.
Faure, Michael G. (2000), 'Product liability and product safety in Europe: harmonization or differentiation?', *Kyklos* **53**(4), pp. 467–508.
The Federalist Papers (1787–8), essays by Alexander Hamilton, John Jay and James Madison, edited by Isaac Kramnick (1987), New York: Penguin Books.
Frey, Bruno S. (1997), 'The public choice of international organizations', in Dennis C. Mueller (ed.), *Perspectives on Public Choice*, Cambridge: Cambridge University Press: 106–23.

Frey, Bruno S. (2001), 'A utopia? Government without territorial monopoly', *Journal of Institutional and Theoretical Economics*, 157: 162–75.

Frey, Bruno S. and Reiner Eichenberger (1995), 'Competition among jurisdictions: the idea of FOCJ', in Luder Gerken (ed.), *Competition Among Institutions*, London: Macmillan: 209–29.

Frey, Bruno S. and Reiner Eichenberger (1996), 'FOCJ: competitive governments for Europe', *International Review of Law and Economics*, **16**(3): 315–27.

Frey, Bruno S. and Reiner Eichenberger (1997), 'FOCJ: creating a single European market for governments', in Dieter Schmidtchen and Robert Cooter (eds), *Constitutional Law and the European Union*, Cheltenham, UK and Brookfield, US: Edward Elgar.

Josselin, Jean-Michel and Alain Marciano (1995), 'Constitutionalism and common knowledge: assessment and application to a future European constitution', *Public Choice* **85**(1–2): 173–88.

Josselin, Jean-Michel and Alain Marciano (1998), 'Une Approche Micro-Economique des Régions Périphériques', *Revue d'Economie Régionale et Urbaine*, 4: 547–64.

Josselin, Jean-Michel and Alain Marciano (1999), 'Unitary states and peripheral regions: A model of heterogeneous spatial clubs'. *International Review of Law and Economics*, **19**(4): 501–11.

Josselin, Jean-Michel and Alain Marciano (2000), 'Displacing your principal. Two historical case studies of some interest for the constitutional future of Europe', *European Journal of Law and Economics*, **10**(3): 217–33.

Josselin, Jean-Michel and Alain Marciano (2001), 'Comportements stratégiques et production de droit: le cas du droit communautaire européen', *Economie Appliquée*, **54**(3): 211–31.

Legrand, Pierre (1997), 'The impossibility of "legal transplants" ', *Maastricht Journal of European and Comparative Law*, 111.

Oates, W.E. and R. Schwab (1988), 'Economic competition among jurisdiction: efficiency enhancing or distortion inducing?', *Journal of Public Economics*, **35**: 333–54.

Ogus, Antony (1999), 'Competition between national legal systems: a contribution of economic analysis to comparative law', *International and Comparative Law Quarterly*, **48**: 405–18.

Rose-Ackerman, Susan (1992), *Re-thinking the Progressive Agenda, the Reform of the American Regulatory State*, New York: The Free Press.

Salmon, Pierre (1987), 'Decentralisation as an incentive scheme', *Oxford Review of Economic Policy*, **3**(2): 24–43.

Salmon Pierre (1995), 'Nations conspiring against themselves: an interpretation of European integration', in A. Breton, G. Galeotti, P. Salmon and R. Wintrobe (eds), *Nationalism and Rationality*, Cambridge and New York: Cambridge University Press, 290–311.

Salmon, Pierre (2000), 'Vertical competition in a unitary state', in G. Galeotti, P. Salmon and R. Wintrobe (eds), *Competition and Structure. The Political Economy of Collective Decisions: Essays in Honor of Albert Breton*, Cambridge: Cambridge University Press: 239–56.

Scott, Anthony (2000), 'Assigning powers over the Canadian environment', in G. Galeotti, P. Salmon and R. Wintrobe (eds), *Competition and Structure. The Political Economy of Collective Decisions: Essays in Honor of Albert Breton*, Cambridge: Cambridge University Press: 174–219.

Steunenberg, B. (1996), 'Agent discretion, regulatory policymaking, and different institutional arrangements', *Public Choice*, **86**: 309–39.

Van den Bergh, Roger (1998), 'Subsidiarity as an economic demarcation principle and the emergence of European private law', *Maastricht Journal of European and Comparative Law*, 129–52.

Van den Bergh, Roger (2000), 'Towards an institutional legal framework for regulatory competition in Europe', *Kyklos* **53**(4), pp. 435–66.

Vanberg, Viktor and W. Kerber (1994), 'Institutional competition among jurisdictions: an evolutionary approach', *Constitutional Political Economy*, **5**(2), 193–219.

Vaubel, Roland (1994), 'The political economy of centralization and the European Community', *Public Choice* **81**(1–2) October, pp. 151–90.

Vaubel, Roland and Thomas D. Willett (eds) (1991), *The Political Economy of International Organisations: A Public Choice Approach*, Boulder, CO: Westview Press.

Vereeck, Lode and Manuela Mühl (2000), 'An economic theory of court delay', *European Journal of Law and Economics* **7**(3), 243–68.

2. On 'Legal Choice' and legal competition in a federal system of justice. Lessons for European legal integration

Sophie Delabruyère[2]

INTRODUCTION

For several decades, European member states have been involved in a progressive and extensive process of integration concerning commercial and economic dimensions, monetary aspects, but also regarding legal and judicial services. The issue of European Legal Integration nowadays takes the form of discussions concerning the emergence of the 'European Judicial Area'. Among the diverse questions that arise in this perspective, one deals with the future shape of this judicial area: does European legal integration necessarily imply a centralized system of justice or, on the contrary, can we consider that the existence and preservation of 'decentralized' legal systems, namely the co-existence of national legal systems in the European Union, is another way, maybe more efficient, to achieve legal integration? It has frequently been argued that the relations between national legal systems on the one hand, and relations between national systems and the European legal order on the other (relations which can be either competitive or cooperative[3]) fully take part in the process of legal integration in Europe.

The achievement of the Single European Market, with the removal of diverse barriers, implies free movement of goods, services, capital and citizens between member states. This mobility of agents, associated with the fact that the national legal and judicial systems remain in force in Europe, contribute to

---

[2] Laboratoire CERAS-EDJ (Economie-Droit-Justice), Université de Reims Champagne Ardenne, UFR de Sciences Economiques, 57 bis Rue Pierre Taittinger, 51096 Reims Cedex, France; E-mail *sophie.delabruyere@univ-reims.fr*; Dipartimento di Economia 'S. Cognetti de Martiis', Università di Torino, Italia.

[3] Indeed, in Europe, we can distinguish several forms of relations between the various courts at two levels, vertical and horizontal, relations that appear to further the process of legal integration (see section 3).

creating a situation of 'competition between jurisdictions'[4]. Using the basis of the economic analysis of fiscal federalism to investigate such a competition in the provision of judicial and legal services, several authors argue that European legal integration can be reached through the competitive process taking place between rules and courts in Europe (among others, Antoniolli Deflorian, 1996; Harnay and Vigouroux, 2002; Kerber, 2000; Mattei, 1997; Ogus, 1999; Smits, 2002; Van Den Bergh, 2002; Woolcock, 1994). In this respect, legal competition should be favoured in Europe: it induces courts to innovate and thus permits the emergence of an efficient set of rules, through an evolutionary process; competitive relations between national courts can thus imply a spontaneous harmonization of legal rules[5]; and lastly, the competitive pressure makes legal jurisdictions more responsive to citizens' preferences regarding legal and judicial services. Nevertheless, this favourable description of such a judicial-legal competition through its potential beneficial effects may become clouded if one takes account of its potential adverse effects, and more precisely of the risk of 'a race to the bottom', that is 'a competition process among regulations in which only the lowest standards survive, and would not fulfil the preferences of the individuals' (Kerber, 2000, pp. 226–7)[6].

Most studies of legal integration through the legal competition process are based on the economics of federalism. Thus as often argued, the achievement of the benefits of interjurisdictional competition in the provision of legal products (or 'regulatory competition') presupposes that diverse conditions must be satisfied. These prerequisites are similar to the assumptions Tiebout (1956) has made in his model of competition between jurisdictions in the provision of local public goods. Briefly, to make the competitive process work, there should be: a sufficient number of providers in this market for legal services, a full knowledge of the features of the diverse legal systems[7], a perfect mobility of 'consumers', firms and individuals, with the underlying conditions of low-cost mobility and absence of externalities. However, as the approaches of regulatory competition acknowledge, all these prerequisites are difficult to

---

[4] The term 'jurisdictions' is generally used with the meaning of 'territorially defined state units' (Kerber, 2000, p. 220). In so far as the legal and judicial services are concerned in this chapter, the term can here refer to the state units providing legal services.

[5] Concerning the issue of European legal integration, this process is deemed more efficient than an *ex ante* harmonization of national legislations, which could be imposed through European directives.

[6] However, few authors like Vanberg (2000, pp. 98–9) argue that the 'race to the bottom' problem is not due to competition *per se*, namely to interjurisdictional competition, but it results from 'the inadequacy of the pertinent rules of the game'.

[7] This assumes in particular the spreading of comparative law studies in order to produce such information concerning the divergences and convergences between the various available systems.

fulfil in the case of the provision of law and justice, considering the essential features of judicial and legal services[8].

Besides, these analyses of legal competition rely on a particular assumption concerning 'consumers of judicial and legal services' (that is firms and individuals); these agents are supposed to adopt a 'voting by feet' behaviour[9]: in the face of several states which offer their own legal system in the 'market of legal and judicial services'[10], individuals and economic operators can choose (either by a physical migration as in Tiebout's model, or by contract in the specific case of commercial firms) the legal system fitting their preferences in order to govern their legal problems[11].

The purpose of the present chapter is to examine more precisely this presumed behaviour of the 'consumers' of legal services, either citizens or firms, in a particular judicial framework, namely a federal system of justice. This interest concerning the behaviour and motivations of those 'consumers of law' is justified in several respects: to administer justice 'legal producers' can need information about consumers' preferences; moreover, the shaping of the 'European Judicial Area' largely depends on the interaction between the strategies of the various agents involved in the process of European legal integration (namely, national judges, judges of the European Court of Justice, lawyers, litigants); and most of all because 'without individual litigants, there would be no cases presented to national courts and thus no basis for legal integration' (Mattli and Slaughter, 1996, p. 12). Our main question here concerns the relevance of the argument that consumers of judicial services, as rational individuals, can select (by physical mobility or by contract) among the diverse available legal systems the one that best fits their needs, and then by this choice reveal their judicial and legal preferences. We can show that various dimensions must be taken into account and that, depending on the case, the implications on the expected effects of the legal competitive process may vary. In short, given the insights on legal consumers' behaviours in their diversity, are the conclusions of models applying fiscal federalism to the provision of

---

[8] These elements will be presented in section 1.

[9] This behaviour of 'voting by feet' was first introduced by Tiebout (1956, p. 420) regarding the provision of local public goods: 'the consumer-voter moves to the community that satisfies his preference pattern. The act of moving or failing to move is crucial. Moving or failing to move replaces the usual market test of willingness to buy a good and reveals the consumer-voter's demand for public goods'.

[10] In these approaches, law is considered as a product that agents, private individuals and firms can choose.

[11] We must point out that, for individuals and firms, there can be an alternative to mobility: instead of moving among local legal jurisdictions or states to select the regulatory jurisdiction they most desire, agents can put pressure on the legislative and judges of their jurisdiction to make law evolve in the way they would like. We refer to the role of pressure groups in the evolution of legal systems. However, for the purpose of our study, we leave aside the possibility of pressures on legal producers.

legal products still relevant? Then we will try to investigate how these reflections could shed light on some aspects of European legal integration.

The chapter is organized as follows. Section 1 outlines the distinctive features of judicial and legal services, features that contribute to explain the peculiarity of federalism regarding the administration of justice and their consequences on agents' behaviours. It also mentions some elements on the notion of 'judicial and legal preferences'. Section 2 deals with the diverse situations which can entail a 'legal and judicial choice', a notion we will explain. By focusing on a central element in the consumption of legal services, that is 'uncertainty', we attempt to draw a typology of cases of 'legal choice'. With this classification, we aim at introducing an additional limit in the use of regulatory competition models. Section 3 examines how these elements can be used to study the process of legal integration in Europe. More precisely, we intend to show that according to the judicial matters and other elements we insist on, the type and intensity of the competitive process may be different, which means that several 'levels', 'speeds' and 'paths' of legal integration could be distinguished in Europe. A concluding section ends the chapter.

1.   AN ECONOMIC APPROACH TO 'SERVICES OF JUSTICE' AND LEGAL PREFERENCES

This section contains some observations on the nature of the judicial and legal services, in order to examine which implications these features can have on the application of economics of federalism to the judicial and legal function. And then we reflect on the notion of 'legal and judicial preferences'.

The Characteristics of Legal and Judicial Products

It seems relevant to mention the distinctive features of judicial and legal services[12], in so far as they permit us to stress the specificity of the economics of fiscal federalism when this approach is applied to legal products. First, judicial and legal services are 'mixed goods' in the sense that they present at the same time private and public characteristics. Indeed, at first sight, a judicial decision may be considered as a private good because it results in individual effects on the person(s) directly affected by the decision. First of all, a judge produces a decision to resolve a particular conflict, and thus the decision is intended to affect the parties involved in the trial. It is also the case when an

---

[12] For further analyses of the characteristics of judicial and legal services, see Barrère (2001). Here, we only take account of the features that are relevant to analyse judicial and legal competition, and the issue of 'legal choice'.

individual addresses a legal question to a court: the magistrate formulates a decision fitted to the specific case he faces (for instance, a request of naturalization). However, the product 'justice' must also be regarded as a public good, in so far as a judicial decision, though fitted to a particular and single legal case, contributes to the general process of affirmation and respect of law. This twofold dimension of the 'services of justice', individual and collective dimensions, has been emphasized by Cooter and Rubinfeld (1989, p. 1070) in the following terms: 'Adjudication by the courts has two distinct products: dispute resolution and rule making. From the private viewpoint, trials are a method of resolving disputes between rational self-interested plaintiffs and defendants. But, from a social viewpoint, trials are a mechanism of collective choice for interpreting and creating laws to regulate and govern society'.

Therefore, the public characteristics of judicial services come from their external effects, more precisely from their spatial and temporal externalities, as judicial decisions may have effects on individuals not directly involved. A judgement can *belong to* the jurisprudence; moreover, a decision in a particular legal dispute gives some information to persons (who are not parties in the present trial) on the outcome they can expect of a conflict in a similar case. Linked to this twofold dimension, the provision of legal and judicial services can result in spill-over effects[13]. As defined by the economic analysis of federalism, spill-overs are said to exist when 'the decisions and actions of individuals within one jurisdiction can have effects on individuals located in other jurisdictions that are not accurately reflected in the marketplace' (Inman and Rubinfeld, 2000, p. 668); they are kinds of spatial externalities. This implies that the principle of 'fiscal equivalence', namely the 'match between those who receive the benefits of a collective good and those who pay for it' (Olson, 1969, p. 483), which is a condition for efficient provision of local public goods, is not met as regards the provision of legal and judicial services. Spill-over effects can be found, for instance, in environmental regulation, since the behaviour of one jurisdiction is likely to have effects not only on the individuals and firms located in its territory, but also on the citizens of the adjoining jurisdiction(s). If state J1 allows a higher rate of pollution for firms than state J2, this legislation may also have effects on agents located in jurisdiction J2, although state J2 can enforce a stricter environment standard. Such externalities result in market failures and allocative inefficiency regarding environmental protection.

Moreover, it proves essential to lay stress on another feature of judicial

---

[13] Certain regulatory fields are not affected by this problem of spill-overs. '. . . The degree of uninternalized externalities may, in fact, vary widely from one field of regulation to the next (. . .) successful acid rain abatement, for instance, requires broad-scale governmental intervention and a healthy measure of interjurisdictional cooperation, while regulation of toxic waste sites (localized harm) benefits from increased regulatory competition' (Esty and Geradin, 2000, p. 241).

services: this concerns the implications of these services on the individuals' utility. Unlike standard goods, the 'consumption' of legal and judicial services can provide not only satisfaction to the agent(s) concerned by this action but also a loss of utility. Indeed, in general, a judicial decision implies at the same time positive effects for one of the parties involved in the trial and negative effects for the other party. As a consequence, a judgement can result in a gain of utility for one agent and a loss of utility for the other, as in most of the cases the judge produces it to resolve a conflict between private individuals or between an individual and society (represented by the public prosecutor's room, in a penal case for instance). This effect on one agent's utility depends on the outcome of the trial, that is a win for the plaintiff or for the defendant. As a matter of fact, for example, when a judge determines an indemnity for the victim of an accident, this decision results in a positive effect on the victim's utility (or at the least to restore his utility), but also a cost for the defendant, that is a loss of utility[14].

Besides, a distinction has to be drawn between 'voluntary consumption' and 'constrained consumption' of legal and judicial services, a distinction linked to the different status that an individual can have in a trial: he may be plaintiff or defendant, it depends on whether he has the initiative of the judicial process. This dimension of 'constraint' is permitted by the coercive power of the State. Public justice can impose consumption of its services on the persons for whom these judicial services mean a loss of utility, that is the defendants. In this sense, judicial services can be considered as a 'good of constraint'. Thus, we can conclude by mentioning that 'justice' is a good with distributional effects, since a judicial decision entails some modifications on agents' resources and rights. In most of the cases, these effects on the distribution of resources between individuals can be interpreted as a 'zero-sum game'; as, for instance, compensation for a victim is also a cost for the defendant, the affirmation of an agent's right can imply an obligation for another individual. So, judicial decisions are likely to affect the distribution of rights and resources between individuals.

This presentation of the essential features of judicial and legal products will permit us to lay stress on the particularity of economics of federalism when this approach is applied to the provision of justice. As has often been argued, the economic models of federalism cannot be applied directly, without taking account of the nature of the judicial function itself and its participation in the process of affirmation and respect of law. Moreover, the characteristics of

---

[14] See Barrère (2001). But, in some situations, the defendant's attorney makes use of a strategy which permits the amount of damages his client must pay to the victim to be lowered. In such a case, the loss of utility is less high than it could have been in the event of failure of the lawyer's strategy.

these services have essential implications on individuals' behaviours and their legal and judicial preferences, as we examine in the subsection that follows.

Some Remarks on Legal and Judicial Preferences

On the basis of the observations on the nature of judicial and legal services, it is reasonable to develop diverse hypotheses about legal and judicial preferences. In this subsection, we do not claim to examine the individual preferences on judicial and legal services from all points of view. We only want to insist on the elements that can prove useful and essential for our study of 'legal choice' situations. The notion of 'legal and judicial preferences' itself would require a specific analysis (how can these preferences be defined?, which elements are determining? and so forth). We suggest that the notion of 'legal and judicial preferences' concerns all the individual preferences regarding legal systems and judicial institutions: it can concern a rule on a specific legal question as well as Justice as a whole, but also particular judicial procedures.

First, we must insist on the heterogeneity of legal and judicial preferences. As for other goods and services, the individual preferences concerning legal services are likely to vary significantly among the agents. For instance, on the issue of liability (either product liability or civil liability), some individuals may prefer strict liability standards whereas others may prefer negligence liability rules. In the same way, private individuals and economic operators might have varying preferences regarding social legislation, environment standards, antitrust law, corporate law and administrative law, that is in the diverse legal fields.

In addition, it is relevant to mention a distinctive characteristic of legal-judicial preferences: these are likely to vary for the same agent when he faces distinct situations. In other words, regarding a given legal issue, an individual can prefer the rule R_1 in one situation, whereas in a different case, he could prefer the rule R_2. His choice depends on the expected gains in each situation. Taking again the issue of liability standards and concerning driver–pedestrian accidents, it is possible (and maybe certain) that the same person can have distinct preferences depending on whether he is a driver or a pedestrian. As a driver, he is likely to prefer a 'negligence liability rule', in so far as under such a negligence rule, he would only be liable for damage for negligent acts; then, since the driver would choose to drive moderately, the pedestrian would bear his own losses. But, as a pedestrian, his preference would not be the same: he would probably encourage the enforcement of strict liability standards, because under such a liability system, the driver would compensate the victim for any damage caused. This variability of preferences for the same agent according to the situation he faces proves essential in our analysis, insofar as it is likely to affect the process of revelation of preferences. Are the individuals encouraged to reveal their preferences concerning a legal question when these depend on the situation faced by them?

Therefore, judicial and legal preferences are heterogeneous on two levels: first, they can vary among individuals, and besides, for the same person, his own preferences may also be different according to the situations. The second feature of these preferences is essential in our discussion because it permits us to distinguish two types of legal questions, therefore two sorts of situations. Thus, we can attempt to classify the legal fields according to this criterion of stability or 'flexibility' of individual preferences.

First, consider the legal issues for which there is stability of preferences for a given individual. Whatever the situation he faces, this agent maintains the same legal preference concerning a particular legal question. It means that the problem faced by one person does not have influence on his legal choices. Since individual preferences on these issues are stable, what matters here is the heterogeneity of preferences among individuals. In most of the cases concerned, two (or more) groups of agents with specific preferences (maybe conflicting) could be distinguished. Various examples can illustrate such an assertion. Indeed, as a simplification, concerning labour standards and social legislation, there are two distinct groups with their own interests and thus their own preferences: the firms and the workers. For firms, minimum wage law, for instance, can induce costs, and then, if firms are assumed to be perfectly mobile, they are inclined to set up in the jurisdiction providing the least restricting rules for their activities, 'ceteris paribus' (that is, independently of the other factors that can explain their location: tax system, the presence of competitors, etc.). On the other hand, workers (if assumed to be perfectly mobile, and not considering the other factors explaining their location choice) would prefer 'restricting' legislation in social matters which contributes to protect social rights, and so legal systems that impose constraints to firms. In the same way, as regards product liability standards, we can draw a distinction between manufacturers' interests and thus their preferences, and consumers' preferences in this matter. In these diverse cases, agents are likely to reveal their preferences if they can choose among distinct legal systems or rules, because these preferences are stable and can be defined 'ex ante', that is before a specific legal problem arises.

Now let us reflect on the legal issues that are characterized by varying preferences. In other words, according to the situation he faces, and most of the time depending on whether he is plaintiff or defendant, an individual can have distinct legal preferences concerning a particular legal question. This assertion can be summed up in the following way: in situation 1, the individual i prefers rule R_1 to rule R_2, whereas in situation 2, for the same individual i, the rule R_2 is preferred to rule R_1. This means that the rule maximizing this agent's expected gains changes with the situation effectively faced. As noted above, this specific feature of legal preferences, namely their 'flexibility', can be encountered in various legal fields such as contract law, civil liability standard (as has been illustrated above), competition law, etc. For instance, concerning competition law fields, a firm can have distinct preferences concerning rules of merger controls and rules governing cartel agreements and abuses of dominant position; it depends on the gains this firm can get in such situations, and moreover, a firm does not know 'ex ante' if such opportunities can appear. In such situations, agents are not likely to reveal any legal preferences 'ex ante' since they face uncertainty regarding the potential legal problems they could encounter.

This distinction between legal fields according to the 'stability' or 'flexibility' of legal preferences will be linked to an essential element in section 2: the presence or absence of uncertainty. Consequently, the individual preferences concerning legal issues must not be taken as given (as exogenous) because, to some extent, these preferences are endogenous.

In most of the cases presented in the models of 'regulatory competition', the product proposed in this market structure is law: 'consumers' are searching the legal rules that satisfy their needs and preferences concerning specific legal issues. This choice process first concerns firms: these choose to produce under a specific standard or rule (for example, concerning a standard of pollution, or a corporate law), that is a particular legal environment which enables them to maximize their expected gains. Private individuals are supposed to adopt the same behavioural model of 'forum shopping' concerning legal products. In this respect, it appears interesting to discuss this process of 'legal choice'. We mean by the general terms 'legal choice' the process of choice of a legal rule, a standard or a legal system as a whole. The competitive framework between legislators and courts is deemed to allow firms and private individuals to select which legal rules they want to regulate their legal problems in an efficient way and at the lowest costs[15]. What we want to discuss here is the feasibility of such a choice by the various 'consumers' of legal and judicial services. In other words, given the essential features of these services, the

[15] Hereafter, some extracts of diverse economic analyses of legal competition, which insist on the possibility to choose legal rules according to one's preferences: 'The market of legal products offers a diversity of legal products, and so brings with it the possibility of matching transactional needs with the most suitable set of rules' (Garcimartin Alferez, 1999, p. 258). 'If domestic industries competing in international markets find that their national legal system imposes on them higher costs than those incurred by their foreign competitors operating under a different jurisdiction, they will apply pressure on their lawmakers to reduce the costs. That demand will be strengthened by the threat of migration to the more favourable jurisdiction, assuming that there are no barriers to the freedom of establishment and to the movement of capital' (Ogus, 1999, p. 407). 'Enterprises and citizens may have heterogeneous preferences as to their preferred set of laws: the more legislators compete, the more preferences may be satisfied. Firms and individuals may "vote by feet" (Tiebout, 1956) and choose the jurisdiction which in their view offers the best set of laws' (Van Den Bergh, 2002, p. 29).

insights on judicial-legal preferences and the relative uncertainty concerning the occurrence of a legal issue, can individuals really make a rational choice between the legal systems in order to resolve the legal problem they face or can eventually face?

2. AN ATTEMPT TO DRAW A TYPOLOGY OF SITUATIONS OF 'LEGAL CHOICE' AND CONSEQUENCES FOR THE PROVISION OF LEGAL SERVICES

In this section, we suggest that various situations of 'legal choice' can be distinguished on the basis of a central element (that is whether uncertainty exists or not), each of which having distinct implications on the competitive process between rules and legal systems. In order to do this, we first consider a few situations to take account of the possible diversity of legal choices. And then, we try to draw a typology among cases of 'legal choice'.

Diversity of Situations of 'Legal Choice'

First of all, we consider the following simple situations.

Situation 1.   One manufacturer wants to set up in a region to produce cars. We suppose that he can choose between two locations, each in one state providing and enforcing different tort-liability systems concerning product liability[16]: in state J1, the product-liability system is based on the 'negligence liability rule', whereas state J2 enforces the 'strict liability standard'. In which state will this manufacturer decide to produce, in other words under which product-liability system?

Situation 2.   Two firms, A and B, respectively set up in state J1 and state J2, sign a commercial contract concerning the delivery of raw materials. The two states are supposed to provide different legal systems. After a process of negotiation, the two companies agree to include in their contract a 'choice of law' clause stating that if a conflict arises between the parties, the law of state J1

---

[16] We do not discuss here what liability standard would be recommended by economic analysis in the case of product liability for manufacturers because of their incentives on firms and level of precaution (for further analysis on this issue, refer to Cooter and Ulen, 1997 (1988)). Here, for the purpose of the study, we only assume that at a given time two states provide and enforce distinct product-liability rules in order to analyse the consequences of such a situation.

will be applied to the given transaction, and thus that tribunals of state J1 have jurisdiction over the claims that could arise out of the contract.

Situation 3. Now we consider a private individual who wants to set up, and has the choice between two systems of civil liability (either each system is provided by different states, or as in the framework proposed by Frey and Eichenberger (1999, pp. 3–4), the individual can choose between two FOCJ (Functional, Overlapping and Competing Jurisdictions) providing and enforcing distinct civil liability standards). How will this person make his choice between the two systems?

Situation 4. We consider two individuals, *i* living in state J1 and *j* from state J2. The two states are assumed to enforce distinct systems of liability concerning car accidents, a system of strict liability and a system of liability for harm. Suppose that an accident occurs between the two motorists *i* and *j* in another state, J3. Which liability standard is likely to apply, and thus who will be held liable for the accident?

Although these diverse situations imply choices of rules and legal systems, they appear different in several respects. First, concerning the number of individuals affected, two different questions must be considered: (1) how many persons are involved at the moment of the legal choice? and (2) is this number likely to be modified in the future? In cases 1 and 2, there is no potential modification in the number of individuals involved, whereas in situations 3 and 4, the individual legal choice is likely to be confronted with another agent's legal choice. Second, we must question whether a contractual relation exists between the two parties concerned by the legal problem. A distinction has to be drawn between two kinds of disputes: conflicts arising between agents linked by a contract, what Polinsky (1989) names 'contractual disputes' as in situation 4, and 'disputes between strangers'[17] as in situation 2. Finally, questions arise concerning the occurrence of the legal issue: is it presently faced by the party (or parties) or is it only potential? In situation 4, the legal problem is presently faced by the individual whereas in the other cases mentioned disputes are only probable. This latter feature must be connected with another essential element in this respect, the temporal dimension: does the choice of a legal system occur 'ex ante' (namely, before the occurrence of a legal problem) or, will it only be made 'ex post' (when a legal question arises)? These few examples shed light on the

---

[17] '. . . It will be useful to distinguish between legal disputes in which the parties are in some kind of contractual relationship, including a market relationship, and disputes in which the parties are, in effect, 'strangers' prior to the dispute. The breach of contract and product liability examples would be characterized as *contractual disputes*, while the nuisance law, automobile accident, and pollution control examples would be described as *disputes between strangers*' (Polinsky, 1989, pp. 121–2).

uncertainty associated with the consumption of the judicial and legal services. It is precisely on this 'uncertainty' we want to focus in order to draw a distinction among the situations in which individuals face the question of legal choice.

A Typology of Situations of 'Legal Choice'

It may be relevant to distinguish different kinds of situations implying a choice of legal system or legal product, insofar as it can permit us to introduce distinctions into the effects of regulatory competition. To do so, the assumptions are specified first. The kinds of uncertainty and their different effects on the competitive process are discussed in turn.

Assumptions

Several assumptions are made here to examine the diverse situations of legal choice. First, it is an accepted fact that economic models of fiscal federalism can apply to the study of regulatory competition, and thus, the conditions required by these models (briefly presented in the introduction) are supposed to be satisfied. We examine the legal choice in a federal structure of justice, that is a situation in which different legal and judicial systems exist, and where agents have the freedom to choose between them. Thus, concerning the assumption on individuals' mobility, it does not necessarily mean a physical migration to an alternative legal system, insofar as, for example, two firms can choose to sign a contract governed by a specific legislation. Moreover, if the principle of FOCJ is adopted, the judicial and legal services could be provided by jurisdictions defined in terms of 'function' (and not according to a particular territory), in the present case the legal and judicial function. Therefore, an entrepreneur could select the legislation (of his country or from a foreign state) to which he would like to submit his activity independently of his location. For instance, 'a German firm wishing to produce under Portuguese law . . . does not need to go to Portugal, but can adopt the Portuguese law while staying in Germany' (Frey and Eichenberger, 1996b, p. 347).

In some respects, the present discussion focuses on the legal and judicial dimensions motivating the locational choice for private individuals and firms, but undoubtedly various criteria as job, environment, public policies and so forth should also be taken into account in this choice procedure. Thus, for the purpose of our analysis, we assume that the distinctions between jurisdictions (in the general sense of 'local governmental units') only concern the characteristics of the judicial and legal products provided by those units, which implies that the other governmental functions and services are supposed to be equivalent (in such a way that, in their choice, the individuals do not consider them as determining variables). Another way of focusing only on judicial and legal dimensions of jurisdictions consists of using the concept of FOCJ mentioned above: thus are considered the jurisdictions competing in the pro-vision of legal services[18].

Concerning the other conditions we presented in the introduction, the number of providers of judicial products is assumed to be sufficient, and the spill-over effects are also supposed to be minimized (that is we assume that each national regulatory system does not have impacts beyond its own juris-diction, which is obviously a simplistic hypothesis). Last, we suppose that individuals are perfectly knowledgeable about the judicial and legal alterna-tives offered by the various jurisdictions. They have information about the laws, the judicial procedures, the local judges' behaviour, etc. that is all the elements characterizing the legal and judicial systems and which can prove determining in the selection of a 'forum' by litigants. Therefore, it is assumed that the conditions to make competition work are fulfilled in order to focus specifically on one aspect, namely the choice of rule or legal system by indi-vidual litigants and firms (even if, as it has often been argued, these conditions are difficult to satisfy as regards the legal and judicial products).

A determining element in our typology: uncertainty

As mentioned above, an element can prove to be essential in an attempt to differentiate various situations of 'legal choice': the existence or absence of uncertainty. The uncertainty that individuals have to face in a situation of legal choice can come from several elements. First, uncertainty could result from insufficient information available for 'consumers' concerning the alternative legal systems. In such a case, the agents would not have enough elements to compare the services offered by each system. Nevertheless, hereafter the legal information is supposed to be perfect. Let us examine more precisely the uncertainty stemming from the interactions between individuals.

On the one hand, uncertainty concerning the emergence of a conflict may appear, since 'ex ante' a person is unaware of the legal disputes he could have in the future with other agents. This uncertainty is strengthened in a way if we consider the distinction between plaintiff and defendant, the former being more informed at first of the probability of legal proceedings than the latter. Moreover, on the basis of the hypotheses made regarding the variability of individual legal preferences[19], the uncertainty also comes from the agent's status in a particular dispute.

---

[18] Indeed, Frey and Eichenberger argue that their concept can be used for the diverse govern-mental services, therefore for the provision of legal and judicial products. 'The overlap between jurisdictions may also extend to a governmental service not mentioned so far: namely, the provi-sion of law. Each individual or firm has the freedom to choose which law it wants to apply to its respective transactions, thus inducing competition among different forms of law' (Frey and Eichenberger, 1996b, p. 346).

[19] See the earlier example of the liability rule in the event of a pedestrian-driver accident.

On the other hand, the uncertainty can relate to the rule which will be used in a particular legal dispute. This kind of uncertainty, regarding the consumption of legal and judicial services, results from the interactions between individual agents because these are likely to challenge the 'legal choice' made by other agent(s). Thus, the relations among individuals imply a potential confrontation of their respective judicial and legal preferences. And if a conflict arises between two persons, the confrontation of their preferences becomes real as they are affected by the same legal issue. Considering the heterogeneity of individuals' preferences, it is likely that a legal conflict implies different legal rules (if these have been chosen 'ex ante'). To put it simply, an individual i can at first choose the rule R_1 because he deems that this one is best fitted to his situation and to his preferences. But, his relations with other persons (whatever these relations may be[20]) can induce a particular dispute with another individual j. The most probable situation is that individual j has distinct legal preferences from agent i's ones, and thus that he has chosen at first a different rule, for instance rule R_2. Consequently, in addition to the uncertainty surrounding the emergence of a legal question, there is uncertainty regarding the law that would be applied: if a conflict arises effectively between the two agents i and j, which of the two rules, R_1 or R_2, will be considered to resolve the dispute? Therefore, although an individual has his own preferences regarding a legal standard, he can be forced to 'consume' a legal rule different from the one he would select himself to solve a particular legal issue. Under these conditions, is he induced to reveal at first his legal preferences, knowing that he is not sure he will 'consume' the legal product corresponding to his preferences? Then, the question arises: what implications can it have in terms of legal competition?

Nevertheless, there are situations in which uncertainty does not exist or at the least, is limited. Such an element, 'uncertainty', serves to distinguish two main situations of 'legal choice' and their respective implications in terms of competition, since the freedom of choice is likely to create a situation of competition between providers of legal systems. But in many situations, there are constraints limiting these choices and thus introducing uncertainty: freedom of choice faces a constraint due to the other persons' legal preferences. Taking account of these 'uncertainty' elements and the problems they induce for the revelation of individuals' preferences appears all the more important as the shaping of the legal 'landscape' is most of the time supposed to depend on 'consumers' judicial and legal preferences. To some extent, individual preferences are at the centre of the process. Frey and

---

[20] This element must be linked to the process of *judicialisation*, that is the fact that relations between persons increasingly have a legal dimension, and thus a legal issue can arise implying the intervention of a judge.

Eichenberger argue: 'FOCJ form an adaptable federal network of governmental units that depend closely on citizens' preferences and adjust to the "geography" of problems – as long as the citizens dominate the formation process of FOCJ' (1999, p. 4).

By insisting on these aspects, we can identify two main kinds of situations in which individuals face a 'legal choice': on the one hand, the situations with no uncertainty; and on the other, the situations with uncertainty due to the potential interactions between agents, and thus interactions of individual (legal and judicial) preferences. In the subsections that follow, we examine more precisely these situations and their respective results in terms of competitive processes. For each group of situations, we will investigate the likely individual behaviours, and how these strategies could influence the diverse legal systems available in the 'market for law'.

Situations of legal choice with no uncertainty

This denomination serves to indicate the cases in which the confrontation of individual legal preferences (as ensuing from the interactions of agents and if a legal dispute arises between them) is not likely to induce a potential modification of an agent's legal choice. Therefore, there is no uncertainty concerning the use of a legal system when it has been chosen by the individual(s) concerned: the rule applied in the event of a legal problem is the one that has been designed 'ex ante'. This absence of uncertainty is also strengthened by the stability of individual preferences about these legal issues. In short, whatever the status the agent has in the trial (whether he is plaintiff or defendant) and whatever the situation faced, he would prefer rule R_1 to rule R_2, or the legal system of state J1 instead of the one of state J2. As it has been noted, various fields of law are implicated: labour legislation, environmental regulation, etc. More precisely, two typical cases can be identified.

The first case is when the 'legal choice' concerns a rule which defines the conditions of a production process or of a transaction (a specific legal context for a contract). In such a case, as in the first of the situations presented above, a firm can select the law it prefers to apply to its activities, comparing the advantages and drawbacks of each legal system concerning a specific question (corporate law, contract law, standard of pollution, product-liability standard and so forth). Thus, the agents are supposed to choose the legal system that best fits their legal and judicial preferences concerning a specific legal question[21].

The second case is when the conditions under which a specific rule (or law)

---

[21] As an example, we note the competition among states for a corporate charter in the United States: more than 40 per cent of the firms listed in the New York Exchange have chosen the corporate law of Delaware.

applies are precisely specified, so that there is no uncertainty concerning this aspect. The typical situation is the clause of 'choice of rule' in a contract between two (or more) agents in expectation of a conflict between the parties bound by the agreement (as in situation 2 presented above). As O'Hara and Ribstein have analysed, 'contracting for choice of law enables the parties easily to determine what law governs the transaction', and thus 'enforcing contractual choice of law is particularly useful in fostering jurisdictional competition for more efficient laws across states' (2000, p. 643). In such situations (corresponding to 'contractual disputes' (Polinsky, 1989)), there is no uncertainty concerning the rule that will apply because the parties have agreed on a precise legal system or court in the event of a conflict between them. So they can compare the different legal systems available and choose the one that fits the legal and judicial preferences of both parties. The 'legal choice' can be made 'ex ante' because the agents in such a case are bound by contractual relation. Therefore, when a dispute really arises between them, there is no confrontation of their respective legal preferences, as the legal system that should apply has already be chosen and there is no uncertainty.

In both typical situations, since there is no uncertainty, the persons can 'shop' for the rule fitting their preferences, so one could assert that there is 'real' competition between the legal systems available. The models of regulatory competition can help to describe such situations of 'forum shopping', and their consequences (mentioned briefly in the introduction).

Situations of legal choice under the 'veil' of uncertainty

The nature of legal competition, and thus its consequences, may be different if uncertainty appears. Two kinds of situations have to be investigated.

First, uncertainty can appear when the inter-individual relations are taken into account, insofar as if a conflict arises between two persons (who are not bound by a contract, therefore a 'dispute between strangers'. Such a legal dispute implies a 'confrontation' of their respective legal preferences[22]. And consequently, since legal preferences are heterogeneous among individuals, it is possible that the legal preferences of one of the two agents are not satisfied[23].

---

[22] The agents are supposed to reveal their preferences by choosing a rule on specific legal issues.

[23] Obviously, there can be situations in which the two individuals, parties in a conflict, have chosen 'ex ante' the same rule concerning a particular legal question. In such a situation, there would not be problem. The legal dispute does not imply a 'confrontation' of their respective preferences (which are identical) so no confrontation of rules ('conflict of laws'). This situation is the one occurring when two 'national' individuals in the same country are in conflict; it is the national legal system that applies. Nevertheless, considering a federal framework of justice (and, at the extreme, the provision of judicial services by FOCJ), the agents do not know 'ex ante' whether a dispute can arise with someone having chosen or not the same legal system. So individuals must take into account this uncertainty if they select a judicial system 'ex ante': they must take account of the fact that their potential adversary in a conflict can have selected a distinct legal system.

Are individuals induced to select 'ex ante' a legal system, legal rules concerning specific situations, that is to reveal their preferences, given that the law applied in a dispute can be different from the one they have chosen? Thus we consider the case in which the adversaries in a legal dispute have preferences for distinct legal systems. Then, through the confrontation of their respective legal choices the dispute induces a confrontation of two legal systems. Which legal system would apply in such a situation? It depends on the 'institutional' framework for regulatory competition. First, if there is no 'rule of the game' designating the court that should have the jurisdiction to resolve the judicial affair, the uncertainty remains. Under these specific conditions, which behaviour could individuals have in the event they must choose 'ex ante' a legal system or a rule concerning a legal question? It seems that individuals are not induced to reveal their 'real' legal preferences when they select a system: they would demand only general rules. The consequences of such a behaviour on the competition between legal systems may be that these systems are encouraged to provide general legal standards, which can entail a greater role on the part of the judges compared to the legislature's role. Moreover, these situations could lead to a 'denial of justice': as there is a 'conflict of laws', no legal system has exclusive competence to adjudicate the dispute. Thus is emphasized the requirement of 'regulation' of legal competition. Kinds of 'rules of the games' must be adopted: government units are induced to sign agreements regarding the jurisdiction, recognition and enforcement of foreign legal disputes. Some conventions have been signed between countries, at the European level as well as at the international level, to deal, first, with the allocation of competences between courts. For instance, the competent court could depend on the place of the action that implied damages; in other cases, it could be the court first seized. Such conventions also provide rules governing the recognition and enforcement of foreign legal decisions. These sets of rules permit a decrease in uncertainty and this also means that a competition between legal systems can exist 'ex ante'. Therefore, one can argue that, in order to work, competition needs some cooperation, as Woolcock (1994, pp. 24–5), among others[24], claims:

> the absence of effective enforcement of regulations is likely to undermine competition among rules, because of the lack of certainty concerning the rules applied. (. . .) Mutual recognition, or the requirement that regulators in one country accept the good or service produced under another regulatory regime will result in more intensive competition between the national regulatory systems.

[24] Indeed, more and more articles on interjurisdictional competition, and in particular on legal competition, emphasize that regulatory competition and legal cooperation are complementary. 'In a world that is pluralistic, not simplistic, a combination of regulatory competition and cooperation will almost always be optimal' argue Esty and Geradin (2000, p. 1) in a model of *Regulatory Co-opetition*. Similar arguments are introduced by, among others, Kerber (2000), Sykes (2000), Trachtman (2000).

What is the result of this 'limitation' of uncertainty on individual behaviour? Each agent can choose 'ex ante' a legal rule, thus revealing his preferences, but to make sure that this rule will apply in the case of a legal problem, he will have to use strategies. Consider the following situation of interstate legal dispute. Two agents, i and j, are in conflict and they want to go to law, each individual wanting the dispute adjudicated by 'his' legal system respectively in states A and B (corresponding to his preferences). If a convention has been signed between the two countries and states that the court first seized has jurisdiction, it will induce the two litigants, i and j, to set judicial strategies, such as a 'race to the courthouse' or a 'race for a judgment' (Herzog, 1995) in order that it is the legal system they selected at first which will resolve the dispute.

Let us now consider a second kind of situation affected by uncertainty. On the basis of our previous comments, we must point out that this 'uncertainty' element may also come from the 'variability' of preferences for a person according the diverse situations he could face. Indeed, in some respects (that is according the legal problems concerned), individual legal preferences cannot be considered as given. Thus, 'ex ante' an individual totally ignores the problem he could have to face (and more precisely, whether he would be plaintiff or defendant, i.e. his status in a trial), and then what his preferences and his legal choice would be in such a particular case. To some extent, in the fields of law concerned (civil liability standard, competition law, etc.), private agents and firms are under a 'veil of uncertainty'. Considering the context, it can prove to be irrational to make a legal choice 'ex ante' because, at the extreme, this choice could turn out to be harmful for the person involved. Indeed, how could an agent select a rule maximizing his expected gains, if he has no information on the possible situations, gains and interests at stake? Consequently, in some legal matters, private individuals and economic operators cannot choose 'ex ante' a legal system or a specific rule that would meet their preferences. Thus, there is no revelation of individual preferences, and no use of the 'exit option' which could generate pressures for improved governmental efficiency in regulation. Since there is no specific demand for particular rules in the legal fields here concerned, we can suppose that there is no real motivation for legal innovation, and thus it is possible that inefficient rules are maintained because of the lack of new rules (maybe more efficient) challenging them. In such a context, one can imagine that legislators will provide only sets of general rules. As a consequence, judges would have an increasing function: they would have to 'create' rules when disputes are submitted to them.

The diverse situations examined show that: first, the degree of the competition between legal systems can differ, and thus the question of harmonization, and, moreover, that the individuals' behaviours can also be different. On the one hand, agents can have a behaviour of 'forum shopping': they select the rule or legal system they deem best meets their preferences and needs concerning a particular legal issue. However, on the other hand, in some situations individuals have to set up strategies, as 'race to the court' for instance.

3. EUROPEAN LEGAL INTEGRATION AND SITUATIONS OF LEGAL CHOICES

The purpose of this section is to investigate how the various elements we have insisted on can shed light on the evolution of law and justice in Europe. A first subsection describes briefly the legal and judicial structure in Europe, insisting on the two levels of legal competition and cooperation. And, then, the issue of European legal integration is examined.

Justice in Europe: National Legal Systems Coexisting with an Increasing Communitary Legal Order

The administration of justice in Europe seems particular as it is organized on two 'levels', national and European: national justices coexist with an increasing communitary legal order. Each member state has its own judicial and legal system, and a supranational legal system has been instituted, the Communitary Law. EC law is enforced by the European Court of Justice (ECJ) and also by the national courts because of the 'direct effect' of EC law[25]. With such a judicial and legal organization in Europe, two levels of regulatory competition and cooperation between courts can be identified. At the horizontal level, concerning the relations between the national courts, there is at one and the same time competition between courts of European member states and cooperation (mainly through convention and council regulations). And, at the vertical level, national tribunals and the ECJ can compete on judicial grounds, but they can also cooperate in some situations, mainly through the process of 'preliminary reference' (article 177 EC)[26]. Such a situation, that is the presence of cooperation and competition between national regulatory systems, is well summarized in the expression used by Arnaud A.-J. (1991): 'simultaneous *polysystem*', namely 'the simultaneous existence, sometimes in harmony, sometimes in confrontation, of several Laws applicable at the same time, in the same place to the same social group' (the translation is ours)[27].

[25] The ECJ proclaimed that doctrine of the 'direct effect' of EC law in the *Van Gend & Loos* v. *Nederlanse Administratie der Belastingen* decision (26/62, 1963, E.C.R.1).

[26] In the new notations of articles of the EC Treaty, the principle of 'preliminary reference' is stated by Article 234. For further analyses of the relationship between national courts and ECJ through the 'preliminary reference', see for example, Harnay and Vigouroux (2002).

[27] *'polysystémie simultanée ... l'existence simultanée, parfois dans l'harmonie, et parfois dans la confrontation, de plusieurs Droits applicables en même temps dans un même lieu à un même groupe social'* (Arnaud, 1991, p. 86).

Economic models of interjurisdictional competition mainly deal with the horizontal legal competition, that is the competitive relationship between national governmental units in the legal fields. Built on these analyses, our discussion concerns the horizontal level, the competition and cooperation between national judicial and legal systems in Europe.

Some Comments on the Process of Legal Integration in Europe

In this subsection, we intend to examine how the observations presented above can prove convenient in analysing the process of legal integration in Europe, a process that combines competition between national legal jurisdictions, cooperation of states in the regulatory realm and harmonization (imposed by the supranational level, through such means as European directives)[28]. More precisely, it deals with the following question: to what extent are member states involved in a process of regulatory competition? In other words, are the various legal fields affected in the same way by interjurisdictional competition? Various categories of legal fields can be differentiated regarding their features (in particular in terms of individual preferences) and their probable evolution (that is the process of legal evolution). Let us thus consider three main groups of legal fields.

First, in some specific fields of law, the integration can be realized through the competition process between national legal orders, because the agents can choose the rules that meet their needs and preferences. To use the terms of our typology, what is at stake are the legal issues for which individuals have 'stable' preferences and for which there is no uncertainty: it concerns corporate law, certain labour standards, pollution standards, etc. Firms search for a favourable legal environment (*ceteris paribus*) which permits them to maximize their gains and minimize their legal risks and costs. The competitive relationship between national systems in these legal fields corresponds to the typical case of regulatory competition models; the legal governmental units are encouraged to set up efficient rules to attract firms. But, as some legal competition theorists point out, this highly competitive relationship between jurisdictions (because of the assumed mobility of firms) can lead to a 'race to the bottom'. To some extent, competitive pressures force governments to adopt rules more in line with the interests and preferences of firms and which could prove inefficient. For instance, as labour standards can entail genuine costs for firms (for instance, minimum wage laws etc.), a government can be induced to lower these standards to attract business in its jurisdiction. Thus, in order to avoid such a race to the bottom and its adverse effects, a claim for

---

[28] We do not consider here the vertical competition and cooperation which take place between national courts and ECJ. Nevertheless, we recognize that this vertical regulatory relationship furthers the process of legal integration in Europe.

'minimum standards' arises: this justifies an imposed harmonization of some standards at the European level.

Besides, there are situations in which a dispute between two persons coming from two different states results in a 'conflict of laws'. We have pointed out above that in order to work competition needs some cooperation. Thus, in order to organize the coexistence of various national judicial and legal systems and the underlying competitive relations between them, the EC has favoured the setting up of Conventions and Council Regulations, in particular concerning competences, and the recognition and enforcement of foreign judicial decisions. For example, article 27 of the Brussels I Regulation of 22 December, 2000 deals with the allocation of 'adjudicatory' competences between courts involved in the same judicial case in civil and commercial matters[29]: '1. Where proceedings involving the same cause of action and between the same parties are brought in the courts of different Member States, any court other than the court first seized shall of its own motion stay its proceedings until such time as the jurisdiction of the court first seized is established; 2. Where the jurisdiction of the court first seized is established, any court other than the court first seized, shall decline jurisdiction in favour of that court'. In the same way, we can mention the Brussels II Regulation of 29 May, 2000,[30] concerning competence, recognition and enforcement of judicial decisions in matrimonial matters. This regulation is intended to resolve issues such as the divorce of bi-national couples and child custody issues. Therefore, in several legal matters (commercial matters, matrimonial matters and so forth), competition between legal rules in Europe requires cooperation between member states in regulatory fields.

Finally, let us consider fields of law (product liability standards, civil liability in cases of accidents, breach of contract law, etc.) for which an 'instability' of individual preferences according to the agent's status in a particular conflict is observed. As previously mentioned, legal competition cannot really operate, and thus the beneficial effects of competitive pressures cannot be achieved. Thus, the question remains: which evolution can be expected in these legal fields at the European level? In these domains, one could argue that legal integration has to be achieved through a process of harmonization. But new problems arise: who (or which authority) is competent to designate the rules that must be enforced by all the national jurisdictions, and how could these rules be designed? At present, communitary authorities have

---

[29] Council Regulation No. 44/2001 of 22 December, 2000, on jurisdiction and the recognition and enforcement of judgements in civil and commercial matters, entered into force on 1 March 2002. (Official Journal EC, 16/01/2001, L12/1-L12/23).

[30] Council Regulation No. 1347/2000 of 29 May, 2000, on jurisdiction and the recognition and enforcement of judgements in matrimonial matters and in matters of parental responsibility for children of both spouses, entered into force on 1 March, 2001. (Official Journal EC, 30/06/2000, L160/19-L160/36).

these competences, and then impose directives and other recommendations on member states.

The issue of legal integration in Europe can be approached differently in the various legal fields, insofar as the regulatory competition can take distinct forms, and thus the question of harmonization does not have the same importance according to legal matters[31]. Thus, there is no general model to describe the competition process in regulatory realm since diverse factors must be considered according to the legal fields affected by the legal integration.

CONCLUSION

For a few decades, the issue of *competition among rules and judicial systems* at the European level, and at the international level, has been of increasing interest to economists. Their economic analyses of such competition (also called *interjurisdictional competition* or *regulatory competition*) build on the insights of economic theories of federalism and Tiebout's approach to dealing with, on the one hand, the virtues of legal competition, and on the other with the failures of the 'market for legal products'. In this perspective, there is one question that deserves particular attention in our opinion: it concerns the behavioural features of the 'consumers of legal products' in such a competitive framework in the regulatory realm. Indeed, for most of the authors, the 'consumers of law', which are firms and private individuals, are assumed to select among the alternative sets of rules (products of each government) the one that best meets their preferences: in other words, they 'forum shop'. It has then proved to be essential to focus on this choice process, here labelled 'legal choice', and thus on the individual preferences in legal fields. Several aspects concerning these kinds of preferences have been brought to the fore, and more precisely their heterogeneity among persons and their possible 'instability' for individuals (preferences cannot be taken as given). These features, with the inter-individual relations, contribute to introduce uncertainty in legal problems, and thus in the individual legal choice process. On the basis of these comments, a 'typology' of cases of legal choice has been proposed to distinguish several degrees of regulatory competition, and thus of competition results. In so doing, we have then tried to introduce a new kind of limitation in the application of regulatory competition models[32]. We can add that the

---

[31] A further analysis would be necessary to verify the legal integration in each legal field to see if it corresponds, to some extent, to the situations described here.

[32] Esty and Geradin (2000), in a critique of 'the Tieboutian or Neo-tieboutian models of regulatory competition', list the following limitations of such models to show the failures of the 'market for regulation': externalities (or spill-overs), imperfect legal information, lack of mobility, economies of scale and transaction costs savings. (As mentioned, in our study we made assumptions concerning these aspects in order to concentrate on a specific dimension: uncertainty).

problem of uncertainty, due to the heterogeneity and the possible 'flexibility' of legal preferences (and thus the fact that they cannot be considered as given) also represents a 'limitation' of the models. In a final section, we have proposed an analysis of the European process of legal integration through this approach. In order to go further, it would be of particular interest to investigate the European context in detail in different legal fields.

REFERENCES

Antoniolli, Deflorian Luisa (1996), *La Struttura Istituzionale del Nuovo Diritto Comune Europeo: Competizione e Circolazione dei Modelli Giuridici*, Trento: Dipartimento di Scienze Giuridiche.

Arnaud, André-Jean (1991), *Pour une Pensée Juridique Européenne*, Les Voies du Droit, PUF.

Barrère, Christian (ed.) (2001), *La Qualité de la Justice. Une Analyse Economique Exploratoire*, report prepared for the GIP Mission de Recherche Droit et Justice, France.

Benson, Bruce L. (1990), *The Enterprise of Law. Justice without the State*, San Francisco, CA: Pacific Research Institute for Public Policy.

Brand, Ronald A. (1997), 'Recognition of foreign judgments as a trade law issue: the economics of private international law', in Alan O. Sykes and Jagdeep S. Blandari (eds), *Economic Dimensions in International Law. Comparative and Empirical Perspectives*, Cambridge University Press, 592–641.

Brennan Geoffrey and Alan Hamlin (1998), 'Fiscal federalism', in Peter Newman (ed), *The New Palgrave Dictionary of Economics and the Law*, Macmillan Press, tome 2, 144–150.

Buchanan, James M. (1965), 'An economic theory of clubs', *Economica*, **32**, 1-14.

Casella, Alessandra and Bruno S. Frey (1992), 'Federalism and clubs. Towards an economic theory of overlapping political jurisdictions', *European Economic Review*, **36**, 639–46.

Cooter, Robert D. and Daniel L. Rubinfeld (1989), 'Economic analysis of legal disputes and their resolution', *Journal of Economic Literature*, **28**, 1067–97.

Cooter, Robert D. and Thomas Ulen (1997), *Law and Economics*, Addison-Wesley Educational Publishers Inc., United States, 2nd edn.

Cooter, Robert D., Ugo Mattei, Pier Giuseppe Monateri, Roberto Pardolesi and Thomas Ulen (1998), *Il Mercato delle Regole. Analisi Economica del Diritto Civile*, Bologna: Il Mulino.

Dezalay, Yves (1995), 'Des justices du marché au marché international de la justice', *Justices, Revue Générale de Droit Processuel*, Janvier–Juin, **1**, 121–33.

Easterbrook, Frank H. (1994), 'Federalism and European business law', *International Review of Law and Economics*, **14**, 125–32.

Esty, Daniel C. and Damien Geradin (2000), 'Regulatory co-opetition', *Journal of International Economic Law*, **3**(2), 235–55.

Esty, Daniel C. and Damien Geradin (eds) (2001), *Regulatory Competition and Economic Integration: Comparative Perspectives*, Oxford: Oxford University Press.

Frey, Bruno S. and Reiner Eichenberger (1996a), 'FOCJ: Competitive Governments for Europe', *International Review of Law and Economics*, **16**(3), September, 315–27.

Frey, Bruno S. and Reiner Eichenberger (1996b), 'To harmonize or to compete? That's not the question', *Journal of Public Economics*, **60**, 335–49.

Frey, Bruno S. and Reiner Eichenberger (1999), *The New Democratic Federalism for Europe: Functional, Overlapping and Competing Jurisdictions*, Cheltenham, UK and Lyme, US: Edward Elgar.

Garcimartin Alferez, Francisco J. (1999), 'Regulatory competition: a private international law approach', *European Journal of Law and Economics*, **8**, 251–70.

Gerken, Luder (ed.) (1995), *Competition Among Institutions*, New York: St Martin's Press.

Harnay, Sophie and Isabelle Vigouroux (2002), 'Judicial competition, legal innovation and European integration: an economic analysis', in Alain Marciano and Jean-Michel Josselin (eds), *The Economics of Harmonizing European Law*, Cheltenham, UK: Edward Elgar, 87–100.

Herzog, Peter E. (1995), 'Brussels and Lugano, should you race to the courthouse or race for a judgment?', *American Journal of Comparative Law*, **43**(3) 379–99.

Inman, Robert P. and Daniel L. Rubinfeld (2000), 'Federalism', in Boudewijn Bouckaert and Gerrit De Geest (eds), *Encyclopedia of Law and Economics*, volume V *The Economics of Crime and Litigation*, Cheltenham: Edward Elgar, 661–91.

Isaac, Guy and Marc Blanquet (2001), *Droit Communautaire Général*, collection U, Armand Colin, 8ème édition.

Kerber, Wolfgang (2000), 'Interjurisdictional competition within the European Union', *Fordham International Law Journal*, **23**, 217–49.

Mattei, Ugo (1997), *Comparative Law and Economics*, Ann Arbor, MI: University of Michigan Press.

Mattli, Walter and Anne-Marie Slaughter (1996), 'Constructing the European Community legal system from the ground up: the role of individual litigants and national courts', Robert Schuman Centre working paper no. 96/56, European University Institute, Florence.

Mercuro, Nicholas and Steven G. Medema (1997), *Economics and the Law. From Posner to Post-Modernism*, Princeton, NJ: Princeton University Press.

Ministère de la Justice (1999), *L'Espace Judiciaire Européen*, Actes de Colloque d'Avignon (du 16 octobre 1998), Paris: La Documentation Française.

Ogus, Anthony (1999), 'Competition between national legal systems: a contribution of economic analysis to comparative law', *International and Comparative Law Quarterly*, **48**, 405–18.

Ogus, Anthony (2000), 'Legal culture as a (natural?) monopoly', in Alain Marciano and Jean-Michel Josselin (eds), *The Economics of Harmonizing European Law*, Cheltenham, UK: Edward Elgar, 71–86.

O'Hara, Erin Ann and Larry E. Ribstein (2000), 'Conflict of laws and choice of law', in Boudewijn Bouckaert and Gerrit De Geest (eds), *Encyclopedia of Law and Economics*, volume V *The Economics of Crime and Litigation*, Cheltenham: Edward Elgar, 631–60.

Olson, Mancur Jr. (1969), 'Principle of fiscal equivalence: the division of responsibilities among different levels of governments', *American Economic Review*, papers and proceedings, **59**, 479–87.

Parisi, Francesco and Erin Ann O'Hara (1998), 'Conflict of laws', in Peter Newman (ed), *The New Palgrave Dictionary of Economics and the Law*, Macmillan Press, tome 1, 387–96.

Polinsky, A. Mitchell (1989), *An Introduction to Law and Economics*, 2nd edn, Boston, MA: Little, Brown and Company.

Posner, Richard A. (1992), *Economic Analysis of Law*, 4th edn, Boston, MA: Little, Brown and Company.

Rebba, Vincenzo (1998), 'Dalla teoria dei beni pubblici locali al federalismo funzionale', *Economia Politica*, **XV**, 2, 333–97.

Schmidtchen, Dieter and Robert C. Cooter (eds) (1997), *Constitutional Law and Economics of the European Union*, Cheltenham, UK and Lyme, US: Edward Elgar.

Smits, Jan M. (2002), 'How to predict the differences in uniformity between different areas of a future European Law? An evolutionary approach', in Alain Marciano and Jean-Michel Josselin (eds), *The Economics of Harmonizing European Law*, Aldershot, UK: Edward Elgar, 50–70.

Sykes, Alan O. (2000), 'Regulatory competition or regulatory harmonization? A silly question?', *Journal of International Economic Law*, **3**(2), 257–64.

Tiebout, Charles M. (1956), 'A pure theory of local expenditures', *Journal of Political Economy*, **64**, 416–24.

Trachtman, Joel P. (2000), 'Regulatory competition and regulatory jurisdictions', *Journal of International Economic Law*, **3**(2), 331–48.

Vanberg Viktor (2000), 'Globalization, democracy and citizens' sovereignty: can competition among governments enhance democracy?', *Constitutional Political Economy*, **11**, 87–112.

Vanberg, Viktor and Wolfgang Kerber (1994), 'Institutional competition among jurisdictions: an evolutionary approach', *Constitutional Political Economy*, **5**(2), 193–219.

Van Den Bergh, Roger (2002), 'Towards a legal framework for regulatory competition: how to make competition between legal orders work?', in Alain Marciano and Jean-Michel Josselin (eds), *The Economics of Harmonizing European Law*, Cheltenham, UK: Edward Elgar, 27–49.

Woolcock, Stephen (1994), *The Single European Market: Centralization or Competition Among National Rules?*, London: The Royal Institute of International Affairs, European Programme.

3. Harmonization of environmental liability legislation in the European Union

Michael Faure and Kristel De Smedt

INTRODUCTION

In the last decade, the European Union was confronted with cases of severe damage to the environment caused by human activities. The accident in Romania where cyanide caused severe pollution of the Tisza river and the incident, a few years ago, near the Doñana nature reserve in the South of Spain, are only two examples of cases where human activities have resulted in substantial damage to the environment.

A growing interest in a harmonized environmental liability regime could therefore be observed at European level. Up to now, the environmental acquis does not provide in European legislation, either by directive or by regulation, for liability for damage caused to the environment. The member states of the European Union have established national environmental liability regimes that cover damage to persons and goods, and they have introduced laws to deal with liability for, and clean-up of, contaminated sites. However, according to the European Commission, these national regimes have not addressed the issue of liability for damage to nature. Damage to the environment has traditionally been seen as a 'public good' for which society as a whole should be responsible and bear the costs, rather than the individual perpetrator who actually caused the damage.

In February 2000, the European Commission issued the 'White Paper on Environmental Liability'[33]. This White Paper outlines the Commission's view on the key elements of a future environmental liability directive. The proposed regime should not only cover damage to persons and goods and contamination of sites, but also damage to nature. The proposed regime addresses especially those natural resources that are important for the conservation of biological diversity in the Community, namely the areas and species protected under the

[33] Commission of the European Communities, White Paper on Environmental Liability, *COM* (2000) 66 final, Brussels, 9 February 2000.

Natura 2000 network. With the introduction of liability for damage to nature as proposed in the White Paper, the Commission expects to bring about a change of attitude that should result in an increased level of prevention and precaution by European industry. Furthermore, the Commission estimates that a liability legislation would improve the implementation of existing EC environmental laws and the decontamination and the restoration of the environment[34]. On 30 July 2001, the Commission went a step further in the process towards a European liability directive by issuing a 'Working Document on the Prevention and Restoration of Significant Environmental Damage[35]'. The Working Document has been prepared for consultation by the member states and other interested parties and is to a large extent based on the environmental liability regime as proposed in the White Paper. Furthermore, there seems to be an increased emphasis on the duty to clean-up and prevention. Meanwhile, this working document has resulted in a formal draft directive. As this chapter was edited prior to this action, the arguments will mostly refer to the White Paper; however, the reasoning would be the same for the draft directive.

These developments at European level gave rise to this contribution. From a theoretical point of view we will examine whether harmonization of environmental liability legislation is desirable. The question that will be addressed in particular in this contribution is whether there are economic reasons for a harmonization of the environmental liability legislation in the European Union. To answer this question, the literature on the optimal level of regulation within federal systems will be used. It should be clear that this article does not deal with the question concerning the need for environmental regulation. That is undisputed. It should also be mentioned that our chapter does not provide an assessment on the proposed liability regime in the White Paper or the draft directive. It merely examines whether harmonization of environmental liability legislation in the European Union is desirable from a theoretical point of view and uses the White Paper as a case study. In that respect, the arguments brought forward by the Commission will be examined, in particular the traditional European argument of harmonization of conditions of competition, for the functioning of the internal market and compared with our theoretical framework.

The structure of the chapter is as follows: section 1 provides firstly a brief review of the foundations of European environmental policy and the background of the White Paper. Secondly, the arguments of the Commission for harmonizing environmental liability are presented. Then, section 2 discusses criteria for (de)centralization, using the literature on federalism. Section 3 applies this theory to the arguments brought forward by the Commission in

---

[34] White Paper, 5 (foreword), 7 (executive summary).
[35] The document is available on the website of DG Environment: http://europa.eu. int/comm/environment/liability/consulation.htm

its White Paper and section 4 completes this analysis by providing an inter-est-group perspective. Section 5 formulates some policy recommendations and a few concluding remarks will be made.

1. ENVIRONMENTAL LIABILITY AT EUROPEAN LEVEL

European Environmental Policy: Harmonization of Conditions of Competition

The origins of environmental legislation in Europe can be traced to the Paris Summit Meeting of the Heads of States in 1972. At that meeting, the member state leaders supported the idea of a common European environmental policy. By that time the EC had become more than a pure economic cooperation and was aware of social and environmental problems. Consequently, the European Union has drafted a series of Environmental Action Programmes, extending for a four- to five-year period. These programmes can be seen as political 'mission statements' and identify the goals and priorities for European en-vironmental legislation. On that basis, the European Union has worked out a fairly elaborate body of environmental law, in particular by means of direc-tives. On 24 January 2001, the Sixth Environmental Action Programme was published[36]. New environmental priorities include enlargement to the East and environmental liability legislation, which is the subject of this contribution.

The European Commission has given a variety of reasons for legislative action at the European level with respect to environmental law. Although most direc-tives tend to have multiple reasons for their adoption[37], the most important are:

- The *transboundary nature of the environmental problem* to be dealt with. Several directives refer to the transboundary character of the pollution to argue for regulation at the European level. This is the case with, for instance, the directive dealing with the discharge of dangerous substances into the aquatic environment[38].
- The creation of *equal conditions of competition*. It is argued that harmo-nizing conditions of competition is necessary for the functioning of the

---

[36] Communication from the Commission to the Council, the European Parliament, the Economic and Social Committee and the Committee of the Regions on the sixth environmental action programme of the European Community 'Environment 2010: Our Future, Our Choice', COM (2001) 31 final, Brussels, 24 January 2001.

[37] For further details, see Van den Bergh, R., Faure, M. and Lefevere, J., 'The subsidiarity prin-ciple in European environmental law: an economic analysis', in Eide, E. and Van den Bergh, R. (eds), *Law and Economics of the Environment*, Oslo, Jurdisk Forlag, 1996, 128-31.

[38] Directive 76/464, Discharge of Dangerous Substances into the Aquatic Environment, *OJ*, 1976, L 129/23.

internal market. This argument, which is often referred to as the need to create a 'level playing field' for industry in Europe, is not only used in environmental law, but is advanced to harmonize any kind of legislation within Europe[39]. The directive on discharges of dangerous substances into the aquatic environment, mentioned above, was also based on this 'harmonization of conditions of competition' argument. It was argued that disparity between the provisions on discharge might create unequal conditions of competition and thus directly affect the functioning of the internal market[40].

– A third reason advanced for European action with respect to environmental matters can be called a purely 'ecological' one. There are a number of environmental directives that aim at the protection of the 'European environmental and cultural heritage and human health'. An example is the habitats directive[41].

The justifications mentioned above were also brought forward by the Commission in the White Paper in its argumentation in favour of a European environmental liability legislation. According to the subsidiarity principle, the 'community shall take action if and only in so far as the objectives of the proposed action cannot be sufficiently achieved by the member states and can, therefore, by reason of the scale or effects of the proposed action, be better achieved by the community[42]'. Therefore, the Commission had to justify in the White Paper that environmental liability could not effectively be dealt with by the member states. The Commission accordingly devotes special attention in the White Paper to the subsidiarity issue and the need for a harmonized environmental liability legislation[43].

In its paragraph on subsidiarity, the Commission states: 'the EC Treaty requires Community policy on the environment to contribute to preserving, protecting and improving the quality of the environment, and to protecting human health (Article 174(1)). This policy must also aim at a high level of

---

[39] Also the European Directive on Product Liability of 25 July 1985 was justified on the grounds that differing liability rules in the member states would hamper the conditions of competition. The considerations preceding the directive read: 'Whereas approximation of the laws of the member states concerning the liability of the producer for damage caused by the defectiveness of his products is necessary because the existing divergences may distort competition and affect the movement of goods within the common market . . .'.

[40] The same argument was made concerning other directives as well; see Van den Bergh, R., Faure, M. and Lefevere, J., 'The subsidiarity principle in European environmental law: an economic analysis,' in Eide, E. and Van den Bergh, R. (eds), *Law and Economics of the Environment*, Oslo, Jurdisk Forlag, 1996, 129.

[41] Directive 92/43, *OJ*, 192, L 206/7.

[42] Article 5 EC Treaty. See on the issue of subsidiarity also Kimber, C., 'A comparison of environmental federalism in the United States and the European Union', 54, *Maryland Law Review*, 1995, 321–26.

[43] White Paper, § 6, 28.

protection, taking into account the diversity of situations in the various regions of the Community. It shall be based on the precautionary principle and on the principle that preventive action should be taken, that environmental damage should as a priority be rectified at source and that the polluter should pay (Article 174(2))'.

According to the Commission, these principles are currently not being implemented in an optimal way throughout the Community. One reason the Commission provides for this is that there is a gap in most member states' liability regimes concerning bio-diversity damage. Moreover, national legislation cannot effectively cover issues of transboundary environmental damage within the Community, which may affect, among others, watercourses and habitats, many of which straddle frontiers. Therefore, the Commission concludes that an EC-wide regime is necessary in order to avoid inadequate solutions to transfrontier damage. An EC regime should aim at fixing the objectives and results, but the member states should have freedom to choose the ways and instruments to achieve these.

This chapter will attempt to critically address the possible meaning of these reasons for legislative action at the European level from an economic point of view. We will critically analyse these arguments of the Commission to justify European competences in the remainder of this chapter. Let us first turn to the goal and contents of the White Paper on environmental liability.

White Paper on Environmental Liability

Purpose and history
In February 2000, the European Commission issued the long-awaited White Paper on Environmental Liability[44]. In the White Paper the Commission describes its view on the key elements of a future environmental liability directive. In the Commission's opinion, such a directive would improve the implementation of the EC Treaty's grand principles of environmental policy incorporated in the EC Treaty (Article 174(2)), the preventive, precautionary and polluter pays principles. Furthermore it would improve the enforcement of existing EC environmental laws, ensure decontamination and restoration of the environment, better integration of the environment into other policy areas and improved functioning of the internal market. Liability should enhance incentives for more responsible behaviour by firms and thus exert a preventive effect[45].

---

[44] Commission of the European Communities, White Paper on Environmental Liability, *COM* (2000) 66 final, Brussels, 9 February 2000. See also L. Bergkamp, 'The White Paper on environmental liability', *European Environmental Law Review* (EELR), April 2000, 105 and P.E.A. Bierbooms and E.H.P. Brans, 'Het EU Witboek Milieuaansprakelijkheid: de vage contouren van een toekomstig aansprakelijkheidsregime', *Milieu & Recht*, July/augustus 2000 no 7/8.

[45] White Paper, executive summary, 7.

It took the Commission more than a decade before a proposal on an Environmental Liability Directive could be presented[46]. In 1989, the Commission proposed a directive dealing only with liability for damage caused by waste[47]; however, the proposal was quickly abandoned. The Commission subsequently started to examine a broader liability regime covering environmental damage. In 1993, the Commission published a Green Paper on Remedying Environmental Damage[48], which presented some of the broad notions on which an EC liability regime could be based and which was intended to initiate a public debate. For a short time, the Commission played with the idea of the EC joining the 1993 Council of Europe Lugano Convention, but this approach was rejected. According to the Commission the main differences between a Community directive and Community accession to the Lugano Convention are that the scope of Community action can be better delimited and the regime for bio-diversity damage can be better elaborated, in accordance with the relevant Community legislation. Both differences result in more legal certainty than provided by the Lugano Convention. However, even if the Community does not accede to the Lugano Convention, the latter could provide an important source of inspiration for a future Community directive[49].

In November 1997, the Commission issued a working paper on environmental liability[50]. Compared with this paper, the White Paper finally published in February 2000 is somewhat less ambitious and leaves more issues open for further debate. Although the publication of a White Paper is already a more formal step towards EU legislation, it does not provide any guarantee that a directive will be finally adopted. Nevertheless, for this contribution, we will take the provisions of the White Paper as given and use it as a tool to test the economic theory of federalism. Indeed, as we indicated in the introduction, the White Paper has meanwhile resulted in a working document and a subsequent draft directive. However, since the White Paper concerns the most interesting, arguments from the perspective of the economies of federalism, we will use this White Paper as a basis for our analysis.

[46] Bergkamp L., note above, 105 to 106 and P.E.A. Bierbooms and E.H.P. Brans.

[47] Proposal for a Directive on civil liability for damage caused by waste, *OJ* C 251/3 (1989); as amended COM (91) final *OJ* C 192/6 (23.07.91).

[48] Green Paper on Remedying Environmental Damage, *COM* (93) 47 final, Brussels, 14 May 1993.

[49] White Paper, § 5.1, 25.

[50] Commission of the European Communities, Working Paper on Environmental Liability, Brussels, 17 November 1997. For a comment on this draft see e.g. Bergkamp, L., 'A future environmental liability regime', *European Environmental Law Review*, 1998, 200–204 and De Vries, C., 'Community action on environmental liability', in Wiggers-Rust, L. and Deketelaere, K. (eds.) *Aansprakelijkheid voor milieuschade en financiële zekerheid*, Die Keure-Vermande, 1999, 141–47.

Main principles of the White Paper

The Commission suggests that an EC liability regime should be based on Article 175 of the Treaty. In accordance also with the subsidiarity and proportionality principles, the directive should be a framework regime containing essential minimum requirements[51]. This framework directive could be completed over time with other elements that might appear necessary on the basis of the experience gathered with its application during the initial period, called the *step-by-step approach.*

The main features of the proposed liability regime that the Commission outlines in its White Paper are:

- A regime that would not have retroactive effects (application to future damage only). The exclusion of the retroactivity is justified by reasons of legal certainty and legitimate expectation.
- Since the protection of health is also an important environmental objective, and for reasons of coherence, the proposed EC regime should cover both traditional damage (harm to health and property) and environmental damage (site contamination and damage to bio-diversity), which is currently not sufficiently covered by the member states.
- The Commission proposes that contaminated sites and traditional damage are only to be covered if caused by an EC-regulated hazardous or potentially hazardous activity. Damage to bio-diversity will only be covered if the area or species are protected by the Natura 2000 network. These protected areas are or have to be designated by the member states under the Wild Birds Directive of 1979 and the Habitats Directive of 1992. Since many habitats and waterways straddle frontiers between member states, the EC regime would also apply to transboundary damage.
- The EC regime should be based on strict liability (this means that no fault by the polluter is required), when damage is caused by inherently dangerous activities, and fault-based liability for damage to bio-diversity caused by a non-dangerous activity.

[51] For comments on this White Paper see e.g. Betlem, G., 'Commission adopts White Paper on environmental liability', *TMA*, 2000, 58–60 and Bierbooms, P.F.A. and Brans, E.H.P., 'Het EU witboek milieu-aansprakelijkheid: de vage contouren van een toekomstig aansprakelijkheidsregime', *Milieu & Recht*, 2000, 182–88 and Rice, P., 'From Lugano to Brussels via Arhus: environmental liability white paper published', *Environmental Liability*, 2000, 39–45. For the reason that with respect to some issues (e.g. causation or defences) no firm decisions have been taken yet Rehbinder is rather critical of the White Paper. He hopes for 'major improvement of the proposal' (see Rehbinder, E., 'Towards a community environmental liability regime: the Commission's White Paper on environmental liability', *Environmental Liability*, 2000, 85–96); others are critical with respect to the proposals on action rights of NGO's, Hunter, R., 'European Commission White Paper proposals on NGO rights of action: wrongful rights of action', *Tijdschrift voor Milieu-aansprakelijkheid*, 2000, 125–26.

In summary, the White Paper suggests that the most appropriate option for a harmonized environmental liability regime would be a framework directive providing for strict liability for damage caused by EC-regulated dangerous activities, with defences, covering both traditional and environmental damage, and fault-based liability for damage to bio-diversity caused by non-dangerous activities.

Arguments for harmonization advanced in the White Paper

According to the subsidiarity principle (art. 5 of the Treaty), in areas where the EC does not have exclusive competence for jurisdiction, such as environment and hence environmental liability, the EC has to justify why it is in a better position than the member states to set policy or legislation on a specific issue. Thorough review of the White Paper reveals six arguments for harmonization brought forward by the Commission in its introduction, its paragraphs 3, 5 and 6[52]. After discussion of the literature on federalism in section 2, the arguments made will be reviewed in section 3. Let us first reiterate, in more detail[53], the arguments which the Commission uses to justify European action with respect to environmental liability.

Transfrontier damage

In the introduction to the White Paper, the Commission already indicates that harmonization should be accepted under the subsidiarity principle, as the member states cannot adequately deal with transboundary environmental pollution. Paragraph 6 of the White Paper dealing specifically with the subsidiarity issue states that a directive would be necessary 'to avoid inadequate solutions to transfrontier damage'[54]. The Commission firmly states that national legislation cannot effectively cover transboundary environmental damage as various watercourses and protected habitats cross the borders of the member states.

Polluter pays principle

Paragraph three deals with the advantages and hence the necessity of a European environmental liability legislation. First, the polluter pays principle is brought forward. In the Commission's view, the proposed liability regime would realize the three grand environmental principles enshrined in Art 174 (2) of the EC Treaty: the polluter pays, precautionary and preventive principles. In particular, liability is viewed as a way of making the polluter pay. 'If

---

[52] Bergkamp, L., 'The White Paper on environmental liability', *European Environmental Law Review*, 2000, 106.

[53] The arguments were briefly introduced above.

[54] White Paper, § 6, 28.

polluters need to pay for damage caused, they will cut back pollution up to the point where the marginal cost of abatement exceeds the compensation avoided'[55]. The European Commission obviously refers to the economic theory of cost internalization. As a firm will always try to minimize its total costs, forcing the polluter to internalize the costs of pollution resulting from production, obliging him to pay for the damage would result in more precaution and hence in prevention of environmental harm. Furthermore the Commission believes that it may encourage investment in research and development (R&D) for improving knowledge and technologies.

Decontamination and restoration of the environment and better implementation
In its plea for an EC environmental liability regime, the Commission raises two further arguments. A liability legislation would ensure decontamination and restoration of the environment and boost the implementation of, and compliance with, EC environmental legislation[56].

Creating a level playing field
As the next argument, the Commission explains that an EC regime 'may contribute to creating a level playing field in the internal market'[57]. From this statement, it seems that the Commission believes that differences in the various national regimes may result in cost differences and thus in competitive advantages for companies in member states with lax environmental liability regimes.

Principle of equal treatment
Finally, an argument that is rather hidden in paragraph 5.2, deals with the principle of equal treatment. Following the argument of transfrontier damage, the Commission argues that a regime dealing exclusively with cross-border harm 'would leave a serious gap where liability for bio-diversity damage is concerned'. This could have as a consequence that purely national and cross-border cases will be treated differently, which could possibly violate the principle of equal treatment developed by the European Court of Justice[58].

We will now immediately turn to the economic approach by addressing the question: what does economics generally teach about the necessity of harmonization? The remainder of the chapter will deal with the question whether harmonization of environmental liability is necessary from an economic point

---

[55] White Paper, § 3.1, 14.
[56] White Paper, §§ 3.2–3.3, 14.
[57] White Paper, § 3.5, 15.
[58] White Paper, § 5.2, 25.

of view. We will first present the economic criteria of centralization and apply these to environmental legislation generally. These criteria have been developed in the context of the discussion concerning (de)centralization. Then we will apply these criteria to the issue of environmental liability by applying them to the just mentioned arguments the European Commission advanced in the White Paper to defend its intervention in the area of environmental liability.

2.　IS HARMONIZATION NEEDED?: CRITERIA FOR (DE)CENTRALIZATION

Bottom-up Federalism of Tiebout

The question whether regulation should be organized at central (European or federal) level or at a more decentralized level (or, to put it in a more balanced way, what kind of regulations should be set at which level) has been addressed in the economics of federalism[59]. The starting point for the analysis is usually the theory of Tiebout about the optimal provision of local public goods[60]. Tiebout argued that when people with the same preferences cluster together in communities competition between local authorities will, under certain restrictive conditions, lead to allocative efficiency. If there are for example in one community citizens with a high preference for sporting facilities and in another one a majority of citizens with a preference for opera, the first community will probably construct sporting facilities, whereas the second will probably provide an opera house. If someone living in the second community would prefer sporting facilities instead of the opera house, he could then move to the first community, which apparently provides services that better suit his preferences. The idea is that well-informed citizens will move to the community that provides the local services that are best adapted to their personal preferences. Through this so-called 'voting with the feet' competition between local authorities will lead citizens to cluster together according to their preferences. In practice one notices that different communities do indeed offer a variety of different

---

[59] This chapter is based on earlier research, see Faure, M., 'Regulatory competition versus harmonization in EU environmental law', in Esty, D. and Geradin, D. (eds), *Regulatory Competition and Economic Integration,* Oxford, Oxford University Press, 2001, 263–86 and see Faure, M., 'Product liability and product safety in Europe: harmonization or differentiation?', *Kyklos,* vol. 53, 2000, 467–508.

[60] Tiebout, C. (1956), 'A pure theory of local government expenditures', *Journal of Political Economy,* 60, 415–24. For a discussion of this theory, see Rose-Ackerman, S., *Rethinking the Progressive Agenda: the Reform of the American Regulatory State,* 1992, 169–70.

services. The idea is that the citizen can influence this provision of local public goods either by influencing the decision-making (vote) or by moving (exit).

This basic idea applies not only to community services, but also, for example, to fiscal decisions[61], environmental choices[62] and even legal rules. It has been argued by Van den Bergh (1994) that competition between legislators will lead to legal systems competing with each other to provide legislation that corresponds best to the preferences of their citizens. Also Ogus (1999) argued that the various lawmakers in the nation-states would create competitive markets for the supply of law.

The idea therefore is that in an optimal world citizens will cluster together in states that provide legal rules that correspond to their preferences. Well-informed citizens, who may be dissatisfied with the legislation provided, could move (voting with the feet) to the community that provides legislation that corresponds best to their preferences. This idea, assuming that those different legal systems offer different legal rules thus explains the variety and differences between the legal systems (Van den Bergh 1998). Moreover, it also shows that differences between the various legal rules of different countries should not necessarily be judged as negative, as is often the case in Europe today. The idea of competing legal systems can probably best be seen 'in action' in international private law where actors can chose the legal systems that best suits their needs in a choice of law regime[63].

Obviously, assuming that competition between legal orders leads to allocative efficiency in the provision of legal rules works only if certain conditions are met. One condition is that citizens have adequate information on the contents of the legal rules provided by the various legislators, in order to be able to make an informed choice. In addition, exit if often costly, so people may stay even if the (legal) regime does not suit their needs optimally[64]. Moreover, a location decision is obviously made under the influence of a set

---

[61] See e.g. Inman, R.P. and Rubinfeld, D.L., 'The EMU and fiscal policy in the new European community, an issue for economic federalism', *International Review of Law and Economics,* vol. 14, 1994, 147–62; Kirchgässner, G. and Pommerehne, W.W., 'Low-cost decisions as a challenge to public choice', *Public Choice,* vol. 77, 1993, 107–16 and Oates, W.E., *Fiscal Federalism,* New York, Harcourt, 1972.

[62] See Oates, W.E. and Schwab, R., 'Economic competition among jurisdiction: efficiency enhancing or distortion inducing?', *Journal of Public Economics,* 1988, vol. 35, 333–54.

[63] Although the choice for a particular legal regime may not always be related to the quality of the legal system but, for example, to the quality of the court or arbitration system. The latter explains, according to Ogus, A., 'Competition between national legal systems: a contribution of economic analysis to comparative law', *International and Comparative Law Quarterly,* vol. 48, 1999, 408, the popularity of English law in choice of law clauses in contracts.

[64] As Ogus, A., 'Competition between national legal systems: a contribution of economic analysis to comparative law', *International and Comparative Law Quarterly,* vol. 48, 1999, 407, states there should be no barriers to the freedom of establishment and to the movement of capital.

of criteria, whereby the legal regime may not be decisive[65]. Usually the job location and residence are so important that in reality there is often little left for people to choose[66]. Finally, as we will discuss below, this system of competition between legal orders works only if the decisions in one legal order have no external effects on others.

In economic literature, this Tiebout model is used to argue that, from an economic point of view, decentralization should be the starting point, since competition between legislators will lead to allocative efficiency. Van den Bergh (1994) uses this theory as well to provide criteria for centralization/decentralization within the European Union. Taking Tiebout as a starting point and assuming that competition between decentralized legislators will lead to an optimal provision of legal rules, the central question is: why centralize?

Van den Bergh therefore criticizes a part of the current discussion in the European legal literature, which seems to focus on the question why there should be decentralization (referred to by Van den Bergh as 'top-down federalization'). According to economic theory, that is the wrong question. Starting from Tiebout's model, there is reason to believe in what Van den Bergh calls a 'bottom-up federalization', assuming that in principle the local level is optimal, since the local level has the best information on local problems and on the preferences of citizens. Only when there is a good reason, should decision-making be moved to a higher level. Economic theory has indeed suggested that there may be a variety of reasons why the local level is not best suited to take decisions and where central decision-making can lead to more efficient results.

These criteria for centralization will now be applied to environmental liability. In particular, these criteria will provide information on whether a harmonized European environmental liability regime might be required.

Reasons for Centralization

Transboundary character of the externality
The Tiebout argument in favour of competition between local communities obviously works only if the problem to be regulated is indeed merely local.

---

[65] That is one of the reasons why Frey, B., 'FOCJ: competitive governments for Europe', *International Review of Law and Economics,* vol. 16, 1996, 315–27 and Frey, B. and Eichenberger, R., 'To harmonize or to compete? That's not the question', *Journal of Public Economics*, 1996, vol. 60, 441–58, argue in favour of FOCJ: the choice for one legal or institutional regime should not be exclusive; there may be 'overlapping' jurisdictions depending upon the different functions.

[66] Rose-Ackerman, S., *Rethinking the Progressive Agenda: the Reform of the American Regulatory State*, New York, Free Press, 1992, 169.

Once it is established that the problem to be regulated has a transboundary character, there may be an economics-of-scale argument to shift powers to a higher legal order that has competence to deal with the externality over a larger territory. This corresponds with the basic insight that if the problem to regulate crosses the borders of competence of the regulatory authority, the decision-making power should be shifted to a higher regulatory level, preferably to an authority which has jurisdiction over a territory large enough to adequately deal with the problem[67].

This argument in favour of centralization could play a role with respect to environmental problems. It can be argued that these are certainly often transboundary[68]. The transboundary character of an externality is, within the European context, obviously an important argument for decision-making at the European level. Indeed, many environmental problems cross national borders. A great many of the environmental directives fit into this economic criterion for community action. These include the regulation on the transboundary shipment of waste[69], as well as many other directives, which regulate pollution of a transboundary character[70].

Nevertheless the most important reason for community action with respect to the environment is therefore probably not the often-stated argument of the harmonization of conditions of competition, but simply the transboundary character of the pollution problem to be regulated. Many of the environmental directives indeed deal with pollution problems, which cross the borders of one single member state. They can therefore be justified under this first economic criterion. This does obviously not necessarily imply that the contents of every directive on this point has been efficient, nor that the instruments used to cure transboundary pollution have always been optimal.

However, some have warned that the argument that centralized powers are necessary to deal with transboundary problems should not be accepted too

---

[67] Compare: Ogus, A., 'Competition between national legal systems: a contribution of economic analysis to comparative law', *International and Comparative Law Quarterly,* vol. 48, 1999, 414 and Kimber, C., 'A comparison of environmental federalism in the United States and the European Union', 54, *Maryland Law Review,* 1995; Esty, D., *Revitalizing Environmental Federalism,* 95 *Michigan Law Review,* 1996, 625 and Rose-Ackerman, S., *Rethinking the Progressive Agenda: the Reform of the American Regulatory State,* New York, Free Press, 1992, 164–65. See also Arcuri, A., 'Controlling environmental risk in Europe: the complementary role of an EC environmental liability regime', *Tijdschrift voor Milieuaansprakelijkheid,* 2001, 41–42.

[68] See equally Oates, W. and Schwab, R., 'Economic competition among jurisdiction: efficiency enhancing or distortion inducing?', *Journal of Public Economics,* 1988, vol. 35, who also argue that as long as the effects of pollutants are confined within the borders of the relevant jurisdictions, local authorities will make socially optimal decisions of environmental quality.

[69] Regulation 259/93 of 1 February 1993, *OJ*, 1993, L 30.

[70] This is certainly the case as well for Directive 76/464 on the Discharge of Dangerous Substances into the Aquatic Environment. For other examples, see Van den Bergh, R., Faure, M. and Lefevere, J., 131–32.

easily. First, Esty and Geradin have powerfully argued against an 'all or nothing' approach, meaning either all powers with the local authorities or shifting all powers to the central level. They have argued that the transboundary pollution problems can be dealt with via other legal instruments than centralization, in other words via instruments which do not involve a change of the national environmental laws of a particular country[71]. One possibility is the external application of (domestic) high-standard country laws. Another one is the national enforcement of domestic laws with cross-border monitoring. In other words: the transboundary character of the externality may be an argument for cooperation, not necessarily for homogeneity of legal rules. However, Esty and Geradin admit that these alternative approaches have serious limitations as well and might not be effective remedies in all cases[72].

Second, Cohen argued that Coasean bargaining between the polluting and the victim state may lead to negotiated agreements between them[73]. Therefore, Cohen argues that there is no a priori reason to centralize regulatory decision-making[74]. There might, however, be several reasons why the ideal solution from Coase's world might not be possible to solve transboundary pollution problems, e.g. in case of transboundary rivers such as the Rhine or the Meuse. Coase assumes that property rights are clearly defined[75]. Although there are some indications in international environmental law on this point, it might not be certain what the legal rule is: right to pollute or polluter pays. This uncertainty concerning the assignment of property rights might endanger negotiations. In addition, adequate information is needed both on the consequences of pollution and on the possible abatement techniques[76] and moreover, there may be no strategic behaviour. Also, parties need to have the possibility to enforce a negotiated agreement. In that respect the EC framework might have several

---

[71] See Esty, D. and Geradin, D., 'Environmental protection and international competitiveness. A conceptual framework', 32/3 *Journal of World Trade*, 1998, 5–46 and see Esty, D. and Geradin, D., 'Market access, competitiveness and harmonization: environmental protection in regional trade agreements', 21 *Harvard Environmental Law Review*, 1997, 265–336 in which they provide an interesting overview of the various legal instruments to deal with harmonization and apply this in the NAFTA and in the European context. See also Trebilcock, M. and Howse, R., 'Trade liberalization and regulatory diversity, reconciling competitive markets with competitive politics', *European Journal of Law and Economics*, vol. 6, 1998, 5–37.

[72] Esty, D. and Geradin, D., 'Environmental protection and international competitiveness. A conceptual framework', 32/3 *Journal of World Trade*, 1998, 34–35.

[73] See also Van den Bergh, R., 'Economics in a legal strait-jacket: the difficult reception of economic analysis in European law' (paper presented at the workshop Empirical Research and Legal Realism. Setting the Agenda, Haifa, 6–9 June 1999).

[74] Cohen, M., 'Commentary', in Eide, E. and Van den Bergh, R. (eds), *Law and Economics of the Environment*, Oslo, Juridisk Forlag, 1996, 167–71.

[75] Which Cohen, M., 'Commentary', in Eide, E. and Van den Bergh, R. (eds), *Law and Economics of the Environment*, Oslo, Juridisk Forlag, 1996, 168–69, mentions as well.

[76] Cohen, M., 'Commentary', in Eide, E. and Van den Bergh, R. (eds), *Law and Economics of the Environment*, Oslo, Juridisk Forlag, 1996, 168.

advantages. The EC offers an institutional framework that provides legal instruments to enforce an agreement. Moreover, the EC regulatory framework might fix the property rights. Also, the fact that member states within the EC framework are repeat players (an injurer today may be a victim tomorrow) may eliminate the risk of strategic behaviour. If one also looks at the practice of transboundary pollution in Europe, one may argue that indeed the EC approach has achieved far better results so far than all the attempts towards bilateral agreements. EC directives on (transboundary) pollution of waters provided Dutch victims of Belgian pollution of the river Meuse with a powerful tool to force the Belgians to pollution abatement[77], a result which could probably never have been achieved through the long-lasting negotiations between the two countries. Thus, the EC has undoubtedly played an important role as far as providing remedies against transboundary pollution is concerned.

However, Van den Bergh has demonstrated that in some cases, more particularly in the area of private law, European law cannot be considered an effective remedy to the interstate externality problem[78]. In some cases European law goes further than is needed to cure transboundary externalities; in other cases less far-reaching legal instruments than total harmonization could be used to remedy the problem[79]. There is, in other words, always the risk that the cure may be worse than the disease. The first issue relates to the problem that European Directives often cover both local and community wide pollution, without making a distinction between regional and interstate pollution[80]. The second point is that in some cases transboundary externalities may also be internalized by national law. The simple fact of transboundary effects is therefore not sufficient to justify European lawmaking[81]. Nevertheless, there can indeed be cases where one can hold that decentralized legal rule making will not be able to remedy the transboundary externality.

Indeed, in some cases the EC considers the transboundary character of a

[77] See Pâques, M., 'Effet direct du droit communautaire, interprétation conforme et responsabilité de l'Etat en général et en matière d'environnement', in Van Dunné, J. (ed.), *Non-Point Source River Pollution; The Case of the River Meuse*, Den Haag–London, Kluwer Law International, 1996, 89–139. See for the case of the river Rhine: Van Dunné, J., *Transboundary Pollution and Liability: the Case of the River Rhine*, Rotterdam, Erasmus University Institute of Environmental Damages, 1991.

[78] Van den Bergh, R., 'Subsidiarity as an economic demarcation principle and the emergence of European private law', 5 *Maastricht Journal of European and Comparative Law*, 1998, 143.

[79] Van den Bergh, R., 'Subsidiarity as an economic demarcation principle and the emergence of European private law', 5 *Maastricht Journal of European and Comparative Law*, 1998, 144–45.

[80] Van den Bergh, R., 'Economics in a legal strait-jacket: the difficult reception of economic analysis in European Law' (paper presented at the workshop Empirical Research and Legal Realism. Setting the Agenda, Haifa, 6–9 June 1999) 10.

[81] Van den Bergh, R., 'Subsidiarity as an economic demarcation principle and the emergence of European private law', 5 *Maastricht Journal of European and Comparative Law*, 1998, 144–45.

problem as a sufficient justification for centralized rule making without differ-entiating between local and transboundary pollution[82]. Moreover, a great deal of the environmental directives also deal with relatively 'local' problems that do not cross national borders. This seems to be the case as well for environ-mental liability. Many pollution cases giving rise to liability are confined within the borders of one country. Moreover, even if there is transboundary pollution other remedies could be applied (e.g. via international private law) that do not go as far as total harmonization. Note that this 'transboundary externality' argument is a totally different one in a product liability case, since the likelihood of products affecting international trade is obviously quite large[83]. For environmental liability there would only be a case for centraliz-ation if the central rules were to apply only to transboundary pollution and even this question would arise only if this problem could not be remedied by less far-reaching means. However, the European environmental liability regime as proposed in the White Paper supposedly applies to 'damage to bio-diversity', which is not necessarily transboundary. The question therefore arises whether other economic reasons can be found for European environ-mental liability legislation in those cases where the effects of pollutants are confined within the borders of the relevant member states, for example in the case of soil pollution[84].

Race for the bottom
There exist a second economic argument for a centralized regulation of en-vironmental problems. The risk of destructive competition, known as a 'race for the bottom' between countries that could emerge to attract foreign invest-ments with low environmental standards. As a result of this, a prisoners' dilemma could arise whereby countries would fail to enact or enforce efficient legislation. This would mean that local governments would compete with lenient environmental legislation to attract industry[85]. The result would be an overall reduction of environmental quality below efficient levels. This should correspond with the traditional game-theoretical result that prisoners' dilem-mas create inefficiencies. Centralization could be advanced as a remedy for these prisoners' dilemmas.

This 'race for the bottom' argument, that competition among jurisdictions

---

[82] See for instance directive 74/464 which regulates discharges of dangerous substances into the aquatic environment for both transboundary rivers and local pounds.

[83] See R.M. Ackerman, 'Tort law and federalism: whatever happened to devolution?', *Yale Law and Policy Review*, 1996, 429–63 and G.T. Schwartz, 'Considering the proper federal role in American Tort Law', 38 *Arizona Law Review*, 1996, 917–51.

[84] The regime as proposed in the White Paper should typically apply to soil pollution.

[85] Compare Rose-Ackerman, S., *Rethinking the Progressive Agenda: the Reform of the American Regulatory State*, New York, Free Press, 1992, 166–70.

for economic activity will be 'destructive', corresponds to some extent with the earlier mentioned Commission argument in the White Paper that the creation of harmonized conditions of competition is necessary to avoid trade distortions. The trade argument is traditionally used to harmonize legislation of the member states in a variety of areas. Simply stated, the argument is that complying with legislation imposes costs on industry. If legislation is different, these costs would therefore differ as well and conditions of competition within the common market would not be equal. The argument apparently assumes that total equality of conditions of competition is necessary for the functioning of the common market. 'Levelling the playing field' for European industry remains the central message.

The 'race for the bottom' argument has had several supporters as well as opponents in North American scholarship. Law and economics scholars tend to stress the benefits of competition between states and point to the dangers of centralization[86], whereas some legal scholars tend to attach greater belief to the 'race for the bottom' rationale for centralization in environmental matters[87]. In Europe these issues are rarely discussed in the context of the 'race for the bottom' but in the European community dogma of 'levelling the playing field to avoid distortions of competition'. This somewhat confuses the debate. The 'harmonization of conditions of competition' argument could either be interpreted narrowly in 'race for the bottom' terms or more broadly as a general argument to harmonize all kinds of rules and standards. The latter is the usual interpretation in Europe. Let us look at both interpretations more closely and see how they relate to the area of environmental liability.

Risk of the bottom versus common market
The traditional European argument claims that any difference in legislation between the member states might endanger the conditions of competition and therefore justifies harmonization of legal rules. This argument seems particularly weak. From an economic point of view, the mere fact that conditions of competition differ does not necessarily create a 'race for the bottom' risk. There can be differences in marketing conditions for a variety of reasons, and if the conditions of competition were indeed totally equal, as the argument assumes, there would also be no trade according to the theory of specialization.

---

[86] See especially with applications to environmental law Revesz, R., 'Rehabilitating interstate competition: rethinking the race for the bottom rational for federal environmental regulation', 67, *New York University Law Review*, 1992, 1210–54 and Revesz, R., 'Federalism and interstate environmental externalities', 144 *University of Pennsylvania Law Review*, 1996, 2341–2416.

[87] See Esty, D. and Geradin, D., note 39, 'Environmental protection and international competitiveness. A conceptual framework', 32/3 *Journal of World Trade*, 1998 and Esty, D. and Geradin, D., 'Market access, competitiveness and harmonization: environmental protection in regional trade agreements', 21 *Harvard Environmental Law Review*, 1997.

Also, Europe has developed an elaborate set of rules, which guarantee – *inter alia* – a free flow of products and services[88] and thus contribute to market integration without the necessity of harmonizing all rules and standards[89]. In this respect one can think of the case law of the European Court of Justice with respect to the free movement of goods versus environmental protection[90]. This shows that the goal of market integration can be achieved via (other) less far-reaching instruments than total harmonization[91] which can equally remove barriers to trade.

Hence, one should make a distinction between the political ideal of creating one common market in Europe on the one hand and the (economic) 'race to the bottom' argument on the other hand[92]. This political goal of market integration may as such be questioned on economic grounds[93] and may justify the need for rules aiming at a reduction of trade restrictions such as, for example, a harmonization of product standards[94]. The problem in environmental law is that initiatives in that area also aim at a harmonization of process standards 'to harmonize conditions of competition'. That seems questionable on efficiency grounds[95]. What can be said about this 'harmonization of conditions of competition' argument either in its 'race for the bottom' or in its 'Common Market' version?

From an economic perspective, differences in the conditions of competition only pose a problem if it is clear that environmental costs would be considerably different between the member states and that these differences would lead

[88] See the articles 28–30 of the Treaty (formerly articles 30–36).

[89] See generally on the potential conflict between free trade and environmental protection, Esty, D. (1999), 'Economic integration and the environment', in Vig, N. and Axelrod, R. (eds), *The Global Environment,* Washington, DC: CQ Press, 190–209.

[90] For an overview of this case law see Lefevere, J. and Faure, M., 'Introduction to European environmental law', in Kegels, T. (ed.), *Shipping Law Faces Europe: European Policy Competition and Environment,* Brussel, Maklu, 1995, 93–107 and Trebilcock, M. and Howse, R., 1998, 21–28.

[91] See also Esty, D. and Geradin, D., 'Environmental protection and international competitiveness. A conceptual framework', 32/3 *Journal of World Trade,* 1998, 296–99 and Ogus, A., *Regulation, Legal Form and Economic Theory,* Oxford, Clarendon Press, 1994, 177–79.

[92] See also Revesz, R., 'Environmental regulation in federal systems' in *Yearbook of European Environmental Law* (2000), at 24 to 27, who equally argues that these are separate points which should be distinguished.

[93] See Van den Bergh, R., 'Economics in a legal strait-jacket: the difficult reception of economic analysis in European law' (paper presented at the workshop Empirical Research and Legal Realism. Setting the Agenda, Haifa, 6–9 June 1999).

[94] These were the result of directives issued as a consequence of the so-called 'Single Market Initiative'. See Vogel, D. *Trading Up: Consumer and Environmental Regulation in the Global Economy,* Cambridge, Harvard University Press, 1995. See on the need to harmonize product safety Faure, M. 'Product liability and product safety in Europe: harmonization or differentiation, *Kyklos',* vol. 53, 2000, 467–508.

[95] This is also criticized by Revesz, R.

to relocation of firms to the member state with the lowest standards[96]. In that case, the so-called race for the bottom argument, in environmental cases referred to as the 'pollution haven' hypothesis, might be an argument in favour of centralization[97]. The question therefore arises whether there is empirical evidence that states can indeed attract industry by lenient environmental standards.

Empirical evidence of pollution havens
Empirical evidence to uphold this 'race for the bottom' rationale is rather weak. Repetto argues that pollution control costs are only a minor fraction of the total sales of manufacturing industries[98]. Moreover, Jaffe/Peterson/Portney/Stavins[99] argued that empirical evidence shows that the effects of environmental regulations are 'either small, statistically insignificant or not robust to tests of model specification'. They argue that the stringency of environmental regulations might have some effect on new firms in their decision to locate for the first time[100], but that this will not induce existing firms to relocate. They equally argue that other criteria such as tax levels, public services and the unionization of labour force have a much more significant impact on the location decision than environmental regulation. Later this empirical evidence has been somewhat contradicted by Xing/Kolstad[101], who argue that the laxity of environmental regulations in a host country is a significant determinant of foreign direct investment by the US chemical industry. The more lax the regulations, the more likely the country is to attract foreign investment, so Xing/Kolstad argue. Although this somewhat weakens the evidence presented by Jaffe/Peterson/Portney/Stavins[102] as far as the location of new firms outside the US is concerned, it does not contradict the finding that existing firms will not relocate because of the stringncy of environmental regulations.

This material, therefore, weakens the prisoner's dilemma argument.

---

[96] See equally Revesz, R., who argues that given the weaknesses of the 'harmonization of conditions of competition' argument 'it is not surprising that recent European scholarship has sought to recharacterize the quest for harmonization in race to the bottom terms'.

[97] Although Esty and Geradin have rightly pointed to the fact that a whole variety of legal instruments exists which may remedy the problem, whereby the total harmonization of standards would be the most far-reaching (Esty, D. and Geradin, D., 'Environmental protection and international competitiveness. A conceptual framework', 32/3 *Journal of World Trade*, 1998, 282–94).

[98] Repetto, R., *Trade and Sustainable Development*, UNEP, Environment and Trade Series.

[99] Jaffe, A., S. Portney, and R. Stavins, 'Environmental regulation and the competitiveness of US manufacturing: what does the evidence tell us?', 33 *Journal of Economic Literature*, 1995, 132–63.

[100] See Esty, D. and Geradin, D., 'Environmental protection and international competitiveness. A conceptual framework', 32/3 *Journal of World Trade*, 1998, 12–15.

[101] Xing, Y. and Kolstad, C., 'Do lax environmental regulations attract foreign investment' 16–95 (working paper in Economics, University of California, 1995).

[102] See White Paper, § 5.1, 25.

Moreover, it has also been argued that as far as environmental standards are concerned, it is not at all clear that there will be a 'race for the bottom'. There is also some evidence that member states precisely try to strive for high environmental standards, even if this puts extra costs or burdens on their industry. Some countries may therefore be more involved in a 'race for the top' instead of a 'race for the bottom'[103]. One could also question whether European law is at all able to remedy a real 'race for the bottom' risk, given the enforcement deficit.

All these arguments apply to the area of environmental liability as well. It is doubtful that within Europe member states would be able to engage in a game in which they would strive for low-level environmental liability in order to attract industry. There is no proof of such a destructive competition towards lower liability standards and this risk is, moreover, not very realistic. Indeed, as indicated, one can doubt whether environmental liability plays a significant role in attracting or repulsing business to or from a given state. Other elements may be far more important than the level of environmental liability in location decisions of businesses. Moreover, if environmental liability were to have any effect as far as the 'race for the bottom' is concerned, it is even more likely that states would wish to protect victims of environmental pollution instead of corporate interests. Indeed, a lenient environmental liability legislation may well run counter to the states' interests since it would limit the possibilities, for example, recovering of soil clean-up costs from liable polluters. If there is any effect at all one can therefore expect a 'race for the top' rather than a 'race for the bottom' in the area of environmental liability. This would enable states to recover, for example, costs for clean-up of (domestically) polluted soils, also from foreign polluters.

Levelling the playing field

Let us now turn to the other – legal – interpretations of the 'race for the bottom' argument. It should be stressed that this European argument that markets shall be distorted without a harmonization of conditions of competition is not only constantly repeated in a stereotypical way, but its validity is hardly ever questioned. The argument as it is usually presented in Europe, cannot, as was stated above, be fitted into the economic criteria for centralization, since it suggests

---

[103] See Van den Bergh, R., Faure, M. and Lefevere, J., 'The Subsidiarity Principle in European environmental law: an economic analysis,' in Eide, E. and Van den Bergh, R. (eds), *Law and Economics of the Environment*, Oslo, Jurdisk Forlag, 1996, 141–42. Ogus argues that there may be benefits to firms to be located in a high-standard member state, since this may generate technological improvements and thus competitive advantages; that may explain 'race for the top' (Ogus, A., 'Competition between national legal systems: a contribution of economic analysis to comparative law', *International and Comparative Law Quarterly*, vol. 48, 1999, 415). See, generally, Vogel, D., *Trading Up: Consumer and Environmental Regulation in the Global Economy*, Cambridge, Harvard University Press, 1995 and Trebilcock, M. and Howse, R., 1998, 13–14.

that removing any difference in legal systems would be necessary to eliminate the 'race for the bottom' risk, which is neither supported by economic theory, nor by empirical evidence. Also, even if one were to take the (political) 'common market' goal as starting point and environmental regulations were to be harmonized on that ground, this would still not create a level playing field since differences in, for example, energy sources, access to raw materials and atmospheric conditions will still lead to diverging marketing conditions[104].

There is, in addition, a strong counter-argument, in that there are many examples showing that economic market integration is possible (without the distortions predicted by the 'race for the bottom' argument) with differentiated legal orders. Public-choice scholars have often advanced the Swiss federal model as an example where economic market integration goes hand in hand with differentiated legal systems[105]. It is apparently possible to create a common market without a total harmonization of all legal rules and standards[106].

These arguments therefore weaken the prisoner's dilemma argument in the field of environmental law both in its 'race to the bottom' form and in the (disguised) way it is presented in the European debate. The European argument that any difference in legal rules between the member states would endanger market integration and that therefore a harmonization of law is needed in order to harmonize conditions of competition[107] is too general, too unbalanced and not supported by economic theory. Differences between legal systems of member states may, from an economic point of view, constitute a problem if this were to result in an inefficient 'race for the bottom'. But the empirical evidence available suggests that this may not be a serious risk in the environmental field. Even if differences in the stringency of environmental law exist between member states, this will generally not lead companies to relocate to 'pollution havens' within Europe. The least one can argue is that if the European Commission were to use a 'race for the bottom' rationale for centralization, it should prove that without centralization in the specific field a risk of destructive competition would emerge[108]. The debate in Europe has,

---

[104] See Van den Bergh, R., 'Economics in a legal strait-jacket: the difficult reception of economic analysis in European Law' (paper presented at the workshop Empirical Research and Legal Realism. Setting the Agenda, Haifa, 6–9 June 1999) , 10.

[105] Frey, B., 'Direct Democracy: Politico-Economic Lessons from Switzerland', 84 *American Economic Review*, 1994, 338–42.

[106] See equally Revesz, R.

[107] See the formulation in the preamble to the Products Liability Directive.

[108] In that case there may seriously be a valid argument for an intervention by Brussels. Compare – in the US context – the remark by Rose-Ackerman, S., *Rethinking the Progressive Agenda*, 173: 'If state and local laws seem designed to protect local business rather than reflect genuine differences in tastes across jurisdiction, the federal government should take a hard look to determine the possible interference with interstate commerce'.

so far, never focused on that question[109], since it was always argued that any harmonization of legal rules was necessary to achieve market integration, which obviously confuses the debate.

The same applies for the area of environmental liability. It is indeed very possible to create a common market without a total harmonization of all legal rules. The goal of market integration should not necessarily be achieved via this far-reaching instrument of total harmonization. This would only justify, for example, general safety standards that aim at avoiding pointless incompatibilities which could create barriers to trade and distortions of competition within the internal market. The latter argument can, however, not justify a harmonization of rules of private law such as environmental liability. Finally, attempts which have been undertaken so far to harmonize rules of private law, for example, in the area of product liability, have not proven to be able to achieve a total harmonization of marketing conditions (see Faure, 2000).

Transaction costs

There may, however, be one final economic argument in favour of harmonization, based on transaction costs reduction[110]. This argument is often advanced by European legal scholars pleading for harmonization of private law in Europe, and is based on the argument that differences in legal systems are very complex and only serves Brussels law firms[111]. This argument cannot be examined in detail here[112]. It is obviously too simple to state that a harmonized legal system is always more efficient than differentiated legal rules because of the transaction costs savings inherent in harmonized rules[113]. This argument neglects the fact that there are substantial benefits from differentiation whereby legislation can be adapted to the preferences of individuals (Mendelsohn, 1986, 301). Moreover, given the differences between the legal systems (and legal cultures) in Europe the costs of harmonization may be huge – if not prohibitive – as well[114]. The crucial question therefore is whether the possible transaction costs savings of harmonization outweigh the benefits of differentiated legal rules. There is little empirical evidence to support the statement that transaction

---

[109] See equally Esty, D. and Geradin, D., who argue that the risk of a regulatory 'race to the bottom' for environmental reasons has not been a major issue in the EC (Esty, D. and Geradin, D., 'Environmental protection and international competitiveness', 32/3 *Journal of World Trade*, 1998, 308).

[110] A somewhat related but different argument relates to economics and diseconomics of scale in administration, see Rose-Ackerman, S., *Rethinking the Progressive Agenda*, New York, Free Press, 1992, 165–66.

[111] This is one of the arguments made by the Danish scholar Lando in favour of harmonized private law (Lando, 1993, 473–74).

[112] It is further developed and criticized in a recent paper by Van den Bergh (1998).

[113] Compare Rose-Ackerman (1992, 172) who argues that uniform federal regulation may reduce search costs and tends to produce a more stable and predictable jurisprudence.

[114] That point has been made especially by Legrand (1997, 111).

costs savings could justify a European harmonization of all kinds of legal rules. Moreover, the transaction cost savings are likely to be relatively small (Van den Bergh, 1998, note 68, 146–48).

If one addresses the question whether the regime proposed in the White Paper could achieve a reduction of transaction costs one would have to assess whether it can create a uniform regime and provide a legal certainty which would reduce transaction costs. That is highly doubtful.

Indeed, there is one particular point of worry concerning the regime proposed in the White Paper which may endanger the uniformity and increase transaction costs. This has to do with the balanced approach chosen in the White Paper which may make a future liability regime highly complex. A scheme provided in the White Paper itself[115] makes clear that the proposed regime is not only well balanced, but also very complex. Indeed, as the summary shows, the applicable regime will depend upon the type of damage (traditional damage, contaminated sites or damage to bio-diversity) but in addition upon the type of activity (dangerous or not). Moreover, the White Paper argues that it focuses on damage to bio-diversity, since most existing member states' environmental liability regimes would not cover that type of damage. The question, however, arises whether that is generally true; member states certainly have rules on traditional damage and contaminated sites.

This entails therefore a risk of increased legal complexity, which could lead to cases whereby different legal regimes (different European and national regimes) apply to various types of damage, resulting from a single pollution case. That would obviously create legal uncertainty and may hence endanger the reduction of transaction costs. To a large extent, this is due to the fact that the White Paper has not addressed the question how the different regimes proposed should be combined if, for example, a non-dangerous activity causes damage to the soil, to human health and to bio-diversity as well. A future regime should definitely better clarify how these (European and national) rules apply to specific cases if one really wishes to reduce transaction costs.

The transaction costs argument could, however, play a role to justify the so-called negative harmonization, which aims at a co-ordination of, for example, product standards to prevent states from hindering a free flow of products and services (see Vogel, 1995, pp. 52–55). This type of cooperation between States can reduce transaction costs, but does not necessitate a homogenization of process standards, which is often the goal in environmental law.

The conclusion therefore is that the economic arguments to harmonize environmental rules with respect to problems which are not transboundary is relatively weak. Nevertheless, many European directives deal with (e.g.

---

[115] Which we have included in an annex.

drinking water or bathing water) problems which are not typically trans-boundary and for which the European competence is therefore difficult to fit into the economic framework. The question, however, arises whether a non-economic argument can be advanced for regulation at the European level.

European heritage argument

Can an argument be found to protect the environment at the European level as such? The protection of habitats and entire ecosystems comes to mind. This is of particular importance since the White Paper precisely focuses on damage to bio-diversity. A traditional example is the question whether there should be any European jurisdiction to protect an imaginary turtle which has, say, only one habitat, which is in Greece. The traditional economic argument in such a case would be that since the problem is merely local, the Greek population should decide whether or not to protect the Greek turtle. An attempt in the direction of an economic argument for European competence has been made by Wils, who classifies the protection of endangered species as justified by the fact that this endangerment causes 'psychic spill-overs' (Wils, 1994, pp. 85–90). The argument then goes that the endangerment of the Greek turtle would also harm the interests of, for example, a Dutch citizen living in Maastricht who would suffer a psychic spill-over from the fact that the Greek turtle would be endangered[116]. According to this view, the externality would be considered transboundary (although the turtle only lives in Greece) and there would, again, be an economic rationale for centralization[117]. Maybe this argument still holds for turtles or for Italian nature parks, whose well-being also affects other European citizens[118]. But what about a European directive, regulating liability of soil pollution by a certain plant and regulating clean-up standards?

Differences according to preferences

In the case above on soil pollution, centralization seems, at first sight, contrary to basic economic logic. From an economic point of view, the environmental clean-up standards to be provided could differ according to differing preferences of citizens[119]. Again, from an economic point of view, there is no reason for centralization if the externalities are local and no pris-oners' dilemmas exist. This economic argument in favour of differentiation

---

[116] Compare Esty, D., 'The health of ecosystems to which we have no physical connection may enter directly into our utility calculus'.

[117] Compare Ogus (1999, p. 418), who argues that harmonization may be justified if foreigners derive disutility from observing the plight of victims in the offending state.

[118] But then the Greek should probably be compensated for the extra costs involved in this European habitat protection (compare Rose-Ackerman, S., 42–43).

[119] Developed by Ogus (1994, pp. 25–30) and more generally in Ogus (1999, p. 413)

according to the preferences of citizens is not only valid for the question whether or not the Greek turtle should be protected at the European level[120]. It is also valid for the whole body of environmental law, and even for environmental liability standards. This corresponds with the Tiebout framework of competition between legal orders where citizens are free to choose the environmental quality that corresponds optimally with their preferences. The consequence of this economic approach is that it should be for Greece to decide, for example, to prefer economic development over environmental quality[121]. A consequence of this economic argument whereby citizens choose a level of environmental protection according to their preference should obviously be that the environmental quality would vary according to the individual preferences of citizens. This argument is also used at the normative level in the US where there are increasingly pleas in favour of standard-setting by the states rather than by a federal environmental agency (Schoenbrod, 1996). This *economic* argument therefore leads to an environmental federalism in which environmental quality between member states could differ as long as there are no transboundary effects and no 'race for the bottom' risks[122]. For areas related to environmental liability such as soil pollution this would mean that states would be free to choose their own clean-up and liability standards.

Guaranteeing a basic environmental quality
There is, however, an important legal or policy argument that could lead to centralization. This has to do with the idea of guaranteeing all European citizens a similar environmental quality. This is sometimes referred to as the protection of the 'European environmental and cultural heritage and human health'. If this argument is accepted at the policy level, it could be used to harmonize environmental quality. It is, however, important to note that the reason for centralization in such a case would then not be the economic need of market integration, but the ecological desire to guarantee all citizens within the Union a similar, or at least basic, environmental quality. The consequence would then be that, contrary to economic logic, it would not be the preferences of citizens that would prevail, but the policy desire to provide one basic

---

[120] To be very specific: this chapter is not concerned with the normative question whether or not the Greek turtle deserves protection. It is concerned only with the question whether such a decision should be taken in Greece or at the European Community level.

[121] Again, this is not to say that Greece should not protect the environment, but only to argue that, from an economic point of view, this is not a question that Brussels should be concerned about.

[122] However, since firms are in a competitive environment a member state which chooses to impose a high level of protection (and thus high costs on firms) will have to compensate for this with, for example, lower taxes on wages in order to avoid the exit of business, see, Rose-Ackerman, S., 41.

environmental quality in Europe[123]. This corresponds with the point made by Ogus that the preferences of citizens for lower standards at lower costs may sometimes be overruled if it is held that these low standards would infringe widely held perceptions of human rights[124]. In the environmental context this point could take the form of guaranteeing all citizens a basic environmental quality[125].

Again this chapter does not argue at the normative level that this would not be a valid argument for centralization, but it is important to stress that if this argument for centralization is used, it is only for ecological (or policy) reasons, not for economic reasons, that one would strive for harmonization of environmental quality. A serious problem with this 'European heritage' argument is that it may be valid to defend, for example, a European-wide protection of, say, the Coliseum in Rome[126], but less so to guarantee a minimum environmental quality. In that case it would make more sense to strive for a Europe-wide minimum level of public health, which is not the case today.

But if this 'European heritage' reason for centralization in order to guarantee all European citizens a basic environmental quality is accepted, there are several consequences. If externalities are merely local and no 'race for the bottom' risks exist, it is hard to find an economic rationale for centralization. At the policy level, truly ecological reasons can be advanced for centralization to guarantee a similar environmental quality throughout the union. This could take the form of minimum standards which should be achieved after the clean-up of polluted soils. But then this ecological argument, not the 'harmonization of conditions of competition argument', has to be advanced to justify, for example, the guarantee of a minimum environmental quality in Greece[127].

---

[123] Compare Esty, D., who argues in favour of global environmental norms which should represent a behavioural minimum. More critically is Revesz, R., 'Federalism and regulation: some generalizations', in D. Esty and D. Geradin (eds), *Regulatory Competition and Economic Integration, Comparative Perspectives*, 2001, 3–29.

[124] Rights may, in this instance, justifiably 'trump efficiency', see Ogus, A., 'Competition between national legal systems: a contribution of economic analysis to comparative law', *International and Comparative Law Quarterly*, vol. 48, 1999, 418. See also Cohen, M., 'Commentary', in Eide, E. and Van den Bergh, R. (eds), *Law and Economics of the Environment*, Oslo, Juridisk Forlag, 1996, 170 who calls for minimum quality standards at centralized level for reasons of 'equity, justice, or pure paternalism' and Stewart, R., who states that geographically uniform standards ensure every individual a minimum healthy environment even though such uniformity is economically inefficient.

[125] See explictly Kimber: 'An analogy may be drawn here with human rights. It is arguable that certain minimum standards of environmental protection ought to be achieved by all countries and regions, particularly if one accepts that the environment is the common heritage of us all' (1995, 1690).

[126] But there it is the transboundary ('psychic') spill-over which justifies European intervention.

[127] If the idea is accepted that it is for ecological reasons (harmonizing environmental quality in the Union) that centralization is needed, this has consequences for environmental standard setting. This point is further developed in Faure (2001)

Balance

In this section, the economic literature on federalism was used to provide a critical look at some aspects of the harmonization of environmental law in general and environmental liability in particular. The economic arguments were also compared to the arguments advanced in favour of harmonization in Europe. First we sought to provide an economic analysis of the traditional European argument that conditions of competition should be harmonized to 'create a level playing field'. This argument is too general to fit into the economic criteria for centralization. This economic literature provides for a balanced answer with respect to the types of subject matters that should be regulated at the centralized or at the decentralized level. This shows that the questions concerning centralization/harmonization cannot be answered in black or white statements. From the economic literature it appears that there are very few economic reasons for harmonization of environmental liability legislation. Such an argument would only exist if domestic polluters could externalize environmental damage to 'foreign victims'. However, other remedies may be available to cure interstate pollution without the need to harmonize liability. A second economic reason for centralization would exist if it were established that states could attract industry with lenient environmental liability standards. That is, however, very unlikely since states would to the contrary enact legislation to protect domestic victims of environmental pollution with high-standard environmental liability legislation. There could be transaction costs savings of uniform environmental liability law if a directive were able to create legal certainty and achieve full harmonization, which is highly doubtful with the regime proposed in the White Paper.

Nevertheless, some non-economic arguments, for example based on ecological grounds, such as the guarantee of a high environmental quality in the European Union, might be legitimate arguments for a certain amount of harmonization and centralization. Therefore, the question that should be asked is what the goal of harmonization of environmental law should be. If European environmental policy is, as is sometimes stated, to promote uniform environmental quality within the Union, this can be reached by fixing a harmonized environmental quality, to be enforced by the Commission, but with differentiated legislation, for example, on environmental liability. If the goal of environmental policy is to equalize conditions of competition, hence purely economic, it should be examined whether harmonization of environmental liability legislation really improves equal competition, or whether it serves some industries that lobbied to erect artificial barriers to entry. Harmonization in such cases might not be desirable. That issue will be addressed below when we examine the importance of special interest If European environmental policy pursues ecological reasons, a certain degree of harmonization may sometimes well be justified. However encouraging 'green behaviour' combined with clear clean-up standards for the member states might be more effective than punishment by a liability legislation.

3. EUROPEAN ENVIRONMENTAL LIABILITY REASSESSED

Section 3 closes the circle and goes back to the starting point of this chapter, the Commission's White Paper on Environmental liability. So far we found that there are relatively few economic arguments in favour of environmental liability rules (see 'Balance' in the previous section) centralized. However, we have already indicated that, within the framework of the subsidiarity discussion, the European Commission also advanced arguments to justify a European-wide environmental liability regime. These arguments put forward by the Commission for an EC environmental liability regime (see above) will now be confronted with the economic criteria for centralization presented above.

Transfrontier Damage

The first argument of the Commission dealt with transboundary damage. It is held in the White Paper that member states cannot effectively address cross-border pollution. Indeed, as the literature on federalism indicates, the Tiebout model will not yield efficient results if cross-border externalities are not adequately addressed (Faure, 1998). In the case of cross-border externalities, the EC, not the member states should have jurisdiction (Bergkamp, 2000, p. 107). This cross-border rationale, however, provides an explanation for only part of the EC environmental legislation, as the EC acknowledges implicitly: 'the Union's current policies extend far beyond air and water quality to include the protection of soils, habitats and fauna and flora, and the conservation of wild birds[128]'.

However, if cross-border harm is a serious problem in the EC but member states can adequately deal with pollution within their borders, then according to the subsidiarity principle, an EC liability regime would only be justified for cross-border environmental harm instead of an overall liability regime. This would result in a so-called 'transboundary only' regime. In this respect, environmental liability differs from other areas of tort like product liability. Products cross borders all the time, but habitats stay where they are (Bergkamp, 2000, p. 107). Moreover, according to Bergkamp, cross-border

---

[128] (www.europa.eu.int/pol/env.info.en.htm)

externalities by themselves do not necessarily justify a harmonized liability regime: 'additional regulatory initiatives or more effective enforcement mechanisms might cure these as well' (Bergkamp, 2000, p. 107). Indeed, case law in many member states has developed in order to allow an extra-territorial application of domestic law on cross-border pollution. These jurisprudential evolutions may thus remedy cross border externalities without the need for a total harmonization of environmental liability. Therefore, transboundary environmental pollution can occur in certain cases in the EU. However, this argument by itself is not sufficient for a fully harmonized liability regime in the EU. Other remedies may solve this problem. Moreover, even if harmonization were to be considered a preferred legal instrument, it could only justify a European 'transboundary only' regime and not a total harmonization.

Polluter Pays Principle

An argument which seems to be very important for the Commission is the polluter pays principle. The Commission believes that environmental liability may encourage investment in research and development (R&D) for improving knowledge and technologies. What can be said about this argument from an economic perspective?

First, it should be made clear that the polluter pays principle as such does not explain why environmental regulation should be issued at the European level to promote this principle. Indeed, in this respect we should refer to the whole range of regulations that already exist today in the member states. The Commission offers no evidence that the liability regime as proposed will generate more incentives for prevention than the existing national and European liability and regulatory schemes (Bergkamp, 2000, p. 108).

Second, the White Paper's statement that the liability legislation will promote R&D is not supported by empirical evidence either (Bergkamp, 2000, p. 108). According to economic theory, if no adequate intellectual property rights are available, R&D will to a large extent be a 'public good' which private parties will not produce, or produce insufficiently. The reason is that once the investment is made, all competitors will benefit without having to make any research investments. This is the well-known free-rider problem. Furthermore, the firms might have incentives not to invest in R&D because in the future the outcome may become minimum standard (Kolstad, 2000).

Third, the polluter pays principle does not resolve the question as to whether costs should be internalized through 'ex ante' regulatory requirements, rather than through 'ex post' liability rules. Nor does it resolve controversies like forcing innocent or marginal polluters to pay for damage caused by their predecessors, or that any polluter has to pay for unforeseeable or tolerable damage. Liability is a way of making the polluter pay, but it might be a very unattractive option. In short, the polluter principle does not require or justify an environmental liability regime (Faure, 1996, 90 and Bergkamp, 2000, 108). But, most importantly, the principle as such can, at least from an economic perspective, not justify the need for European action.

Decontamination and Restoration of the Environment

The Commission repeatedly expresses its expectations that a liability regime would encourage decontamination and restoration of the environment and improve the implementation of, and compliance with, EC environmental legislation[129]. This consists in fact of a variety of sub-arguments. First, it is argued that a European regime would encourage the restoration of the environment.

Although one could only cheer this result, these expectations are probably more idealistic than realistic. Liability is neither a sufficient nor a necessary condition for pursuing these two objectives[130]. Bergkamp points out that the argument that an EC liability regime is necessary to ensure the restoration of damaged habitats is not sufficient, as member states are already required to do so[131]. He argues that, if the objective of an environmental liability legislation is ensuring the clean-up of contaminated land then EC law should solely impose an obligation on member states to reach that objective. By issuing such a directive, the member states would be free to choose the instruments they will use. This may, but does not have to, involve additional liability rules. According to Bergkamp, 'liability is not the right instrument to promote compliance with environmental regulations, unless it is used as a sanction for damage caused by non-compliance and the regulatory compliance defence is fully recognized'[132].

First we have already pointed out that there are few economic reasons that can be advanced for a harmonized environmental liability regime. However, we indicated that European action might be brought, although for non-economic reasons. If the Commission refers, by the 'decontamination and restoration argument', to the desire of guaranteeing all European citizens a similar (high) environmental quality, this objective might be fulfilled by other means than environmental liability. Whereas liability punishes industry, market-oriented approaches encouraging R&D in greening the industry (by funding), combined with clear clean-up standards for the member states, might be more effective.

---

[129] White Paper, § 3.1–3.2, 14.

[130] L. Bergkamp, 'The White Paper on environmental liability', *European Environmental Law Review*, April 2000, 108.

[131] Council Directive 92/43 on the conservation of natural habitats and wild fauna and flora, *OJ*, L 206 , 7.

[132] Bergkamp L., 'The White Paper on environmental liability', *European Environmental Law Review*, April 2000, 108.

Second, the argument has been made that by using liability law the implementation of EC environmental legislation can be promoted. But, as we have just indicated, European law provides for a wide variety of other legal instruments to stimulate implementation of European law. Liability rules can only play a minor role to that effect.

Third, it should be stressed that the Commission apparently does not propose a European-wide harmonized environmental liability regime, but links the EC liability regime with existing EC environmental legislation. Moreover, the Commission specifically focuses the proposed regime on damage to bio-diversity since most existing member states' environmental liability regimes do not cover this type of damage[133].

From a subsidiarity perspective this approach seems to be rather balanced in that it focuses merely on those areas where member states have apparently not enacted legislation and limits itself largely to liability resulting from activities regulated under EC environmental law. However, several objections could be made to this approach as well. First, the mere fact that member states would not have enacted legislation with respect to a particular subject matter is obviously, under subsidiarity, no justification for European intervention. Second, it simply does not seem correct that the White Paper would merely deal with areas where the member states have not yet enacted legislation. The White Paper for example deals extensively with soil pollution. This issue is also dealt with in the legislation of many member states. Finally, although the balanced approach of not opting for a total harmonization can be defended (although it would have been better to limit the European regime to transboundary damage), a disadvantage is obviously that it has become so complex that the differences in conditions of competition will obviously remain in existence. This shows once more that any approach which chooses to combine European and member state legislation can never lead to a 'level playing field', so that argument cannot justify European competences.

Creation of a Level Playing Field

Although the Commission does not place the argument for the creation of a level playing field in first place in its White Paper, it probably will be one of the main arguments for harmonization. The literature on federalism, however, clarified that the risk of a 'race to the bottom' is very unlikely to occur in the EU. Even if differences in the stringency of environmental law exist between

---

[133] For a critical perspective of the European competence with respect to environmental liability see Niezen, G.J., 'Aansprakelijkheid voor milieuschade in de Europese Unie' in *Ongebonden Recht Bedrijven*, Kluwer, 2000, 165–67 and 168–69.

member states, this will generally not lead companies to relocate to 'pollution havens' within Europe. This argument has been extensively dealt with above.

Moreover, full harmonization cannot be justified either in order to create 'equal conditions of competition'. The reasons have been discussed above. The Commission for its part also admits that there is no clear evidence of such advantages. Studies carried out at the request of the Commission have shown that the effect of liability regimes on competitiveness remain unclear[134]. When the Commission discusses the economic impact of environmental liability at EC level, it states itself in the White Paper that 'no significant impact is discernible and the environmental liability regimes in place in member states . . . have not led to any significant competitiveness problems'[135].

If that is the case, one may wonder how an EC directive can be justified on the grounds of levelling the playing field. Moreover, the White Paper suggest that the directive would be based on Article 175 of the Treaty. This would mean, according to the wording of Article 175 and 176, that member states would be authorized to go beyond the directive's scope and broaden it[136]. Therefore competitiveness reasons cannot justify EC intervention. Bergkamp rightly indicates that any competition distortions that may exist would be likely to continue to persist even after the proposed liability regime is implemented[137].

Moreover, we have indicated that the regime proposed in the White Paper is so complex that it can never have the effect of creating a 'level playing field'. The argument for the creation of a level playing field is therefore not sufficient to allow for a harmonized European environmental liability regime.

Principle of Equal Treatment

The final argument deals with the principle of equal treatment. The equal treatment is discussed in the White Paper in the context of the transboundary externalities argument. In the literature it has been suggested that if interstate externalities are a reason for centralization, the European directive should not necessarily cover both local and community-wide pollution[138]. This idea of a

---

[134] 'Economic aspects of liability and joint compensation systems for remedying environmental damage, summary report', ERM Economics, London, March 1996 (annex to the White Paper).

[135] White Paper, § 7, 29.

[136] Article 176 provides that 'the protective measures adopted pursuant to Article 175 shall not prevent any Member State from maintaining or introducing more stringent protective measures. Such measures must be compatible with this Treaty. They shall be notified to the Commission'.

[137] Bergkamp L., 'The White Paper on environmental liability', *European Environmental Law Review*, April 2000, 106.

[138] Van den Bergh suggested that a distinction should be made between regional and interstate pollution (Van den Bergh, 'Economics in a legal strait-jacket: the difficult reception of economic analysis in European law' (paper presented at the workshop Empirical Research and Legal Realism. Setting the Agenda, Haifa, 6–9 June 1999, 10).

'transboundary only' regime was rejected, since this could lead to inequalities in treatment of victims in member states depending on whether they were victim of transboundary or local pollution[139]. Nevertheless this White Paper on environmental liability shows that the Commission now (the White Paper was issued on 9 February 2000) seems to be aware of the arguments advanced in economic literature in favour of (de)centralization and at least discusses them.

Strikingly, the White Paper – at least implicitly – discusses the criteria advanced by economic analysis for centralization at the European level (more particularly the transboundary character of environmental pollution and the 'harmonisation of conditions of competition' arguments) and rightly points to the fact that these arguments would theoretically lead to a preference for a 'transboundary only' regime. The White Paper, however, rejects this approach on the basis of equality arguments.

At this point, it seems that when referring to equality, the Commission no longer argues within the scope of the subsidiarity principle. It simply argues for uniformity[140]. As we will argue in the next chapter, this argument could fit into the public choice theory which holds that industry in heavily regulated (and probably polluted) areas lobbies (supported by green NGOs) to force their very stringent environmental regulations upon other member states that might not need such stringent measures. In that way, this industry might erect artificial barriers to entry.

However, the subsidiarity principle has been included in the EC Treaty precisely to prevent Community action based mainly on a desire for uniformity or equal treatment. As it is not proven that uniformity is necessary for the member states in order to deal effectively with environmental damage, there is no need for full harmonization. The equality argument against a 'transboundary only' regime is therefore not very convincing, neither from an economic, nor from a legal perspective.

4.   PUBLIC CHOICE CONSIDERATION

So far we have discussed the economic criteria for (de)centralization, applying these to the area of environmental liability (section 2). We compared these to the arguments advanced by the European Commission to justify European competences, as these were advanced in the White Paper (section 3).

We concluded that relatively few economic arguments can be found to

---

[139] White Paper, 25–26.
[140] Bergkamp L., 'The White Paper on environmental liability', *European Environmental Law Review*, April 2000, 107.

justify centralization in the area of environmental liability. This was only the case for transboundary pollution and even then the question arises whether the same result cannot be reached through different, less far-reaching legal instruments than total harmonization.

Nevertheless, we found that there are apparently strong forces in Brussels striving for a European environmental liability regime, at least for damage to bio-diversity. To some extent this can still be explained on public-interest grounds since we also indicated that non-economic, ecological arguments could be advanced, for example, to strive for a minimum quality of clean-up for polluted soils. However, public choice scholars have thought that there is always a risk that regulation in fact serves the interests of particular pressure groups.

Indeed, another non-economic reason why the European Union would harmonize liability legislation can be found in the public choice theory. Public choice theory deals with the role of interest groups in legislation. Lobbying activities at the European level are extremely strong. With respect to environmental standard-setting, intensive rent-seeking behaviour by interest groups can be identified. In Europe, industry may be confronted at state level with 'green' non-governmental organizations (NGOs), whereas these countervailing powers might have less force in Brussels. Moreover, the lack of transparency in the decision-making process, which the European Union is often reproached for, will stimulate European industry to engage in serious lobbying efforts.

The lobbying does not necessarily have to result in lower environmental standards. In particular cases, special-interest groups, representing industry, might, understandably, lobby in favour of harmonization at a higher level of environmental protection[141]. Interest groups in areas which are already heavily regulated may have incentives to extend their strict (national) regulations to the European level, forcing foreign competitors to follow the same strict regulation with which they already comply. The result is that industry will lobby to erect artificial barriers to entry. In addition, green NGOs will be pleased with this lobby and will obviously support the demand to transfer strict national standards to a European standard[142]. Thus, industry in heavily regulated (and probably polluted) areas can (supported by green NGOs) force their very stringent emission-limit values upon their (southern) competitors, although these member states probably would not need these

---

[141] See also Esty, D. and Geradin, D., 'Market access, competitiveness and harmonization: environmental protection in regional trade agreements', 21 *Harvard Environmental Law Review*,1997.

[142] These 'alliances' between environmentalists and domestic producers are also discussed by David Vogel: *Trading Up: Consumer and Environmental Regulation in the Global Economy*, Cambridge, Harvard University Press, 1995, 52–55.

stringent environmental limit values if the policy goal were one of reaching uniform environmental quality.

Thus it becomes clear that the 'harmonization of conditions of competition' argument is used to serve the interests of industries in heavily regulated areas to erect barriers to entry. Hence, environmental law can be used to limit market entry and environmental law is abused to serve private-interest goals. This leads to the conclusion that the 'harmonization of conditions of competition' argument, as presented in European rhetoric, can even be problematic, from both the economic and ecological points of view, and in fact serves the interests of industrial groups in heavily regulated areas[143]. It can be in their interests that 'conditions of competition' are actually harmonized. It is not clear yet whether the White Paper on environmental liability should be considered as an attempt by interest groups to create barriers to entry. One problem is that the contents of the White Paper are still rather vague and specific details of the regime (e.g. clean-up standards) are not known yet.

The Commission argued that the white paper deals with a topic, damage to bio-diversity, which has not been the subject yet of legislation in the member states. That is, however, only partially the case. Most member states may indeed lack specific rules, for example, concerning the way damage to natural habitats has to be calculated. But the White Paper also addressed the area of soil pollution, for which extensive regulations exist in most member states. Thus, theoretically, one could still run the risk that industry in member states with stringent soil clean-up regulations would strive for centralization, creating a barrier to entry for competitors from countries where these strict standards do not yet apply.

It is too early to assess whether the desire to create a European environmental liability regime in fact serves the interests of industry. One should, however, always be aware of the fact that the risk that centralization can be abused to create barriers to entry may always appear in any attempt towards centralization.

5. POLICY RECOMMENDATIONS AND CONCLUSIONS

This contribution has tried to examine from a theoretical point of view whether there are economic reasons for a harmonization of environmental liability legislation in the European Union. As a case study, the arguments

---

[143] This is not to say that there is no risk of regulatory capture resulting in inefficient standards at the level of the member states; compare (in the US context) Rose-Ackerman, S., *Rethinking the Progressive Agenda,* New York, Free Press, 1992, 166 and 173. However, in Europe, it is especially the untransparent Brussels bureaucracy which is feared from a public choice perspective.

brought forward by the Commission in its White Paper on Environmental liability were examined, in particular the traditional European argument that a harmonization of conditions of competition would be necessary in order to create a level playing field. The literature on federalism makes clear that there are very few economic arguments to justify a harmonized liability regulation in the European Union. Even though there may be an argument for centralization in cases of transboundary pollution, this does not justify a total harmonization. Non-economic arguments such as ecological reasons may justify a certain degree of harmonization. However encouraging 'green behaviour' combined with clear clean-up standards for the member states might be more effective than deterrence through liability legislation.

Therefore, the basic question the European Union should ask is what the goal of harmonization of environmental liability should be. European policy-makers should think more thoroughly about the reasons for harmonization or at least about the rhetoric used to justify such a harmonization. More particularly they should realize that they can either opt for the ecological goal of uniform environmental quality or for the goal of harmonizing legislation, but not for both at the same time. One has the impression at the present time that the instruments chosen (harmonization of legislation) do not always match the expressed goals (harmonization of environmental quality). Apparently European legal scholars are coming round to this view to this insight as well. Recently De Witte argued that Europe should now leave the – wrong – rhetoric about harmonization of conditions of competition aside and should clearly state that it wants to achieve a minimum quality for its citizens[144].

Several conclusions can be drawn from the analyses in the previous sections. First, from the analyses it appears that the arguments advanced by the Commission to justify European competences for the area of environmental liability are either weak or insufficient to justify a harmonized liability legislation in Europe. Therefore, if Europe is concerned with ecological goals and wishes to achieve a similar environmental quality in the Union, it should set harmonized target standards. Europe should, in other words, be interested in the end product, being the environmental quality to be reached. This also assumes that Europe would merely receive powerful tools to monitor whether this environmental quality is actually achieved (which is still a major weakness today[145])

---

[144] De Witte, B., 'Carving out a place for European Union law in the legal universe' (paper presented at the conference Ius Commune in a World Context, Maastricht 15 April 1999, forthcoming in the *Maastricht Journal of European and Comparative Law*).

[145] In Europe there is no enforcement agency which possesses police powers, as this is considered by member states to violate their sovereignty (Kimber, C., 'A comparison of environmental federalism in the United States and the European Union', 54, *Maryland Law Review*, 1995, 1685; Ogus, A., *Regulation, Legal Form and Economic Theory*, Oxford: Clarendon Press, 1994, 212–13 and Pfander, J., 72–75.

and to enforce the target in case of non compliance. The fact that it is difficult to monitor the actual quality of the environment may also explain why Europe long preferred directives containing emission standards whereby the Commission only checked whether there was a correct formal implementation in the legislation of the member states.

Second, in order to reach this uniform environmental quality, environmental liability legislation can be differentiated. This differentiation is efficient as long as the benefits of differentiation outweigh the (administrative) costs.

Third, from this it follows that the idea of harmonization of conditions of competition, as it is pronounced as a goal for European environmental action, is wrong for several reasons. It is wrong for economic reasons, since a full harmonization of conditions of competition is not needed to reach the economic goals of the Treaty; it is equally wrong for ecological reasons, since it does not allow for the goal of uniform environmental quality. The conclusion may only be different if externalities are transboundary or there is a serious risk of a run to pollution havens. Those may be arguments to harmonize liability legislation, but then it should be clear that this may not lead to an equal environmental quality. In that case European policymakers will have to make a choice between 'levelling the playing field' through harmonized legislation or ecological harmonization of environmental quality. One way to (partially) reconcile these goals is to shift powers to Brussels because of the transboundary character of the externality, but to recognize differentiated liability rules[146].

It should equally be examined whether a total harmonization of liability standards is needed to reach a common market in Europe. Other, useful, but not that far-reaching (less inefficient) instruments may be available. One can think, for example, of a standardization of procedures within environmental law which still remains useful because of the transboundary character of pollution and industrial operations[147]. This can indeed increase transparency, as was intended to be achieved by the IPPC Directive, and can reduce transaction costs. However, such a harmonization should not necessarily be achieved through formal directives, but can also be achieved through a search for common principles through comparative research, looking for a *ius commune*.

In that respect it should be stressed that economic analysis of federalism provides certainly useful insights concerning the question of centralization,

---

[146] This was rightly suggested by Esty, D. and Geradin, D., 'Market access, competitiveness and harmonization: environmental protection in regional trade agreements', 21 *Harvard Environmental Law Review*, 1997, 291; and Esty, D. and Geradin, D., 'Environmental protection and international competitiveness. A conceptual framework', 32/2 *Journal of World Trade*, 1998, 43.

[147] This is suggested by Esty, D. and Geradin, D., 'Market access, competitiveness and harmonization: environmental protection in regional trade agreements', 21 *Harvard Environmental Law Review*, 1997, 293.

but it does not always provide an answer to the question which of the many possible legal techniques of harmonization has to be chosen to deal with a particular problem. The economic notion of *centralization* is too general to cover all the legal techniques of *harmonization*. It therefore certainly merits further research to find which of these harmonization techniques is best suited to deal with a particular problem like environmental liability. Moreover, in the economic analysis there are unanswered questions which merit further research. One of them is how the need to centralize decision-making in case of transboundary externalities can be reconciled with the ecological goal of a uniform environmental quality. Another is whether industry in heavily polluted areas may be disadvantaged with more stringent emission standards with repect to their competitors in 'cleaner' countries. Some of the questions need further empirical research, for example, concerning the influence of environmental regulation on industry behaviour. In that respect Europe should certainly carefully look at the US experience with environmental federalism[148].

REFERENCES

Ackerman, R.M. (1996), 'Tort law and Federalism: whatever happened to devolution?', *Yale Law and Policy Review*, 429–63.
Arcuri, A. (2000), 'Controlling environmental risk in Europe: the complementary role of an EC environmental liability regime', *TMA*, 37–45.
Bergkamp, L. (1998), 'A future environmental liability regime', *European Environmental Law Review*, 200–204.
Bergkamp L. (2000), 'The White Paper on environmental liability', *European Environmental Law Review*, 105–114.
Betlem, G. (2000), 'Commission adopts White Paper on environmental liability', *TMA*, 58–60.
Bierbooms, P.F.A. and E.H.P. Brans (2000), 'Het EU witboek milieu-aansprakelijkheid: de vage contouren van een toekomstig aansprakelijkheidsregime', Milieu & Recht, 182–88.
Cohen, M. (1996), 'Commentary', in E. Eide, and R. Van den Bergh (eds), *Law and Economics of the Environment*, Oslo: Juridisk Forlag, 167–71.
De Vries, C. (1999), 'Community action on environmental liability', in L. Wiggers-Rust, and K. Deketelaere (eds), *Aansprakelijkheid voor milieuschade en financiële zekerheid*, Die Keure-Vermande, 141–47.

---

[148] See for comparative analyses of environmental federalism in the US and Europe e.g. Kimber, Clíona, 'A Comparison of Environmental Federalism in the United States and the European Union', 54, *Maryland Law Review*, 1995; Esty, D. and Geradin, D., 'Market access, competitiveness and harmonization: environmental protection in regional trade agreements', 21 *Harvard Environmental Law Review*, 1997, and Esty, D. and Geradin, D., 'Environmental protection and international competitiveness. A conceptual framework', 32/2 *Journal of World Trade*, 1998; Pfander, J., note 3 (1996) and Rose-Ackerman, S., *Rethinking the Progressive Agenda*, New York, Free Press, 1992, 37–54.

De Witte, B. (1999), 'Carving out a place for European Union law in the legal universe', paper presented at the conference Ius Commune in a World Context, Maastricht 15 April, forthcoming in the *Maastricht Journal of European and Comparative Law.*

Esty, D. (1996), 'Revitalizing environmental federalism', *Michigan Law Review*, **95**, 625.

Esty, D. (1999), 'Economic integration and the environment', in N. Vig, and R. Axelrod (eds), *The Global Environment,* Washington, DC: CQ Press, 190–209.

Esty, D. and D. Geradin (1997), 'Market access, competitiveness and harmonization: environmental protection in regional trade agreements', *Harvard Environmental Law Review*, **21**, 265–336.

Esty, D. and D. Geradin (1998), 'Environmental protection and international competitiveness. A conceptual framework', *Journal of World Trade*, **32**(3), 5–46.

Esty, D. and D. Geradin (eds) (2001), *Regulatory Competition and Economic Integration, Comparative Perspectives,*

Faure M. (1996), 'Economic aspects of environmental liability: an introduction', *European Review of Private Law*, 85–109.

Faure, M. (1998), 'Harmonisation of environmental law and market integration: harmonising for the wrong reasons?', *European Environmental Law Review*, 169–175.

Faure, M. (2000), 'Product liability and product safety in Europe: harmonisation or differentiation?', *Kyklos*, **53**, 467–508.

Faure, M. (2001), 'Regulatory competition versus harmonization in EU environmental law', in D. Esty and D. Geradin (eds), *Regulatory Competition and Economic Integration,* Oxford: Oxford University Press, 263–86.

Frey, B. (1994), 'Direct democracy: politico-economic lessons from Switzerland', *American Economic Review*, **84**, 338–42.

Frey, B. (1996a), 'FOCJ: competitive governments for Europe', *International Review of Law and Economics,* **16**, 315–27.

Frey, B. and R. Eichenberger (1996), 'To harmonise or to compete? That's not the question', *Journal of Public Economics*, **60**, 441–58.

Hunter, R. (2000), 'European Commission White Paper proposals on NGO rights of action: wrongful rights of action', *Tijdschrift voor Milieu-aansprakelijkheid*, 125–26.

Inman, R.P. and D.L. Rubinfeld (1994), 'The EMU and fiscal policy in the new European community, an issue for economic federalism', *International Review of Law and Economics,* **14**, 147–62.

Jaffe, A., S. Peterson, S. Portney and R. Stavins (1995), 'Environmental regulation and the competitiveness of US manufacturing: what does the evidence tell us?', *Journal of Economic Literature*, **33**, 132–63.

Kimber, C. (1995), 'A comparison of environmental federalism in the United States and the European Union', *Maryland Law Review*, **54**, 321–26.

Kirchgässner, G. and W.W. Pommerehne (1993), 'Low-cost decisions as a challenge to public choice', *Public Choice*, **77**, 107–16.

Kolstad, C.D. (2000), *Environmental Economics*, Oxford: Oxford University Press.

Lando, O. (1993), 'Die Regeln des Europäischen Vertragsrecht', in P. Müller-Graff (ed.), *Gemeinsames Privatrecht in der Europäischen Gemeinschaft*, Baden-Baden: Nomos, 473–74.

Lefevere, J. and M. Faure (1995), 'Introduction to European environmental law', in T. Kegels (ed.), *Shipping Law Faces Europe: European Policy Competition and Environment,* Brussels: Maklu, 93–107.

Legrand, B. (1997), 'The impossibility of "legal transplants"', *Maastricht Journal of European and Comparative Law*, 111ff.

Mendelsohn, R. (1986), 'Regulatory heterogeneous emissions', *Journal of Environmental Economics and Management*, **13**, 301.

Niezen, G.J. (2000), 'Aansprakelijkheid voor milieuschade in de Europese Unie' in *Ongebonden Recht Bedrijven*, Kluwer, 165–67 and 168–69.

Oates, W.E. (1972), *Fiscal Federalism*, New York: Harcourt.

Oates, W.E. and Schwab, R. (1988), 'Economic competition among jurisdiction: efficiency enhancing or distortion inducing?', *Journal of Public Economics*, **35**, 333–54.

Ogus, A. (1996), *Regulation, Legal Form and Economic Theory*, Oxford: Clarendon Press.

Ogus, A. (1999b), 'Standard setting for an environmental protection', in M. Faure, J. Vervaele and A. Weale (eds), *Environmental Standards in the European Union in an Interdisciplinary Framework*, Antwerpen: Maklu, 25–30.

Ogus, A. (1999), 'Competition between national legal systems: a contribution of economic analysis to comparative law', *International and Comparative Law Quarterly*, **48**, 408.

Pâques, M. (1996), 'Effet direct du droit communautaire, interprétation conforme et responsabilité de l'Etat en général et en matière d'environnement', in J. Van Dunné (ed.), *Non-Point Source River Pollution; The Case of the River Meuse*, Den Haag and London: Kluwer Law International, 89–139.

Rehbinder, E. (2000), 'Towards a community environmental liability regime: the commission's white paper on environmental liability', *Environmental Liability*, 85–96.

Repetto, R., *Trade and Sustainable Development*, UNEP, Environment and Trade Series.

Revesz, R. (1992), 'Rehabilitating interstate competition: rethinking the race for the bottom rational for federal environmental regulation', *New York University Law Review*, **67**, 1210–54.

Revesz, R. (1996), 'Federalism and interstate environmental externalities', *University of Pennsylvania Law Review*, **144**, 2341–2416.

Revesz, R. (2001), 'Federalism and regulation: some generalizations', in D. Esty and D. Geradin (eds), *Regulatory Competition and Economic Integration, Comparative Perspectives*, 3–29.

Rice, P. (2000), 'From Lugano to Brussels via Arhus: environmental liability white paper published', *Environmental Liability*, 39–45.

Rose-Ackerman, S. (1992), *Rethinking the Progressive Agenda: the Reform of the American Regulatory State*, New York: Free Press, 169.

Schoenbrod, D. (1996), 'Why states, not EPA, should set pollution standards', *Regulation*, **4**, 18–25.

Trebilcock, M. and R. Howse (1998), 'Trade liberalization and regulatory diversity, reconciling competitive markets with competitive politics', *European Journal of Law and Economics*, **6**, 5–37.

Van den Bergh, R. (1994), 'The subsidiarity principle in European Community law: some insights from law and economics', *Maastricht Journal of European and Comparative Law*.

Van den Bergh, R., M. Faure and J. Lefevere (1996), 'The subsidiarity principle in European environmental law: an economic analysis,' in E. Eide and R. Van den Bergh (eds), *Law and Economics of the Environment*, Oslo: Jurdisk Forlag, 128–31.

Van den Bergh, R. (1998), 'Subsidiarity as an economic demarcation principle and the emergence of European private law', *Maastricht Journal of European and Comparative Law*.

Van den Bergh, R. (1999), 'Economics in a legal strait-jacket: the difficult reception of economic analysis in European law' paper presented at the Empirical Research and Legal Realism. Setting the Agenda workshop, Haifa, 6–9 June.

Van Dunné, J. (1991), *Transboundary Pollution and Liability: the Case of the River Rhine*, Rotterdam: Erasmus University Institute of Environmental Damages.

Vogel, D. (1995), *Trading Up: Consumer and Environmental Regulation in the Global Economy*, Cambridge: Harvard University Press.

Wils, W. (1994), 'Subsidiarity and the EC environmental policy: taking people's concerns seriously', *Journal of Environmental Law*, 85–90.

Xing, Y. and C. Kolstad (1995), 'Do lax environmental regulations attract foreign investment'?, working paper in economics 16–95, University of California.

ANNEX 3.1   POSSIBLE SCOPE OF AN EC ENVIRONMENTAL LIABILITY REGIME

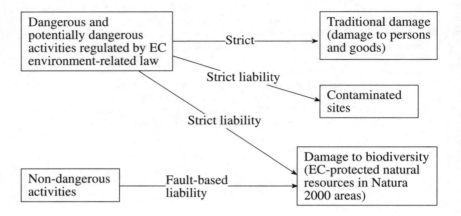

4. Resale price maintenance for books in Germany and the European Union: A legal and economic analysis

Jürgen G. Backhaus and Reginald Hansen

INTRODUCTION

'I fail to see how a regime that keeps book prices higher than they need to be promotes culture.' EU Commissioner designate Mario Monti

List prices and end price maintenance agreements between producers and vendors are not uncommon in some industries. Typically, such agreements occur when a brand name needs to be protected by specific services for maintenance of the product, by large stocks of materials necessary for the use of the products or if particularly high skills are required for the service to the customer in relation to the product. While, for instance, in the United States it is not uncommon for booksellers to discount[149], in the German language area there has traditionally been a book price maintenance binding the booksellers not to discount (except under very specific conditions). Since Germany as a cultural entity extends over several sovereign states of which two are members of the European Union, an issue of cross-border traffic arises (between the Federal Republics of Austria and Germany), and a suit had been brought by the Austrian book chain 'Libro-Amadeus' which signalled that it would settle its suit in exchange for 100 German railroad station book stores.[150] During the very last meeting of the European Commission under its president Jacques Santer, the Belgian Commissioner for Competition, Karel van Miert, had

---

[149] The arrival of the Internet book trade has brought additional turbulence to book prices. Amazon.com Inc. for one has started to offer 50 per cent discounts on best selling books, where a best-seller is defined as being listed on the *New York Times* best-seller lists. (The use of that list has sparked an additional legal dispute that has been resolved in the following way: Amazon can use the copyrighted list in exchange for sharing sensitive sales data with the *New York Times*. Other sellers such as barnesandnoble.com have kept book discounts very steady at the 20–40 per cent level, and this also applies to Dalton with its real, as opposed to virtual, book stores. See Anders (1999).

[150] Michael Naumann, 'Was Bücher von Kartoffeln unterscheidet', *Welt am Sonntag*, 29, 13.7.1999, p. 19 (The Difference between Potatoes and Books).

pushed for a measure to prohibit the German resale price maintenance agreements in honouring Libro-Amadeus' claim on the basis of an expert opinion
by the London-based research group EuropeMonitor. Due to strong opposition
from some of his colleagues, he failed to receive the 11 commissioners' majority of the requisite vote. This was due in particular to the opposition from the
Commissioner for Cultural Affairs, the Spaniard Marcelino Oreja, who based
his argument on article 151 of the Treaty of Amsterdam which re-affirms that
the commission has to respect the cultural differences of the various member
states. This issue is by no means a spurious one. During the formal interviews
of the candidate commissioners under the designated commission president
Romano Prodi, the designated commissioner for Competition, Mario Monti,
re-affirmed and even strengthened his predecessor's position, granting
however that for the German book trade there may be a cultural aspect of
which he yet had to be convinced. On the other hand, the candidate from
Luxembourg for cultural affairs, Viviane Reding, made the cultural issue with
respect to the German book trade a major plank of her pitch, along with an
emphasis on preserving minority languages in the different member states. In
the meantime, the German Book Traders Association and its Austrian counterpart have tried to come to an agreement largely modelled upon the French
system based on the Lois Lang. While the Commission in a press release of 23
February 2000 reported that the German and Austrian book publishers have
now accepted the Commission's position implying that the cross-border
system of fixed prices will be replaced by separate but co-ordinated German
and Austrian systems of fixed prices, the same press release also stated that the
solution obtained was now fully supported by Ms. Reding, the present
Commissioner for Culture and Education. On the other hand, the Commission
has also tried to enlist the support of the Swiss Cartel Authority. In principle,
issues of cultural affairs in Switzerland rest with the cantonal authorities; only
antitrust policy is a matter of the federal level. Hence, the same problem resur-
faces for Switzerland that is also playing out in Germany. If the cultural issue
is of equally significant importance, the antitrust aspects would likewise have
to be dealt with at the level of the Länder, i.e. by the 16 Länder antitrust
authorities. Given these circumstances, a law and economics analysis of the
effects and their desirability of the end price maintenance agreements in the
German language book trade is by no means a straightforward affair. Typically
in the fields of law and economics we can safely assume that there is an aspect
to a broader issue that can be reasonably claimed for economic analysis. In this
particular case, however, disentangling the economic and cultural issues is the
first major task for addressing the problem. The consultancy work of the
EuroMonitor group had readily been criticized for not taking into account relevant features of the German language book trade. The researchers, who had no
command of German, were, of course, in a most peculiar position. The mate-

rial on the German language book trade is totally locked into the German language. However, the organization of the book trade has a long history and both are very complicated. Hence, a thorough description with a view towards economic analysis is needed before any standard analysis can be applied[151]. Accordingly, the background chapter consists in an analytical description of the structure of the German book trade with a view to understanding the functional role of the end sale maintenance agreements.

That part of the analysis has five sections. The first section deals with the role of competition and the development of the German book trade. The second deals with the development of the current organizational structure of the German book trade. The third part is devoted to the cultural mission of the German book trade as an exception in EU competition law. Fourth we deal with the change of position in the European Directorate General on competition with respect to the German book trade. Finally, the fifth section of part I looks at the position of the German Book Trade Association with respect to the European Commission initiative.

In the second part of the chapter, we are trying to lay the groundwork for a sensible law and economics analysis that takes the historical and organizational history of the German book trade seriously and looks at its specific role in the development and care for German literary culture. One part of that culture is, of course, science and scholarship, which is why we need to look at the scholarly publishers separately. Part two therefore starts with a brief history of one of these originally German-based publishers and its role in the international community of science publishers. This provides an additional dimension to the problem of understanding competition and the institutional order in which such competition can take place with respect to the production, availability and sale of books. The analysis in the second part yields a set of propositions which necessarily have to underlie any type of decision-making on the part of the European Commission. In the conclusion, we summarize our major findings and identify work still to be done.

The focus of this chapter is not an analysis of the structure of the German language book trade as such. It is hard to measure the impact of the current system of resale price maintenance on quantity and quality (including composition and cultural diversity) of book production, in particular since the sector is currently undergoing deep technological change. The question explored here is whether regulatory action on the part of the European Commission can conceivably be welfare-enhancing. The Commission lacks authority where the cultural identity of member states is involved; hence, it is important to explore whether the current structure of the German language book trade, of which the system of resale price maintenance is only a part

---

[151] Backhaus, Jürgen G. and Reginald Hansen, 1999.

and which has evolved over several centuries, is intertwined with the cultural identity of the German language literary institutions in such a way that a link can be established. It is immaterial in this context to provide quantitative data (such as the number of books published per head of the population) because, first, such data do not give any information about quality and, secondly, there is no apparent link between such data and the cultural institution of a particular people.[152]

1.   THE HISTORY AND ORGANIZATION OF THE GERMAN BOOK TRADE

The current debate about the end price maintenance for German language books has to be seen in the context of the larger organization of the German book trade, which has to be looked upon as path dependent and therefore different from organizational structures that have developed in some (but not all) of the other member states of the European Union. It is therefore sensible to look at this organizational history more closely.

The Function of Competition and the Development of the German Book Trade

Currently, the industry of book publishing, wholesaling and retailing, as well as readers' behaviour, is undergoing deep technological change. This will likely lead to new forms of marketing and production and new forms of packaging of what we now refer to as a book. In this sense, it is likely that the current system of resale price maintenance as it has evolved in Germany over time will undergo changes quite independent of action taken by the European Commission. After all, since the invention of technical printing, the German book trade has undergone various technical innovations which, although ultimately welfare-enhancing, have sometimes taken some time to materialize due to the social frictions that they caused.

When using the term book trade, we refer to the entire industry of media-based information, from the conception by the author and his surroundings (in either a corporate- or a government-based working environment or in a home-based industry) in terms of a put-out system targeted ultimately at the consumer, including production, processing, distribution, consumption or use and storage. This industry is now facing several challenges, both technical and

---

[152] The respective figures are per 1 million head population: in the German-language area, the number of books currently available is 8323; in the United States and Great Britain, this number is clearly lower at 5771. For details please see Backhaus and Hansen, 1999.

institutional. At the technical level, there is substantial uncertainty about the future of the book itself. There are some who believe that the book in its present form will disappear and be replaced by some type of electronic file or site. There are, however, others who believe that the traditional book does have a future, side by side with new electronic media, files, sites, disks and the like. Also, next to the production and storage of the media involved, publishing itself is becoming a more and more international and integrated activity in the sense that publishing houses merge across borders and language barriers. Hence, the traditional book becomes part of a multi-media and multi-language product menu. This process is furthermore facilitated (but not caused) by the common European market. Similar developments can be expected in the other common markets, NAFTA and MercoSur. In addition, the European Union has now challenged the traditional form of the German-language area book trade which, as one of its significant features, has the rule of contractually based fixed-end (as opposed to intermediate) book prices. This intervention is all the more surprising since the traditional book trade is currently being replaced by a virtual book trade over the Internet. This development already poses a substantial challenge to the traditional bookstore. In Germany alone, there are about 2000 independent bookstores and more than 20 000 licensed booksellers.[153]

Technological and social change has indeed not come easy to the German book publishing and processing industry in its history. Here is one example. The publisher F.A. Brockhaus, whose name today stands for the most important German encyclopaedia (comparable to the Encyclopaedia Britannica in the English-language world) is a company that had been founded in Amsterdam in 1805, in 1811 moved to Altenberg (Saxony), and in 1817–18 moved again, to Leipzig. In 1826 the company wanted its three wooden book presses built in 1816 to be replaced by a newly-developed, much more efficient express press. The printers who had been trained on presses with the wooden technology resisted bitterly. Actually, on 4 September 1830, a mob stormed the printing facility in order to destroy the express presses, their leaders indicating their belief that the new technology took away the livelihood of many workers.[154]

---

[153] Booksellers are organized as a craft, that is to say there is an apprenticeship, a period of journeyman and an examination in order to obtain the master's degree. Although based on state regulations, the system is administered by the chamber of commerce which also handles the exams. The curriculum is a mixture of those of a librarian and those of a merchant (Kaufmann), both professions also being similarly regulated. There are no restrictions on entry, and wages of employed booksellers tend to be depressed; the same holds for incomes of self-employed booksellers. The profession tends to attract highly intrinsically-motivated persons; it has traditionally served as a niche for political minorities and outsiders, notably when political freedom was endangered. This may partly explain why opposition to the European Commission's initiative has been so widespread and across party lines in Germany.

[154] F.A. Brockhaus, '1805–1940. Aus der Arbeit von fünf Generationen', Zum Gutenberg-Jahr 1940. F.A. Brockhaus, Leipzig, 1940, p. 14 and p. 67 f.

These luddites saw the technology as a menace to their own livelihood. Similarly today, the elements outlined above are seen and experienced as endangering the livelihood of the more than 20 000 German booksellers and all those who depend on them; since booksellers traditionally tend to be an important multiplier and opinion leader in the political community, the issue should not be underestimated from the point of view of the political feasibility of this European Union initiative. It is from this point of view that we urge a thorough analysis including the entire spectrum of historical, cultural and economic issues.

As a consequence of her complex history, Germany has cultural institutions which are very different from those found in other countries that form part of the European Union. (See the detailed overview in Backhaus and Hansen, 1999.) The book as a commodity appeared, of course, almost simultaneously with the Lutheran Reformation (started in 1517), and not surprisingly some of the first printed works were translated Bibles. However, that same event, the Reformation, ultimately led to the disastrous Thirty Years' War which was concluded with three treaties in 1648. As a consequence, Germany had many fairly independent states making up the whole German empire, and hence it also had many capitals competing one with the other, very often in terms of cultural affairs. Censorship would be practised in some states but there were always exceptions of more lenient rulers, and hence sometimes very small states produced a blooming publishing landscape, such as the tiny Thuringian Duchy of Saxony-Hildburghausen, the capital of which, i.e. Hildburghausen, became a centre of publishing, and the site of the first German-language encyclopaedia. Since trade between these many centres of book publishing had to be facilitated, early on the German booksellers developed their own fair with its own rules, regulations, overseeing boards etc., organizing the biannual book fair originally in Leipzig, which also houses the main German central depository library. This non-state association, which is still in existence and organizes the book fairs in Frankfurt and Leipzig on an annual basis now, also became a pioneer in establishing authors' property rights (copyrights). It is important to emphasize the non-state nature of this entity, as German culture, due to German diversity in statehood, could develop unified structures only separate from state organization.

This cultural peculiarity proved to be a big advantage during the reign of the national socialists, who could not break the stern independence of independent publishing houses despite their very best effort and hence failed in totally suppressing basic freedoms of expression, despite trying hard.[155] From this point of view, it is not far-fetched to emphasize the cultural aspect of the

---

[155] On aspects of this policy see the essay on the Springer-Verlag, forthcoming in *Business Library Review*.

German book trade organization over and against issues of simple models of competition. The current system that has grown up is a path-dependent structure with a long history, and this history is deeply steeped in German culture. Any European decision will have to take account of the priority of the cultural aspect over the competition aspect; hence the main question that has to be addressed is exactly that which Commissioner Monti raised: what is the connection between the cultural diversity of German book publishing due to its peculiar history-based organization on the one hand and the end price maintenance agreements on the other?

PART II   THE STAGES OF PRODUCTION OF A BOOK

At the heart of the German-language area book price agreements lies the question as to whether the institution is primarily a cartel with the effect of reducing output and increasing prices, or whether it has primarily the effect of promoting cultural diversity. On the basis of the historical description of the organizational structure of the German book trade, this section provides a preliminary economic analysis. In order to reflect the complex structure of the German book trade, six different stages of market interaction are being distinguished, and for each stage the question is asked whether an end to the book price agreements would lead to a price effect (either an increase or a decrease) or have some effect on cultural diversity. It should be mentioned from the outset that it is possible that the destruction of the agreements by the European Commission would lead to an ultimate increase in book prices in addition to an adverse effect on cultural diversity. In principle, three outcomes are possible. The policy change can lead to an increase, a decrease or no change at all; and two characteristics need to be observed, prices and cultural diversity. This yields in principle nine possible outcomes. Hence it is the purpose of this section to narrow down the nine possible outcomes for each of the six distinguished stages, thus yielding a total of 12 predictions, since for each stage there are two variables (prices and cultural diversity) for which the likely outcome needs to be established.

The purpose of this exercise is straightforward. If the analysis yields the result that there are significant effects on cultural diversity (irrespective of the price effects), then the issue at hand is not simply a competence of the Competition Commissioner. It is important to emphasize at this point that a focused economic analysis not looking at the effects on cultural diversity is not sufficient for this project.[156] Before one can look at the appropriate decision

---

[156] For such an analysis see Henning Stumpp, 'Die Preisbindung für Verlagserzeugnisse: Wettbewerbsbeschränkung oder Regulierung zur Beseitigung von Marktunvollkommenheiten?' Baden Baden: Nomos 1999, pp. 2 and 6.

itself, it has to be established in which political realm and hence political competency the decision has to fall. Despite recent moves in Germany to establish an office in the Chancellery, cultural affairs are a matter of the 16 constituent states of the Federal Republic of Germany and cannot be claimed by the European Commission. In Austria, it is the federal government's responsibility; in Switzerland it is a cantonal prerogative, except for the possibility that the issue of the end price agreements is primarily and overridingly an economic matter. In that case, this Swiss antitrust agency would be responsible.

In addition to the initiatives by the European Commission, the book trade in Germany (but not in Austria or Switzerland) is faced with the effects of a planned tax reform and the book trade worldwide may undergo deep change as a consequence of the emergence of the Internet and the possibility of printing on demand. Since the first electronic publications have already appeared which are not derivatives of the traditional book, the impact of this electronic revolution on the book trade broadly conceived is largely uncertain. It is very likely that the traditional German book trade will be affected, but it is uncertain in which way. Many licensed booksellers have taken to an extensive use of the Internet already, and quite a few bookstores, notably some in remote communities, derive a substantial part of their revenue from Internet sales. Under these circumstances, the timing of the European Commission's initiative complicates a thorough analysis of the long-term consequences of any considered change in the rules affecting the German-language book trade.[157]

There are six stages or levels on which the analysis has to concentrate.

Stage 1

At the heart of every creative project leading to a published result there must be an idea and hence by necessity an author. The author may be embedded in a productive context such as a corporation, a governmental environment, a not-for-profit organization or a private environment, since much creative work is still taking place in the traditional form of home-based production.[158] The diversity of book and related media production implies that books are not

---

[157] Strangely enough, the European Commission takes the deep technological change currently affecting the book trade worldwide as a reason for its intervention in the historically-grown German structures. In support, it cites the 1997 decision of the British Restrictive Practices Court.

[158] Among the almost 80 000 (in 1997 77 900) titles produced in Germany, 12.2 per cent are literary productions as such, 7.2 per cent fall into the category of mathematics and the natural sciences, 7.2 per cent of arts, music and sports, 5.7 per cent of medicine, another 5.7 per cent of economics and business, 5.4 per cent are books for children and adolescents, 5.3 per cent cover law, 5 per cent religion, 4.9 per cent make up the important market for school books, another 4.9 per cent are devoted to history, 4.6 per cent to philosophy and psychology, 4.4 per cent to languages, 4.2 per cent are maps, 3.2 per cent geography and travel, and the remainder of another 20.1 per cent is spread widely over other areas of knowledge and entertainment.

homogenous products for which simple demand curves can be drawn. We rather have to think of singular products and unique processes and circumstances of production when a culturally diverse landscape of books is to be envisaged. This distinction, although difficult to quantify, is important for the issue at hand. It is, in principle, possible to manufacture a book or documentary on any conceivable topic according to certain guidelines. As soon as creativity is involved and discoveries need to be made, such manufacturing turns into a craft. For manufactured products, market demand can be projected beforehand. In order to put out craftwork, entrepreneurial judgement is necessary and a personal relationship between the put out entrepreneur, that is to say the publisher, and the author or team of authors of the craftwork in question. This is not only the case with fine literature, it is also the case with scholarly work, and this is why the large scholarly publishers have developed highly diversified company structures with many independently operating publishers within them.

As demand cannot readily be established for any particular piece of craftwork, just for a particular style or area or discipline of scholarship according to its own criteria of quality, for each individual piece it is hard to 'ex ante' calculate the demand and likely business success. It is an entire line of work which identifies a particular publishing venture which has its own market segment and therefore can be assessed for its value. In order to have some basis for calculation, a fixed price allows for a precise contract with the author, establishing royalties and some expectation on which to base the extension of work and effort. Likewise, the fixed end price allows for appropriations of budgets on the part of the publisher to each particular venture. In fact, the fixed end price results in a cross-subsidization of less successful projects by more successful ones, where it is not known beforehand which project will be successful and which will be less so. If the end price were not fixed, the entire calculatory basis would change. Then, one would first have to establish the demand for a particular product (and not line or class of products), conceivably establishing the demand by appropriate marketing methods beforehand. After that the manufacturing of such a product could take place and manufacturing authors would be recruited to fulfil the task. Those would be able to command high honoraria. The end result would be a smaller number of highly successful products with the downside that the large diversity of products would suffer. For the American market, this has been well documented for scholarly books, which have all but disappeared in entire sub-disciplines.[159]

Interestingly enough, the end price agreements in the international financial

---

[159] See William C. Dowling (1997), 'The crisis in scholarly publishing, in *The Public Interest* 129, pp. 23–37. The crisis is identified as 'the drying up of resources for intensive studies of small but worthwhile subjects in favour of trend-driven publishing' (p. 23).

literature are routinely referred to as the Austro-German book cartel. A cartel in the broadest sense can be defined as 'a group of producers that acts collectively'.[160] Generally, the implication is that the collective action involves agreement upon a price with the effect of reducing output and increasing the price above the competitive level. As has become apparent by now, the end price agreements result in fixed prices but not in an output reduction. In addition, the agreements do not result in a uniform price; the individual publishers remain free to set their prices at whichever level they desire, and they compete among each other with both prices and the quality of their product or better product lines. Hence, speaking of a cartel overextends the appropriate meaning of the economic term and does not add to clarity. In conclusion, we note that the book end price agreements do not eliminate price competition, but that they do have a cultural effect in that through cross-subsidization cultural diversity is being supported. This diversity implies that some books, the trend-driven publications, may be priced higher, but that a large number of books will also be priced lower than otherwise they would be. The overall price effect is not an increase, and ending the agreements would therefore not result automatically in a decrease of the overall book price levels.

Stage 2

Besides the books and their derivatives, there is, of course, also the market for copyrights. Here the question arises as to whether the end price agreements affect the value of copyrights. Again, we have to look for both a possible price effect and a conceivable effect on cultural diversity, in this case a quantity effect (number of copyrights granted and protected). In stage 2, when we look at the relationship not between the publisher and the author but the question of how many books will be marketed (and hence copyrights requested), the only effect the end book price agreements have on these decisions is to add an element of certainty and hence allow for a better calculatory basis. The price itself can be anything – it is a means of competition. Yet the price is a fixed one, not an uncertain figure oscillating over time and place. The better calculatory basis allows for a broader and longer catalogue of books, and hence there is, again, an impact on cultural diversity. There is no discernible price effect at this stage.

   An unrelated issue, which has, however, had a potential impact on the two variables discussed so far, concerns the planned repeal of accelerated depreciation of books held in storage by publishers. Under the current system in the Federal Republic of Germany, books printed and put in storage can depreciate

---

[160] See Robert S. Pindyck and Daniel L. Rubinfeld (1998), *Microeconomics*, Upper-Saddle River, New Jersey: Prentice Hall, p. 10.

rapidly and hence will show up as profit only when sold. This allows for large catalogues of books actually held in storage over very long periods of time. A traditional science publisher, for instance, proudly emphasizes that every book published since 1945 is still available. (The company lost its entire stock of books and its archive during the last war.) This policy will be hard to continue if accelerated depreciation can no longer be applied. This would lead to shorter durations of storage, shorter catalogues and in this sense a dampening effect on cultural variety. Some selected titles would be kept in storage, and there would then likely be an upward price effect for those cases. However, it should be emphasized that this measure is in principle unrelated to the European Commission initiative, although it impacts in similar ways.

The remaining four stages can be largely seen as being driven by the interests of the consumer. Here we have to look consecutively at the wholesale stage, the retail sale stage, the household decisions involving consumption and the impact of government initiatives with respect to cultural diversity.

Stage 3

As a vital link between the several thousand book publishers with almost 100 000 titles in German alone per year on the one hand and the more than 20 000 licensed booksellers in more than 2000 bookshops serving a population of about 100 million in the German-language area, there is the vital link of the wholesalers. These can quickly locate hard-to-find books and publishers and have the desired items shipped to the requesting bookstore in a matter of a few days, sometimes just hours. This system is by far superior to anything one can experience outside the German trade area, for instance in the United States. Since their turnover is so much larger than that of any one bookstore, even large ones in choice locations, the wholesalers can also maintain very large stocks of books, up to substantial fractions of all the books in print, the most frequently demanded ones in substantial quantities. This system of wholesale intermediacy owes its existence to the very large number of titles and publishers involved and operates under the umbrella of the fixed end price on the basis of which the customer has already made a choice and commissions the provision of the book. The end price contains information provided on the one hand by the publisher and on the other, together with the first volume of orders, by the customer. Both of these sources of information substantially facilitate the decisions of the wholesaler. If that fixed end price were no longer available, wholesalers would have to make their own guesses as to which books might be requested and with what frequency, and they would necessarily have to specialize in subject areas such as the ones mentioned in the quantitative survey. That would lengthen the process between ordering the book and receiving it, which is all-important for the consumer at the end of the chain. We can therefore see clearly that there is a connection between the end price and the extent of cultural diversity, with the end price primarily reducing transaction costs in the interest of speed and diversity. Instead of searching for the best price of any specific book, booksellers can search for the closest availability of a particular book, quoting a fixed price to their customers. Some books will be more expensive to ship than others, some searches will take longer than others, but overall the cost minimization can be done on the basis of the sales figures these wholesalers have and which guide their policies of how to stock and which channels of communication to maintain and use. Abolishing the end price agreements would have to lead to a substantial reorganization of the wholesale book industry, and some of these wholesalers would probably try to reach a segment of end customers bypassing the retailers. Such a move might bring price advantages to a select group of book users (institutional purchasers such as libraries come to mind) but retail presence in smaller locations would necessarily suffer.

Stage 4

Much of the current debate focuses on the future of the more than 20 000 licensed booksellers whose existence is seen as endangered by the Association of the German Book Trade. The connection between the end price agreements and the operation of these booksellers is not quite obvious for the outsider, but can be readily gleaned from the history and organization of the book trade described above and the discussion of the first stages of the book trade in this section. The discussion needs to start by a clarification of terms. The retailers are not involved in a cartel designed to fix the price and reduce the input. They are not even involved in some kind of collective agreement, as many retailers fiercely compete with each other in local markets. Any local book market is highly contestable. Due to their large number and regulation of entry through a licensing system that requires schooling but not the demonstration of some need for a bookstore in a local area, each store is faced by the ready entry of local competitors and needs to compete by satisfying customers with their specific wishes. That requires obviously to have an attractive collection ready for the casual up-to-date reader who may not be a repeat customer; this would be the strategy, for instance, in an American airport.[161] However, just serving up current novels and other similar literature would only at most cover 12 per cent of the entire book market available. The local bookstore will try to cater to the wishes of the different professional groups, adding their various

---

[161] The complaint against the German system was actually brought by a large Austrian chain, operating some 200 stores, mostly in railroad stations and generating total annual sales of DM 0.5 billion. This chain is comparable to operators at, for instance, American airports.

demands in the sciences, the arts, medical literature, business and economic literature, children's books and books for youths, law, religion, school books and the like, carefully adding segment upon segment of these various demands according to local conditions. In this way, it becomes clear that the competition between the booksellers can become fierce without even having to involve price competition. (Price competition does happen with respect to special occasions, returned copies and the like.) By excluding price competition in normal cases, the large number of booksellers are forced into quantity and quality competition that can only be won if as large a spectrum as possible of the total available can be projected onto the local market. This is exactly what cultural diversity is about, and it is surprising to what detailed extent the training of booksellers (which regularly takes three years) focuses on skills not only in retail management and business practice, but notably in identifying and finding titles in many different areas of knowledge and expertise. The more precisely sometimes vaguely described books can be identified by the local bookseller, the more precise can be the order to the wholesaler and the more promptly can it be fulfilled. Here, these skills of identifying items that the bookseller cannot possibly know as such, but can locate by using the correct categories of research, pay off in winning customers' orders for items that are not in stock. These skills of selling what cannot possibly be held in stock are emphasized in the training, hence the unmistakable link between cultural diversity and the function of the bookseller as documented in the training regulations. In addition, the end price agreements allow for a low transaction cost relationship between the retailer and the wholesaler in the interest of speed and diversity. We can therefore conclude that the end price agreement does fulfil an important role with respect to cultural diversity. Removing it would have an adverse effect on cultural diversity.

Stage 5

Cultural diversity can only be obtained if a book is not only purchased but also consumed. It is in this context that the question arises as to the relative importance of price and quality competition in the book trade. It is, of course, readily conceivable that price competition can be organized on the basis of such lists as the New York Times best-seller list with some 20 or even 50 titles that are readily identified by a large number of people. This we can see on the Internet and can expect to continue as a phenomenon. However, cultural diversity is not about 50 current books, but it is about the accumulated annual stream of some 100 000 books only in the German-language area. The purpose is to keep this stream flowing and to have it available not only as a stream but also as the stock of the past streams of annual production. If it is primarily those books that require a substantial amount of time for their consumption that we are concerned with, the overriding concern is not the price paid for the book in the bookstore, it is the ease with which it can be obtained and the ease with which it can be consumed. The time involved here in terms of opportunity costs is easily worth ten, 50, even a 100 times the price of the book in the local store. Yet here lies the catch. If there is no local store available and getting the book requires an annual ritual of travel to a major city, conceivably even to a foreign country, the cost of book acquisition even in the presence of price competition becomes an obstacle to cultural diversity. It is this implicit calculus of the efficient reader which points us to the relative irrelevance of price competition in this area as compared to diversity competition. We hence have to draw the conclusion again that cultural diversity is served by the end price maintenance agreements and an insistence on price competition will substantially reduce cultural diversity.

Stage 6

The final stage involves the regulatory environment and government options with respect to promoting cultural diversity. At present, the view prevails in the European Commission that cultural diversity is best promoted or at least not harmed by fierce price competition. We have seen by now that this view is hard to defend. However, even despite the strong relationship between non-price competition and cultural diversity demonstrated for the first five stages, it is conceivable that governments may resort to even more effective means to promote cultural diversity. For instance, the Allende government in 1971 resorted to a policy of putting a book into everybody's hand and opened bookstores with deeply discounted paperbacks bought on the international (Spanish) market. The entire Spanish classical literature was readily available, as was an impressive set of socialist tracts originally of many different persuasions. As so many similar such initiatives, this policy was short-lived because the supply of these rock-bottom paperbacks, even in such a large market as the Spanish language, is limited. More diversity would only have been added by freeing substantial foreign-exchange reserves, as local publishers, not only due to paper shortages but a general environment hostile to free and unhampered book publishing, moved elsewhere or into specialized niches. The episode demonstrates the difficulty of policies in this area. If the price is used as a policy instrument and discounts are sought for government purposes, this can be sustained for stock but with more difficulty for new books to be generated. A different market is that of schoolbooks, which through the prescription (that is to say state adoption decision) immediately receive an inelastic demand curve and contain no element of cultural variety. Here, a bidding scheme involving the provision of a schoolbook together with a

price quotation might allow a state committee to base a choice on both quality and price. Likewise, public libraries can be used as instruments to
promote cultural diversity, and since they do not need the specific services
of the book trade, the idea can be entertained to give them direct access to
wholesalers and thereby win discounts. This practice does exist. Overall,
however, the options for a more effective promotion of cultural diversity by
a state agency are extremely limited. It appears that simply granting the
exemption for the time-honoured practice is the most attractive choice,
given that cultural prerogatives are scattered over different levels of
government in the German-language area and given that the cultural
element clearly overrides conceivable benefits to be had from price competition in the book trade.

CONCLUSION

In this chapter on the organization of the German book trade, it has been
argued that the cultural and historical aspects of its organization are in all
respects more important than the anti-trust aspects. By way of summary, we
can offer the following table. Looking at the six different stages as identified
in the production of books and other similar media of communication, the
question is whether this peculiar organization of resale price maintenance
agreements has an impact on the end price and on cultural diversity. As the
table shows, our argument has been that in each of the six stages, the impact
of the agreements on cultural diversity is clearly positive. The impact on prices
is irrelevant or nil in three of the stages identified, and it is (due to cross-subsidization) undeterminable with different effects in opposite directions at the
other three stages.

*Table 4.1   Price agreements with positive/negative/uncertain effect on
prices/cultural variety*

Stages	1	2	3	4	5	6
Price	±	=	±	=	=	±
Cultural diversity	+	+	+	+	+	+

REFERENCES

Albert, H. (1998), 'Bemerkungen zur Wertproblematik', in *Schriftenreihe des Max-
Planck-Instituts zur Erforschung von Wirtschaftssystemen*, Jena: Akademischer
Buchhandel, Fachbuchservice.

Albert, H. (1967), *Marktsoziologie und Entscheidungslogik. Ökonomische Probleme in Soziologischer Perspektive*, Neuwied: Luchterhand.

Anders, George (1999), 'Amazon to offer discounts of 50% on popular books', *The Wall Street Journal Europe*, 17 May, 16.

Backhaus, Jürgen G. (1999), 'Springer-Verlag 1842–1999: a review essay', *Business Library Review*.

Backhaus, Jürgen G. and Reginald Hansen (1999), 'Die Streit um der Aufhebung der Buchpreisbindung in Deutschland', working paper, Maastricht University.

Börsenverein des Deutschen Buchhandels e.V., press information.

Börsenverein des Deutschen Buchhandels e.V. (1998), 'Erwiderung der anmeldenden Verlage auf die Beschwerdepunkte der Europäischen Kommission gegen die grenzüberschreitende Preisbindung zwischen Deutschland und Österreich – Zusammenfassung', Sonderdruck zu dem Börsenblatt für den Deutschen Buchhandel, No. 54, 7 July.

Böhm, Franz (1933), *Wettbewerb und Monopolkampf, Eine Untersuchung zur Frage des wirtschaftlichen Kampfrechts und zur Frage der rechtlichen Struktur der geltenden Wirtschaftsordnung*, Berlin: Heymann.

Brockhaus, F.A. (1940), *1805–1940. Aus der Arbeit von fünf Generationen, Zum Gutenberg-Jahr 1940*, Leipzig: F.A. Brockhaus, 14 and 67 f.

Bücher, Karl (1904), *Der deutsche Buchhandel und die Wissenschaft, Denkschrift im Auftrage des Akademischen Schutzvereins*, 3rd edn, Leipzig: Teubner.

Bücher, Karl (1903), 'Buchhandel und Wissenschaft. Eine Antwort', in *Jahrbücher für Nationalökonomie und Statistik*, III Folge, 26 Band, 237 ff.

Dowling, William C. (1997), 'The crisis in scholarly publishing', *The Public Interest*, **129**, 23–37.

Ersch, J.S. and J.G. Gruber (eds) (1824), *Allgemeine Encyclopädie der Wissenschaften und Künste in alphabetischer Folge von Schriftstellern bearbeitet, Dreizehnter Theil*, Leipzig: Gleditsch.

Estermann, Monika and Michael Knoche, (eds) (1990), *Von Göschen bis Rowohlt. Beiträge zur Geschichte des deutschen Verlagswesens, Festschrift für Heinz Sarkowski zum 65. Geburtstag*, Wiesbaden: Harrassowitz.

Frankfurter Allgemeine Zeitung (FAZ).

Frankfurter Rundschau (FR).

Goldfriedrich, Johann (1908), *Geschichte des deutschen Buchhandels vom Westfälischen Frieden bis zum Beginn der klassischen Literaturperiode (1648–1740)*, Leipzig: Verlag des Börsenvereins der deutschen Buchhändler.

Goldfriedrich, Johann (1909), *Geschichte des deutschen Buchhandels vom Beginn der klassischen Literaturperiode bis zum Beginn der Fremdherrschaft. (1740–1804)*, Leipzig: Verlag des Börsenvereins der deutschen Buchhändler.

Goldfriedrich, Johann, (ed.) (1918), *Aus den Briefen der Göschensammlung des Börsenvereins der Deutschen Buchhändler zu Leipzig*, Leipzig: Gesellschaft der Freunde der Deutschen Bücherei.

Goldfriedrich, Johann (1904), *Denkschrift betreffend die Bearbeitung einer Geschichte des deutschen Buchhandels der neueren Zeit*, Leipzig.

Goldfriedrich, Johann (1915), *Geschichte des deutschen Buchhandels vom Beginn der Fremdherrschaft bis zur Reform des Börsenvereins im neuen Deutschen Reiche. (1804–1889)*, Leipzig: Verlag des Börsenvereins der deutschen Buchhändler.

Hasbach, Wilhelm (1891), *Untersuchungen über Adam Smith und die Entwicklung der politischen Ökonomie*, Leipzig: Duncker & Humblot.

Kapp, Friedrich (1886), *Geschichte des deutschen Buchhandels bis in das siebzehnte Jahrhundert*, Leipzig: Verlag des Börsenvereins der deutschen Buchhändler.

Koch, C.F. (1856), *Allgemeines Landrecht für die Preußischen Staaten. Unter Andeutung der obsoleten oder aufgehobenen Vorschriften und Einschaltung der jüngeren noch geltenden Bestimmungen, mit Kommentar in Anmerkungen*, 3rd edn, Berlin: Guttentag.

Liefmann, Robert (1904), 'Der deutsche Buchhandel in der Kartellenquete, nebst Untersuchungen über seine Organisation und voraussichtliche Weiterbildung', in *Jahrbücher für Nationalökonomie und Statistik*, III. Folge, 28 Band, 200.

Meerhaeghe, M. van (1995), *The Information Policy of the European Commission*, Heft 4, Centre for the New Europe, CNE, Zelik.

Meyer, Julius (1843), *Conversations-Lexikon für die gebildeten Stände*, 6. Bd. Hildburghausen: Bibliographisches Institut.

Müller-Armack, A. (1948), *Wirtschaftslenkung und Marktwirtschaft*, 2nd edn, Hamburg: Verlag für Wirtschaft und Politik.

Myrdal, G. (1932), *Das politische Element in der nationalökonomischen Doktrinbildung*, Berlin: Junker und Dünnhaupt.

Naumann, Michael (1999), 'Was Bücher von Kartoffeln unterscheidet' (The Difference between Potatoes and Books), *Welt am Sonntag*, 29, 13 July, 19.

Pindyck, Robert S. and Daniel L. Rubinfeld (1998), *Microeconomics*, Upper-Saddle River, NJ: Prentice Hall, 10.

Sarkowski, Heinz (1995), *Gustav Weiland Nachf.: Einhundertfünfzig Jahre Buchhandel in Lübeck 1845–1995*, Lübeck: Weiland.

Sarkowski, Heinz (1992), *Der Springer-Verlag. Stationen seiner Geschichte. Teil 1: 1842–1945*, Berlin: Springer.

Steinfeld, Th. (1999), 'Die Marktheiligen. Van Miert plant letzten Schlag gegen die Buchpreisbindung', *Frankfurter Allgemeine Zeitung*, 10 June, 49.

Stumpp, Henning (1999), *Die Preisbindung für Verlagserzeugnisse: Wettbewerbsbeschränkung oder Regulierung zur Beseitigung von Marktunvollkommenheiten?*, Baden Baden: Nomos, 2 and 6.

Wissowa, Georg (1903), 'Buchhandel und Wissenschaft', in *Jahrbücher für Nationalökonomie und Statistik*, II Folge, 26 Band, 218.

Zedler, Johann, H. (1733), *Großes-vollständiges Universal-Lexicon Aller Wissenschaften und Künste, welche bisher durch menschlichen Verstand und Witz erfunden und verbessert wurden*, Halle und Leipzig: Zedler.

5. Tax mimicking among regional jurisdictions

Lars P. Feld, Jean-Michel Josselin and Yvon Rocaboy

INTRODUCTION

Since Tiebout (1956), the focus of models of fiscal federalism has been mainly on the mechanisms and properties of market-like competition between institutions or jurisdictions. In a survey of the literature, Wilson (1999) has pointed out that such a competition for mobile production factors between jurisdictions may well lead to a race to the bottom in tax rates. However, authors like Salmon (1987) and Besley and Case (1995) have used alternative or complementary explanations of public decision-making processes in a setting of fiscal federalism. A tool of labour economics (Holmstrom, 1982) and of the economics of the firm (Shleifer, 1985), yardstick competition thus has gained attention as a very insightful concept in the field of public economics.

In a world of imperfect and asymmetric information, voters have restricted possibilities to assess the performance of the representatives in their polity. Selfish representatives aim at obtaining political rents and hence have incentives to keep information about their opportunistic behaviour hidden from voters. However, voters can draw inferences on politicians' behaviour by comparing it to the performance of governments and parliaments in neighbouring jurisdictions. Other things being equal, these neighbours serve as yardsticks for the voters' evaluation. A worse performance in their own jurisdiction compared to other jurisdictions could lead to the punishment of representatives by throwing them out of office in the next elections. As a consequence, public choices would not only be driven by information gathering from neighbouring jurisdictions, but also by mimicking behaviour. Representatives may indeed anticipate the yardstick mechanism, thereby adapting their policies to those of their neighbours.

As this intuition has progressively made its way, a number of significant articles (Ladd, 1992; Case, 1993; Case, Rosen and Hines, 1993; Heyndels and Vuchelen, 1997; Figlio, Kolpin and Reed, 1999; Brueckner and Saavedra, 1999; Saavedra, 2000) has contributed to the better understanding of the mechanism of yardstick competition in public decisions. For instance, mimicking behaviour of competing jurisdictions in the case of the US welfare system are investigated by Brueckner (2000). The empirical relevance of the hypothesis in the political market has also been assessed, particularly in the American case (Besley and Case, 1995).

The present chapter follows this wake and its contribution is original in three ways. First, we start with an empirical glance on the tax rates at the regional level in France since the decentralization reform of 1986. This reform has devolved extended tax prerogatives to regions and the aim is to derive some information as to whether a 'race to the bottom' in tax rates can be observed (section 1). If this is not the case, then other explanations than the traditional tax competition must be developed. The theoretical part of the chapter then proposes an agency model in the spirit of Besley and Case (1995) which depicts a multi-period relationship between the decisive voter and her agent, the elected representative (section 2). Yardstick competition with neighbouring jurisdictions induces an interference in this agency setting. The agent in one jurisdiction wants to take advantage of shocks that are not observed by principals. The claimed shock on the cost of provision of the public goods would then result in an increase in the tax rate without endangering the prospects of re-election. However, the ability of the principal to observe the situation in neighbouring jurisdictions affected by similar shocks threatens to alleviate the possible strategic use of private information by the agent. Our model here substantially differs from that of Besley and Case (1995) since opportunistic or 'bad' behaviours are not constituent of the nature of the agents (they being 'bad' or 'good' in the model of Besley and Case). Opportunism is here simply one of the possible strategies that can be checked by comparison with the behaviour of agents in other jurisdictions.

The third contribution of the chapter is to provide an econometric test with data on French regions (section 3). The French decentralized level is particularly interesting, because *régions*, *départements* and local jurisdictions have non-negligible tax-setting power since the decentralization of 1986. The analysis thus provides a test of tax-mimicking in a country engaged in a significant devolution process. Concluding remarks are in the final section.

1.   DEVOLUTION TO THE FRENCH REGIONS AND THE EVOLUTION OF TAX RATES

Since the decentralization reform of 1986, the French sub-national administrations are allowed to set tax rates in a widened band fixed by the central government in Paris. The corresponding taxes are the *taxe d'habitation* as a tax on housing (independent from the property status), the *taxe professionnelle*

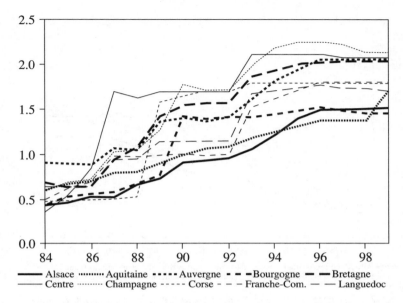

Figure 5.1   Tax rates of the 'taxe d'habitation' in selected French regions, 1984 to 1999

as a local business tax, and the *taxes foncières sur les propriétés bâties et non-bâties* as two property taxes on developed and non developed sites. There is thus new room for manœuvre for regions. Figure 5.1, where the development of the *taxe d'habitation* is drawn for a selection of regions, reveals an interesting pattern. Immediately after the decentralization of 1986 the variance of the *taxe d'habitation* increases considerably. The coefficient of variation of this tax for all 22 regions increases from 37.78 in 1985 to 46.85 in 1987. Afterwards, convergence is observable for the regions in Figure 5.1. For all 22 regions the coefficient of variation decreases from 46.85 in 1987 to 23.13 in 1995 which corresponds to a reduction of about 51 per cent. Hence, in the ten years after decentralization, tax rates of the *taxe d'habitation* have considerably converged. However, and in contrast to the predictions of the theory of tax competition, no race to the bottom occurs, but these tax rates converge to a higher and still increasing level.

A similar pattern of tax-rate convergence between the French regions is observable in the case of the local business tax. Figure 5.2 illustrates this convergence for the same seven regions as before. For all 22 regions, the coefficient of variation increases from 39.84 in 1985 to 40.98 in 1987 and decreases afterwards to 19.92. Local business tax rates increase continuously from 1987 to 1999. While convergence of tax rates is also observable for both

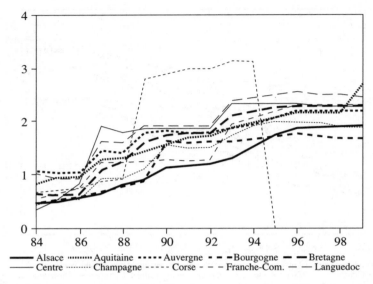

Figure 5.2   Tax rates of the local business tax in selected French regions,
1984 to 1999

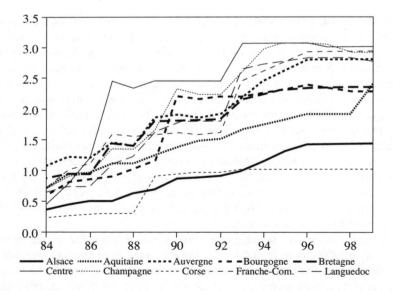

Figure 5.3   Property tax rates (developed sites) in selected French regions,
1984 to 1999

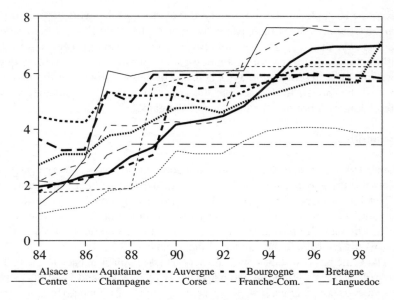

Figure 5.4   Property tax rates (non-developed sites) for selected French regions, 1984 to 1999

property tax rates, it is less pronounced than in the two previous cases, as Figures 5.3 and 5.4 indicate. For all 22 regions, the coefficient of variation decreases from 53.43 in 1987 to 37.55 in 1995, a reduction of 30 per cent in the case of the property tax on developed sites, and decreases from 47.68 in 1987 to 34.31 in 1995, a reduction of 28 per cent in the case of the property tax on non-developed sites. Both tax rates increase as well continuously over time. Given this development of tax rates at the French regional level, an explanation on the basis of traditional tax competition models does not seem to be appropriate. An alternative explanation is necessary in order to be able to explain such a 'race to the top'.

2.   BASIC THEORETICAL FRAMEWORK

The framework of the model consists of two jurisdictions providing public goods financed through local taxation. In each of them, an agency mechanism describes the working of collective decisions. The decisive voter is the principal while the local government is mandated as the agent. Rather than strictly focusing on the largely discussed principal agent relationship, the model examines how decisions within a given agency are influenced by the observation of what happens in the other community. If the principals have the opportunity to compare the actions of their respective agents, how will it shift their strategies? How will the agents take this possible comparison into account? What will be the results of the corresponding game? In order to answer these questions, the first step of the analysis consists in the description of the assumptions of the model. In this setting, the agents will develop strategies whose interactions will provide the outcome of the game.

Assumptions

The first assumption is that of a non cooperative framework. Neither the principals nor the agents can build coalitions. In particular, the agents cannot try collectively to deceive the principals, for instance by consciously shirking in the same way so as to blur any signals of cheating that the principals could catch. The latter, in the same way, cannot create a common agency by which they would coordinate the control of the agents.

The game has two stages, with an election taking place at each of them. The two jurisdictions are represented respectively by agents i and j and the principals wish to obtain at each stage the same quantity of public good $g_i = g_j = \bar{g}$. By assumption, this quantity is equivalent to the public expenditure. To finance it, each local government (each agent) relies on the taxation of a base B that can take two values according to the current budgetary conditions. The first one is low, $B = B^-$, and it corresponds to a negative shock, which may occur with probability p. The second value of the tax base is high, $B = B^+$, with probability $(1 - p)$ for this positive shock. The agents do observe this variation in their tax bases but the principals do not. However, the latter know that both jurisdictions are similarly affected by the shock whatever its direction.

Distinctions between the two jurisdictions thus reduce to tax rate policies t_i and t_j, which helps concentrate the analysis on possible mimicking behaviours. Agent i, for instance, elected in period one, is by construction of the model re-elected in period two if $t_i \le t_j$. He fails to be re-elected if it happens that $t_i > t_j$. Since both jurisdictions face the same budgetary conditions, the opportunism of agent i is exposed whenever the agent in the other community is 'honest'. The range of values for the tax rates is assumed to be such that, in each jurisdiction, $t \in [t^-, t^+]$ with $\bar{g} = t^+ B^- = t^- B^+$. The maximum rate t^+ allows just to finance public expenditures $\bar{g}$ in unfavourable budgetary circumstances, whilst good economic conditions make it possible to use the lowest rate t^- to finance $\bar{g}$. An external and exogenous authority is assumed to have the capacity of controlling and preventing any attempt to pick a rate outside $[t^-, t^+]$.

We have seen that, elected in the first period, an agent can be re-elected in the second one only if the tax rate he plays is lower than or equal to the one played by the agent of the other jurisdiction. By assumption, the number of mandates is limited to two. During the second one, having nothing to lose, the re-elected representative is assumed to systematically behave strategically by always choosing the highest tax rate t^+, whatever the budgetary conditions. Finally, there is no discounting from one period to the other. If an agent intends to maximize his expected gain over the two periods, then which rate must he choose in the first one?

Strategies of the Agents

We consider for instance the strategies of agent i who must determine the tax rate t_i that will provide the best possible answer to a given tax rate t_j from agent j. Two cases may arise.

First case: strategy of re-election: $t_i = t_j + \varepsilon$ with $\varepsilon \leq 0$

Agent i is in this case re-elected. Let EP_1 denote his expected payoff over the two periods. It can be calculated as follows. In the first period, the tax base takes its low value with probability p for a gain of $(t_j + \varepsilon)B^- - t^+B^-$. With probability $(1 - p)$, the shock on budgetary conditions is favourable and the corresponding gain amounts to $(t_j + \varepsilon)B^+ - t^-B^+$. In the second period, the agent is re-elected but whether he obtains a strictly positive gain depends on the nature of the shock. In the situation of an unfavourable environment, the representative cannot take advantage of his position, even if he uses the upper value of the tax rate. Providing $\bar{g}$ yields t^+B^- but costs as much. On the contrary, a favourable shock provides a positive gain of $t^+B^+ - t^-B^+ = t^+B^+ - t^+B^- = t^+\Delta B$, this with probability $(1 - p)$. On the whole, the expected payoff is:

$$EP_1 = p[(t_j + \varepsilon)B^- - t^+B^- + (1 - p)t^+\Delta B]$$
$$+ (1 - p)[(t_j + \varepsilon)B^+ - t^-B^+ + (1 - p)t^+\Delta B]$$

If the elected representative maximizes this payoff, then he solves the program

$$\max_{t_i} EP_1 = \max_{\varepsilon} EP_1,$$

which implies $\varepsilon = 0$. He models his behaviour on that of his counterpart in the other jurisdiction and thus obtains:

$$EP_1 = p[t_jB^- - t^+B^- + (1 - p)t^+\Delta B] + (1 - p)[t_jB^+ - t^-B^+ + (1 - p)t^+\Delta B]$$

which amounts to:

$$EP_1 = t_j EB - \bar{g} + (1 - p)t^+\Delta B$$

where $EB = pB^- + (1 - p)B^+$ represents the expected tax base in the community. This strategy of re-election can be contrasted with the other option consisting in playing straightforward opportunism from the first period onwards, even if this leads to non re-election in the second period.

Second case: strategy of non-re-election: $t_i = t_j + \varepsilon$ with $\varepsilon > 0$

At first glance, it may seem surprising that a politician would seek defeat in an election. Everything else equal, it is nevertheless a rational strategy if it brings about a higher expected gain than what the other option can offer. If $t_i = t_j + \varepsilon$ with $\varepsilon > 0$, agent i is not re-elected and he of course cannot expect any reward during a second mandate. At the end of the first period, the payoff is:

$$EP_2 = p[(t_j + \varepsilon)B^- - t^+B^-] + (1 - p)[(t_j + \varepsilon)B^+ - t^-B^+]$$

Solving

$$\max_{t_i} EP_2 = \max_{\varepsilon} EP_2,$$

amounts to choosing $\varepsilon = t^+ - t_j$ and hence the maximum rate t^+, which brings an expected payoff of $EP_2 = (1 - p)[t^+B^+ - t^-B^+] = (1 - p)t^+\Delta B$. Those strategies are of course played non cooperatively with the other agent. The actual payoffs to the representatives then depend on the possible outcomes of these interactions.

Interactions and Mimicking

We first construct the reaction functions in order to compute the Nash equilibria of the game between the agents in a second step.

Reaction curves
The strategy of re-election, namely the case where $t_i = t_j + \varepsilon$ with $\varepsilon < 0$, rationally leads to mimicking. Should this strategy be preferred to the second one ($t_i = t_j + \varepsilon$ with $\varepsilon > 0$) where the agent plays all his cards during the first period? In the latter case, the representative cannot claim a second mandate and he rationally chooses the maximum rate t^+. The strategy of re-election is preferable if $EP_1 > EP_2$, that is to say if $t_j \geq \bar{g}/EB$. The elected agent in jurisdiction i will thus adopt a mimicking behaviour ($t_i = t_j$) if the rate set in the other community is greater than or equal to the rate required to finance

public expenditures, taking into account the expected tax base. On the contrary, if $t_j < \bar{g}/EB$, then $EP_2 > EP_1$ and player i should play the maximum rate $t_i = t^+$.

Nash equilibria

As is illustrated in Figure 5.5, the Nash equilibria of this symmetrical game can be computed as follows. For values of the tax rate in the interval $[t^-, \bar{g}/EB]$, the Nash equilibrium is in $t_i = t_j = t^+$. If jurisdiction j plays a rate $t^- < \hat{t}_j < \bar{g}/EB$, then agent i had better play the maximum rate $t_i = t^+$ since he knows that the electors will systematically sanction any rate higher than that of the neighbour. The reaction of agent j then consists in playing the maximum rate as well. If the latter were to play $\tilde{t}_j$ such that $\bar{g}/EB < \tilde{t}_j < t^+$, then agent i would adjust his own rate so as to obtain $t_i = \tilde{t}_j$.

The computation of the Nash equilibria of the game reinforces the intuition behind the assumption of mimicking. At least, this assumption cannot be rejected. The combination of the reaction curves of the players displays an infinite number of mimicking equilibria such that $t_j = t_i$ for $[t_i, t_j] \in [\bar{g}/EB, t^+]$. Non-opportunistic behaviours represented by $t_i = t_j = \bar{g}/EB$ do provide a Nash equilibrium which consists in playing the rate that finances public expenditures for the expected tax base, but it is only one of the possible equilibria. Moreover, this 'honest' equilibrium is dominated by all the others in

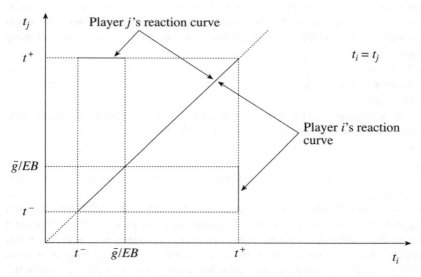

Figure 5.5   Nash equilibria of the game of mimicking

terms of Pareto efficiency (if the domain of validity of this criterion is restricted to the set of players). Any move along $t_j = t_i$ from $t_i = t_j = \bar{g}/EB$ onwards is Pareto improving and leads to a unique Pareto efficient situation in $t_i = t_j = t^+$. This provides a strong incentive to collusion, which is precluded by the non-cooperative setting of the model but which real-world games cannot fully prevent.

3.　AN ECONOMETRIC ANALYSIS FOR FRENCH REGIONS

The first step is the description of the specification. The results are then presented and discussed.

Specification

The theoretical model suggests that the payoffs of representatives in each region depend on tax rates of competing jurisdictions. In the case of the French regions, this means that the level and the changes in the *taxe d'habitation*, the local business tax and both property taxes in region i are a function of the respective tax levels and tax changes in the other regions. In the econometric specifications used here, we assume that those taxes in region i are influenced by the unweighted average of taxes in geographically neighbouring regions only. For instance, representatives of the Île-de-France consider the tax policies in the regions of Haute-Normandie, Picardie, Champagne-Ardenne, Bourgogne and Centre when they decide upon changes in tax rates. By taking the unweighted average of neighbours' tax rates, we weight each neighbour of each region equally. In our example, the region of Picardie does not have more influence on tax rate decisions in the Île-de-France than the regions of Bourgogne or Centre.

In addition to the neighbours' taxes, other economic and demographic variables may have an impact on tax policies at the French regional level. The estimation equation is thus:

$$t_T^* = \beta_1 \hat{t}_T + \beta_2' X_T + \varepsilon$$

where t_T^* is the optimal tax rate in a region for year T. Scalar β_1 measures the influence of the tax policies of neighbouring regions ($\hat{t}_T$ is the average of their tax rates). Vector X_T describes k economic and demographic variables of the region. The associated vector β_2 thus measures their influence on its tax policy. Finally, ε is an error term which is assumed to be normally distributed with zero mean and constant variance.

A further assumption is that the adjustment to the optimal tax rate is not instantaneous, which can be formalized in the following way:

$$t_T - t_{T-1} = \lambda(t_T^* - t_{T-1}) \text{ with } \lambda \in (0,1)$$

Combining the two equations gives:

$$t_T = (1 - \lambda)t_{T-1} + \lambda\beta_1\hat{t}_T + \lambda\beta_2'X_T + \lambda\varepsilon$$

which is the estimation equation. Vector X_T contains variables like the density and structure of the population, grants received from the state level. A trend is also included in order to control for the evolution of the rates since 1986.

Endogeneity cannot be completely precluded, however. The tax policy of a given region i may indeed be influenced by the neighbours, but the neighbours themselves are simultaneously influenced by the policies of their own neighbours, including i. The solution proposed by Kelejian and Prucha (1998) and Kelejian and Robertson (1993) is used here. It consists of using the economic and demographic variables of the neighbouring regions (with a lag of one period) as instruments.

Estimations

Table 5.1 provides the results of the fixed effects model for the 22 French regions over the period 1986–98. About 90 per cent of rate variation is explained by the model. The coefficient of adjustment λ is significant. It is higher for the local tax on housing and business tax (about 0.38) than for the property taxes (about 0.28). This would suggest that the adjustment to the desired level is quicker for the first two taxes. This is consistent with the intuition that property taxes in France have a lesser political and economic impact than housing and business taxes.

Tax rates in a given region are significantly and positively influenced by those of the neighbours. This is particularly true for the housing and business rates, which corroborates the tighter convergence that we previously observed. In this respect, the local business tax is the more likely to prompt mimicking. At short term (respectively at long term), that is to say when we consider the parameter $\lambda\beta_1$ (respectively β_1), an increase of one point in the average rates of the neighbours of a given region induces an increase of 0.225 (respectively 0.6) point of the rate in this same region. At the same time, however, property tax rates do not seem to imply important mimicking behaviours. The estimated coefficient reaches only 0.081 at short term and 0.29 at long term. Robustness tests do not change the results. They consist in including the weighted average of tax rates of all regions using the inverse of the distance between the regional

Table 5.1 Model of tax mimicking among the 22 French regions (fixed cross-sectional effects), 1986 to 1998

Dependent variables	Tax rate of the local housing tax	Tax rate of the local business tax	Property tax rate (developed sites)	Property tax rate (non-developed sites)
Average household income	-0.004	-0.012**	-0.009**	-0.002
	(-1.33)	(-3.82)	(-3.86)	(-0.19)
Regional unemployment rate	-0.004	0.007	-0.013	0.036
	(-0.55)	(1.10)	(-1.47)	(1.37)
Population density	-1.053	-0.829	-0.411	1.317(*)
	(-0.67)	(-0.45)	(-0.32)	(1.84)
Population	-0.103	-0.015	-0.055	-2.083**
	(-0.95)	(-0.11)	(-0.48)	(-3.45)
Share of population younger than 20	0.042**	0.080**	0.027(*)	0.290**
	(2.90)	(3.45)	(1.73)	(3.70)
Share of population between 60 and 75	0.087**	0.121**	0.076**	0.303**
	(3.37)	(4.33)	(2.89)	(3.06)
Share of population older than 75	0.013	0.107**	-0.029	0.121
	(0.46)	(3.67)	(-0.94)	(1.20)
Current expenditures grants (per inhabitant)	-0.076	-0.351	-0.094**	-0.195
	(-1.40)	(-1.03)	(-4.36)	(-1.13)

	(1)	(2)	(3)	(4)
Invest grants (per inhabitant)	0.946**	1.317**	1.017**	1.781*
	(4.12)	(3.99)	(5.36)	(2.50)
Trend	0.013	0.026	0.019*	0.033
	(1.47)	(1.60)	(2.03)	(0.89)
Dependent variable$_{t-1}$	0.620**	0.625**	0.724**	0.733**
	(11.58)	(9.80)	(15.90)	(15.49)
Local housing tax: tax rate of the neighbouring regions	0.174**	–	–	–
	(6.35)			
Local business tax: tax rate of the neighbouring regions	–	0.225**	–	–
		(8.42)		
Property tax (developed sites): tax rate of the neighbouring regions	–	–	0.081**	–
			(4.96)	
Property tax (non-developed sites): tax rate of the neighbouring regions	–	–	–	0.152**
				(5.21)
$\bar{R}^2$	0.93	0.87	0.91	0.94
SER	0.15	0.24	0.29	0.57
d.f.	252	252	252	252

Note: The numbers in parentheses are the absolute values of the estimated t-statistics (with a White correction). '**', '*' or '(*)' indicate that the estimated parameter is significantly different from zero at the 1, 5, or 10 per cent, respectively.

capitals (in kilometres) as a weight. Regional tax rates do appear as strategic complements.

As to the other variables, they do not always have a significant effect. The impact of the average income is negative and statistically significant for the local business tax and the property tax on developed sites. Since the income of the households is indeed an indicator of the value of the local tax bases, the higher it is, the lower is the tax rate required to finance a given level of public services (ceteris paribus). In the same way, current expenditure grants received from the government are as many resources that replace taxation. Investment grants have a positive and significant impact on tax rates. Public investment by regional authorities brings about further current expenditures, which necessitates increases in tax rates (ceteris paribus). Finally, demographic variables may play a role in the variation of tax rates. For instance, the share of population younger than 20 has a positive effect on rates since investment in secondary education is now devolved to the regions.

All in all, the results indicate that tax rates at the French regional level are positively influenced by the tax policy in neighbouring regions. Basically, this evidence is compatible with traditional tax competition models as well as with yardstick competition models. Given the fact that tax rates of the four regional taxes considered in the analysis are steadily increasing over time since the decentralization, a yardstick competition model allowing for convergence in increasing taxes is more consistent with the estimates.

CONCLUSION

In a setting of yardstick competition, voters compare the fiscal policy of their government to that in neighbouring jurisdictions in order to evaluate the fiscal performance of their representatives. This may generate a convergence of fiscal policies. The difference with tax competition is that such a 'copycatting' may also lead to a convergence of tax rates at a higher level.

The theoretical model implies that tax rates in a jurisdiction under consideration are influenced by tax rates in neighbouring jurisdictions and that this may either lead to a convergence to optimal tax rates or to inefficiently high tax rates. This implication of the model is tested econometrically with panel data of the 22 French regions from 1984 to 1995. The French decentralized level is particularly interesting, because French regional jurisdictions have non-negligible tax-setting power since the decentralization of 1986. Moreover, the relevant regional tax rates have converged on a higher level than the starting point in each case. The econometric panel results show that tax mimicking at the French regional level cannot be rejected. Competition patterns thus take on many forms and the ongoing devolution process may well help develop them further.

REFERENCES

Besley, T. and A.C. Case (1995), 'Incumbent behavior: vote-seeking, tax-setting, and yardstick competition', *American Economic Review*, **85**, 25–45.

Brueckner, J.K. (2000), 'Welfare reform and the race to the bottom: theory and evidence', *Southern Economic Journal*, **66**, 505–25.

Brueckner, J.K. and L.A. Saavedra (1999), 'Do local governments engage in strategic property tax competition?', unpublished manuscript, University of Illinois at Urbana-Champaign.

Case, A.C. (1993), 'Interstate tax competition after TRA86', *Journal of Policy Analysis and Management*, **12**, 136–48.

Case, A.C., H.S. Rosen and J.R. Hines Jr (1993), 'Budget spillovers and fiscal policy interdependence. Evidence from the states', *Journal of Public Economics*, **52**, 285–307.

Figlio, D.N., V.W. Kolpin and W.E. Reid (1999), 'Do states play welfare games?', *Journal of Urban Economics*, **46**, 437–54.

Heyndels, B. and J. Vuchelen (1997), 'Tax mimicking among Belgian municipalities', *National Tax Journal*, **51**, 89–101.

Holmstrom, B.R. (1982), 'Moral hazard in teams', *Bell Journal of Economics and Management Science*, **13**, 324–40.

Kelejian, H.H. and I.R. Prucha (1998), 'A generalized spatial two-stage least squares procedure for estimating a spatial autoregressive model with autoregressive disturbances', *Journal of Real Estate Finance and Economics*, **17**, 99–121.

Kelejian, H.H. and D.H. Robertson (1993), 'A suggested estimation for spatial interdependent models with autocorrelated errors, and an application to a county expenditure model', *Papers in Regional Science*, **72**, 297–312.

Ladd, H.F. (1992), 'Mimicking of local tax burdens among neighboring counties', *Public Finance Quarterly*, **20**, 450–67.

Saavedra, L.A. (2000), 'A model of welfare competition with evidence from AFDC', *Journal of Urban Economics*, **47**, 248–79.

Salmon, P. (1987), 'Decentralisation as an incentive scheme', *Oxford Review of Economic Policy*, **3**, 24–43.

Shleifer, A. (1985), 'A theory of yardstick competition', *Rand Journal of Economics*, **16**, 319–27.

Tiebout, C.M. (1956), 'A pure theory of public expenditures', *Journal of Political Economy*, **64**, 416–24.

Wilson, J.D. (1999), 'Theories of tax competition', *National Tax Journal*, **53**, 269–304.

6. Harmonization of judicial interest payments and litigation in a federalist state

Manuela Mühl and Lode Vereeck

INTRODUCTION

Justice is not served unless it is rendered swiftly. Delay is therefore a problem that clearly undermines the functioning of the court system and may even threaten its very existence. In a recent article,[162] an extended Shavellian (1982) model clearly demonstrated how court delay negatively affects social welfare. Court delay is not only unjust and unlawful,[163] it is also inefficient. Since Gravelle (1990) observed that the time-elasticities of the demand for trials from plaintiffs and defendants are negatively correlated, conventional supply-side policies to reduce delay are considered inadequate. Rationing trials by court fees is then the only alternative left. Judicial interest payments are meant to compensate litigants for waiting and the depreciation of their stakes. But what is the impact of such awards on the level of litigation?

With the European Community came free intra-European trade and movement of persons, yet also more conflicts between parties of different nationalities. If a federalist constitution permits mobility of litigants, post-conflict resolution opportunities might be described in terms of Tiebout competition between different court systems. This appears to be the case since litigants have some freedom in choosing the place of court (e.g. the residence of the plaintiff or defendant or the place of accident or failed transaction). Unintended competition between national court systems will be the result and can take many forms. Timely resolution of conflicts is an attractive, yet self-destructing competitive factor. Since judicial interest payments have the same effect as shortening the trial period, delay-ridden courts will resort to high interest rates thus expectedly plunging the European Union into excessive litigation.

The chapter is structured as follows. Section 1 looks briefly at the economic

---

[162] See Vereeck and Mühl (2000).

[163] The European Convention on Human Rights, article 6, requires trials to be concluded within a 'reasonable' period of time.

121

characteristics of verdicts and defines the precise meaning of court delay and
judicial interest. The next section discusses the impact of delay and interest
payments on the demand for trials by plaintiffs and defendants. Section 3
examines the effect of judicial interest-rate competition on the level of litigation in a federalist state before the fourth and final sections conclude with
policy recommendations.

1.   COURT PRODUCTION

Verdicts as Public Goods

The growing industry of private dispute resolution services, e.g. commercial
arbitration, clearly demonstrates that the 'private' net benefits of resolving
conflicts are substantial. Nevertheless, the production of justice has some positive side-effects which go beyond the interests of the parties seeking to settle
their dispute. Third parties who are not directly involved in the conflict may
learn from the outcome and avoid similar conflicts and costs. The use of the
information embodied in a verdict is non-rivalrous and the exclusion of future
litigants from that information is undesirable. Court decisions can thus be cat-
egorized as public goods (Samuelson, 1954). These characteristics make
dispute resolution particularly well-suited for production by states because
they can best capture the 'external' benefits. Therefore, all European states
provide court services at subsidized prices. Subsidization leads to an increasing demand for trials which is often not met by supply. The growing backlog
of cases in many European countries leads to considerable waiting periods
which not only undermines the perfomance of their court systems but also the
actual value of the stakes of plaintiffs. The fact that trials are rationed by waiting lists is inefficient because time spent waiting imposes an opportunity cost
on the litigants not offset by any gain to the court system (Barzel, 1974;
Cheung, 1974). Although occupants of waiting lists wait, they do so *in absen-
tia*. Therefore, the opportunity cost is not the value of the time wasted, but the
depreciation of the good waited for (Lindsay and Feigenbaum, 1984). The
award of judical interests restores the value of the stakes. But what are the
implications for the demand for trials, in other words for court delay and
performance? How do different judicial interest rates in the countries of a
federalist state affect litigation behaviour of the citizens.

Definition of Court Delay and Judicial Interest

The legal process of resolving a dispute includes four different time periods.
First, there is the negotiation time between parties before the plaintiff issues a

suit by registering at the court's office. Next, there is the procedural time necessary to prepare the trial. Third, the waiting time between the final procedural moment of registering at the court and the actual start of the trial. And finally, the time period of the trial itself (between the first trial day and the final verdict). Only the third period is defined as court delay since it depends on the performance of the courts. While the first and second period are determined by the behaviour of the parties themselves,[164] the fourth period or actual trial depends on the complexity of the case. When studying the effects of awarding judicial is on litigating, the relevant stretch of time comprises all four periods. For the purpose of this chapter, the time period causing the depreciation is irrelevant.

Interests awarded by courts in order to compensate the winning party for the depreciation of the stake due to the passage of time are of two different kinds pending on the legal nature of the case. *Compensatory interests* are awarded in addition to compensatory damages stemming from tort cases. When awarded, they are computed starting from the actual occurence of the damage. *Overdue payment interests* are awarded when a conflict over the performance of a contract has led to non-payment or overdue payment. The starting point upon which the interest payments are computed is the moment of sending a reminder or filing the case. The two terms differentiate the legal nature of the case, but from an economic point of view, this distinction is irrelevant. Therefore, we will use the term *judicial interest payments* to indicate both. The term *legal interest* is often used as a synonym for judicial interest, but it can also designate the interest rate fixed by law. We will use it in the latter sense.

2.   DEMAND FOR TRIALS

The demand for trials over private matters under a code law system or civil cases under a common law system is a two-step process in which a party first decides to bring suit and then considers the room for settlement. Following Shavell (1982), a suit will be launched when the plaintiff believes that the net expected benefits of a trial (NEB) are positive and he can credibly threaten his opponent. The expected benefit depends on the chance of prevailing (p_x) and the value of the award by the court (V). The legal costs (C) consist of the costs borne by the litigant, i.e. court and lawyer fees.[165] In the European Union, legal cost allocation follows the indemnity rule by which most legal costs are borne by the loser

---

[164] Spier (1992) and recently Fenn and Rickman (1999) discuss the causes of delay in settlement negotiations.
[165] The costs of operating the courts are called trial costs.

of the trial.[166] Hence, the expected legal costs are the sum (2C) of the plaintiff's and the defendant's costs discounted by the probability of losing $(1 - p_x)$.

$$NEB = p_x V - (1 - p_x)2C > 0 \Leftrightarrow p_x^* > 2C/(V + 2C) \tag{1}$$

If the likelihood of prevailing p_x is above the critical point p_x^*, the plaintiff will sue. Shavell concluded that, whereas the American system attracts more risky, high-stake cases, the indemnity system induces suits when the chance of winning is high because the legal costs are more heavily discounted by the low probability of losing.

After bringing suit, the parties may still settle. This depends on their negotiation skills and the room for settlement (SR). The latter is equal to the difference between the maximum offer by the defendant, i.e. the total expected legal costs of the trial (TEC) saved, and the minimum amount acceptable to the plaintiff, i.e. the net expected benefit of a trial. Equation shows that the settlement range is equal to the legal costs. When the defendant's probability to win is $p_y = 1 - p_x$,[167] we find that:

$$SR = TEC - (NEB) = p_x V + p_x 2C - (p_x V - (1 - p_x)2C) = 2C > 0 \tag{2}$$

Indeed, when they decide to settle, parties win the legal costs (2C) saved. That is why, among others, economists prefer settlements over trials.[168] The chances of a negotiated agreement increase the larger the settlement range. The likelihood of settlement seems to suffer most from the parties' optimism about the outcome of the trial $(1 < p_x + p_y = p)$[169]. The minimum acceptable offer for the plaintiff increases while the maximum offer by the defendant decreases, hence the room and likelihood of settlement diminish.

$$SR = (1 - p_y)V + (1 - p_y)2C - (p_x V - (1 - p_x)2C)$$
$$= 2C + (1 - p)(2C + V) < 2C \tag{3}$$

The demand for trials is determined by the number of suits that are not settled, which in turn depends on the magnitude of the settlement range. Legal

---

[166] In contrast, in the US, each party bears his own costs.

[167] Rational litigants will assume that their chance to win is the inverse of the opponent's. Therefore, the sum of their probabilities to win equals 1. This is the case when there is no optimism. Parties are said to be optimistic when the sum of their subjective probabilities to prevail exceeds 1.

[168] Moreover, it is reasonable to assume that the parties themselves are more knowlegeable on the value of the disputed stake or specific business practices, in other words have superior information over third parties, in particular a judge. Settled outcomes are thus preferred over adjudicated ones.

[169] See footnote 167.

costs, the way they are allocated and the perceived chances to prevail seem to determine the demand for trials. So far we have neglected time aspects which necessitate plaintiffs and defendants to discount the costs. Time and judicial interest payments are thus crucial determinants of the demand since they bear an effect on the number of suits and trials, as we will show in the next paragraph.

Demand of the Plaintiff

Waiting affects the net expected benefit of a trial for the plaintiff in various ways. Firstly, the net value of a judgement simply falls by a subjective discount factor of time ($\delta = (1 + d)^{-t}$), thus reducing the willingness to sue. Secondly, the plaintiff's chances to win are reduced ($\pi_x = p_x - \alpha$) by time because it leads to a deterioration in the quality and availability of evidence (α). Since costs are typically borne at the beginning or during the trial while the award is granted at the end, the net expected benefit will drop.

$$NEB = \pi_x V\delta - (1 + \delta - 2\pi_x\delta)C < p_x V - (1 - p_x)2C \qquad (4)$$

$$(\partial NEB/\partial\delta)(\partial\delta/\partial t) < 0 \qquad (5)$$

The indemnity system is relatively sensitive to waiting. The deterioration of evidence α, which reduces the likelihood of prevailing π_x, makes it less certain to recoup the stake as well as the legal costs. However, the award of judicial interests (j) restores to greater or lesser extent the actual value of the plaintiff's stake which was prone to depreciation. With $(1 + j)^t\delta = \rho$, the net expected benefit of a trial should be defined as:

$$NEB = \pi_x V\rho - (1 + \rho - 2\pi_x\rho)C \qquad (6)$$

$$(\partial NEB/\partial\rho)(\partial\rho/\partial j) > 0 \qquad (7)$$

The effect of judicial interest on the net expected benefit of a trial for the plaintiff, hence on his ability to threaten his opponent and, conversely, his willingness to sue, depends on the value of ρ. There are three scenarios: ρ is equal to, lower or higher than 1. In all three cases, a rise of the judicial interest rate may result in a positive net expected benefit of some trials thus increasing the number of suits (equation 7). To make their threats towards the defendants more credible, plaintiffs have an interest in shifting their cases to the jurisdiction where courts award high judicial interest payments. If such mobility is permitted, this will lead to an increase of suits in the whole territory.

Perfect compensation ($\rho = 1$ or $j = d$)
When the plaintiff is perfectly compensated for the depreciation of the stake, the judicial interest equals his subjective discount rate, hence $\rho = 1$. It follows that the plaintiff's discounted net expected benefit of the trial becomes almost the same as if the conflict was resolved without any delay.

$$NEB = \pi_x V - (1 - \pi_x)2C$$

$$(\partial NEB/\partial\rho)(\partial\rho/\partial t) = 0$$

The demand for trials is negatively affected, however, by the deterioration of evidence (α) which is typically not comprised of the judicial interest.

Incomplete compensation ($\rho < 1$ or $j < d$)
But when the judicial interest is lower than the subjective discount rate, the depreciation of the plaintiff's value at stake will increase with time and court delay.

$$NEB = \pi_x V\rho - (1 + \rho - 2\pi_x\rho)C$$

$$(\partial NEB/\partial\rho)(\partial\rho/\partial t) < 0$$

Consequently, the demand for suits and trials from the plaintiff will be lower compared to perfect compensation. However, we need to recall that $\rho > \delta$. This implies that the mere award of judicial interests leads to more suits because it boosts the plaintiff's credibility to threaten the defendant with a trial.

Overcompensation ($\rho > 1$ or $j > d$)
In this scenario, the court awards judicial interests at a rate above the plaintiff's discount rate. As a result, the discounted net expected benefit of a trial, hence the number of suits, increases the longer it takes to end the conflict. When $j > d$ substantially, rational plaintiffs may start to 'invest' in a trial.

$$NEB = \pi_x V\rho - (1 + \rho - 2\pi_x\rho)C$$

$$(\partial NEB/\partial\rho)(\partial\rho/\partial t) > 0$$

Whether the award of generous judicial interests boosts the demand for trials above the level in which courts resolve disputes instantaneously ultimately depends on the value of α. Briefly, we can state that the impact of judicial interest payments on the demand for suits and trials from the plaintiff is ambiguous and depends on the interest-discount rate gap adjusted for α.

Demand of the Defendant

The award of the verdict (V) is a probable cost for the defendant borne entirely at the end of the trial. The depreciation of the value at stake caused by waiting thus lowers his costs of litigation. Time has an inverse effect on the defendant's demand. Moreover, the likelihood of losing decreases $(1 - \pi_y < 1 - p_y)$ because the quality of the evidence brought forward by the plaintiff erodes $(\pi_y = p_y + \alpha)$. This evolution increases the chances of recouping the legal costs borne at the beginning of the trial.

$$TEC = (1 - \pi_y)V\delta + (1 + \delta - 2\pi_y\delta)C \qquad (8)$$

$$(\partial TEC/\partial\delta)(\partial\delta/\partial t) < 0 \qquad (9)$$

Consequently, the more time goes by, the more will the total expected discounted costs of trial for the defendant decrease. Hence, he is likely to make a smaller settlement offer and be more inclined to go to court. However, the granting of judicial interests changes his behaviour dramatically. The actualized costs will increase and may become even larger than in a zero-delay situation. This is true when the judicial interest exceeds the defendant's subjective discount factor.

$$TEC = (1 - \pi_y)V\rho + (1 + \rho - 2\pi_y\rho)C \qquad (10)$$

$$(\partial TEC/\partial\rho)(\partial\rho/\partial j) > 0 \qquad (11)$$

The award of judicial interest payments adds to the costs of trial for the defendant making him more willing to settle (equation 11). But given the judicial interest rate, we need to distinguish between three scenarios to know the overall effect of delay: ρ is equal to, lower or higher than 1.

No depreciation ($\rho = 1$ or $j = d$)
When the judicial interest rate equals the defendant's subjective rate, the discounted total expected costs of trial become (almost) the same as if the dispute would have been resolved by the court without any time lost. In other words, there is no depreciation of the award by the court.

$$TEC = (1 - \pi_y)V + (1 - \pi_y)2C = (1 - p_y - \alpha)(V + 2C)$$

$$(\partial TEC/\partial\rho)(\partial\rho/\partial t) = 0$$

The defendant finds himself in a situation in which he considers the costs of the trial as if there was no time wasted between the suit and the court's decision. However, the equations clearly show that his chances of prevailing have improved due to the lower quality of evidence brought against him.

Depreciation ($\rho < 1$ or $j < d$)
In this scenario, the subjective expected legal costs fall with time since the depreciation of the award is not entirely offset by the judicial interest payments.

$$TEC = (1 - \pi_y)V\rho + (1 + \rho - 2\pi_y\rho)C$$

$$(\partial TEC/\partial\rho)(\partial\rho/\partial t) < 0$$

Time reduces the actualized cost of a trial since the defendant discounts the future at a higher rate than the court. As a consequence, he will make a lower settlement offer and be less dissuaded from going to court. Again, we need to recall that still $\rho > \delta$ so that the defendant's willingness to settle is improving when judicial interests are awarded, no matter how small they are.

Appreciation ($\rho > 1$ or $j > d$)
In this case, the judge is inflicting extra costs on the defendant by awarding judicial interests at a rate above the subjective discount rate. The total expected costs of a trial are thus increasing with time.

$$TEC = (1 - \pi_y)V\rho + (1 + \rho - 2\pi_y\rho)C$$

$$(\partial TEC/\partial\rho)(\partial\rho/\partial t) > 0$$

It follows that these comparatively high judicial interest rates have a benign effect on the defendant's willingness to settle. In other words, it lowers his demand for trial.

We can now conclude that the effect of judicial interest payments on the demand for trails from the defendant is ambigous, contrary to the plaintiff's and dependent on the interest-discount rate gap as well as the degree of deterioration of evidence with time.

3.   AGGREGATE DEMAND FOR TRIALS

With these opposing tendencies for plaintiff and defendant, how do time and judicial interest payments affect the 'aggregate' demand for trials? The demand for trials depends on the number of suits that are launched minus the number of conflicts that are settled before trial. The former is determined by the number of conflicts which have a NEB > 0,[170] the latter depends on the settlement range (SR). The larger the range, the higher the likelihood that parties reach an agreement. The settlement range is determined by the maximum offer of the defendant which is equal to the total expected costs of a trial he is hoping to save by settling and by the minimum settlement amount acceptable to the plaintiff, which is equal to his net expected benefit of the trial. With $p = p_x + p_y$ and $\pi = \pi_x + \pi_y$, hence $p = \pi$, it can be easily deduced that:

$$SR = TEC - NEB = 2C + (1 - p)\delta(2C + V) \tag{12}$$

$$SR = 2C \Leftrightarrow p = 1 \tag{13}$$

$$\partial SR/\partial p < 0 \tag{14}$$

$$(\partial SR/\partial \delta)(\partial \delta/\partial t) = 0 \Leftrightarrow p = 1 \tag{15}$$

$$(\partial SR/\partial \delta)(\partial \delta/\partial t) > 0 \Leftrightarrow p > 1 \tag{16}$$

It should be noted that waiting only has some effect on the likelihood of settlement when there is optimism (equation 16). Indeed, when there is no optimism ($p = \pi = 1$), the reduced willingness to settle by the defendant is precisely offset by the plaintiff's increase regardless of time (equation 13). Only when $p > 1$ does the depreciation of the stake play a role in the settlement behaviour of parties. Luckily, the negative effects of optimism on the likelihood to settle are mitigated by time (equation 16). Since $(1 - p) < 0$, it follows that the second term in equation 12 gets smaller over time. The reason is straightforward. A settlement always saves the parties the legal costs borne at the beginning of the trial, 2C. Optimism narrows the gap between their expectations of the verdict. Each party may be confident to win the case, obtain their claim and even recoup most legal costs under an indemnity system. But when time passes, the discounted value of the verdict is reduced, leaving the litigants only with the starting costs to be saved. Their settlement range will increase since the future and expected gains, which troubled the settlement negotiations, gradually vanish.

We can learn from the analysis above that, when we introduce judicial interest payments into the economic model of settlement behaviour, we need to distinguish carefully between cases in which optimism prevails or not. The mere award of interests (which has the same impact as shortening the trial time) only has an impact on the likelihood to settle and the demand for trials

---

[170] See supra **Demand of the Plaintiff**.

when the subjective perception of the chance to win takes the best of both parties (equation 18). One disturbing result is that the negative effects of optimism are amplified by judicial interest payments (equation 14).

Following equation 12, we can redefine the settlement range as:

$$SR = 2C + (1 - p)\rho(2C + V) \tag{17}$$

$$SR = 2C \Leftrightarrow p = 1 \tag{13}$$

$$\partial SR/\partial p < 0 \tag{14}$$

$$(\partial SR/\partial \rho)(\partial \rho/\partial j,t) = 0 \Leftrightarrow p = 1 \tag{18}$$

$$(\partial SR/\partial \rho)(\partial \rho/\partial j) < 0 \Leftrightarrow p > 1 \tag{19}$$

$$(\partial SR/\partial \rho)(\partial \rho/\partial t) > 0 \Leftrightarrow p > 1 \text{ and } j < d \tag{20}$$

Thus, when there is optimism, the award of judicial interest payments has a negative on the likelihood to settle (equation 19). When there is a positive gap between the judicial interest and the subjective discount rate, i.e. $j > d$ or $\rho > 1$, the settlement range will shrink over time (equation 20). Since judges tend to award high judicial interest payments (reflecting efficient compensation for the risk of α), it seems reasonable to argue that $j > d$ in practice.

However, this conclusion cannot be maintained under all circumstances because it presupposes identical subjective discount rates of the plaintiff and the defendant. This assumption seems unrealistic. Therefore, following equations 6 and 10, we need to define the SR as:

$$\begin{aligned} SR = TEC - NEB &= (1 - \pi_y)V\rho_y + (1 + \rho_y - 2\pi_y\rho_y)C \\ &- \pi_x V\rho_x + (1 + \rho_x - 2\pi_x\rho_x)C = \mathbf{2C} + (\rho_y + \rho_x)C \\ &- 2(\pi_y\rho_y + \pi_x\rho_x)C + (\rho_y - (\pi_y\rho_y + \pi_x\rho_x))V \end{aligned} \tag{21}$$

As mentioned earlier, the impact of time and judicial interest on the demand for trials depends to a large extent on the occurence of optimism in the legal market.

No Optimism ($\pi = 1$)

When the parties hold objective views on their chances of prevailing, i.e. $\pi_y = 1 - \pi_x$, we can rewrite equation 21 as:

$$SR = 2C + (\rho_x - \rho_y)C - 2(\rho_x - \rho_y)\pi_x C - (\rho_x - \rho_y)\pi_x V \qquad (22)$$

Four scenarios need to be distinguished in which the subjective discount rates of the litigants hold different values.

3.1.1. Uniform discount rates with perfect compensation ($\rho_x = \rho_y = 1$ or $j = d_x = d_y$)
It follows directly from equation 22 that:

$$SR = 2C \Leftarrow \rho_x - \rho_y = 0 \qquad (23)$$

$$\partial SR/\partial t = 0 \qquad (24)$$

Perfect compensation make the litigants act as if there was no waiting period. The deterioration of evidence α is as much a gain for the defendant as it is a loss for the plaintiff. So, under these circumstances, time nor judicial interest payments have any impact on the settlement range or the demand for trials.

3.1.2. Uniform discount rates with imperfect compensation ($\rho_x = \rho_y \neq 1$ or $j \neq d_x = d_y$)
The same results are obtained if we assume imperfect compensation. It should be noted that incomplete and over-compensation yield the same outcome. Whether the judicial interest rate is above or below the discount rates of the parties has no bearing on the likelihood to settle. Again, we can easily deduce from equation 22 that the settlement range is equal to:

$$SR = 2C \Leftarrow \rho_x - \rho_y = 0 \qquad (23)$$

$$\partial SR/\partial t = 0 \qquad (24)$$

$$\partial SR/\partial j = 0 \qquad (25)$$

In other words, judicial interest payments have no effect on the likelihood to settle when parties hold objective probabilities to win and equal discount rates. The change in the net expected benefit of a trial for the plaintiff is precisely offset by the defendant's change of total expected costs. Although the respective minimum and maximum offers for settlement change, they do so in the same direction and with the same amount, hence the remainder is unaffected.

3.1.3.   Negative plaintiff–defendant discount rate gap
$$(\rho_x > \rho_y \text{ or } d_x < d_y)$$

For reasons of analytical simplicity, let us first rewrite equation 22 to assess the effect of differing subjective discount rates between plaintiff and defendant.

$$SR = 2C + (\rho_x - \rho_y)(C - 2\pi_x C - \pi_x V) \qquad (22)$$

Since $\rho_x - \rho_y > 0$, the effect of a negative discount rate gap on the settlement range is negative when the following condition is fulfilled: $(C - 2\pi_x C - \pi_x V) < 0 \Leftrightarrow \pi_x > C/(2C + V)$. This condition always holds since $\pi_x > 2C/(2C + V)$ for NEB > 0, i.e. to have a suit to start with. The reason for the negative relationship is straightforward. On the one hand, the plaintiff gains from the interests awarded and will get tougher in the settlement negotiations. The defendant, on the other hand, will observe a rise of his actualized costs and be more eager to try and strike a deal before trial. Unfortunately, his eagerness to settle has not strengthened as much as the plaintiff's stubbornness since $\rho_x > \rho_y$. The overall conclusion is that the likelihood to settle decreases when the defendant discounts future payments more heavily than his opponent.

$$\partial SR/\partial j < 0 \qquad (26)$$

$$\partial SR/\partial t < 0 \qquad (27)$$

We noted earlier that time *in se* does not affect the settlement range, but that it does have a positive effect when there is optimism (equation 16). However, even when $\pi = 1$, this benign consequence is overturned (equation 27) if the plaintiff takes a different, more patient attitude at the passage of time. His higher valuation of future awards by the court makes him an increasingly tough negotiator during the settlement talks. The same logic applies to the negative effect of judicial interest payments which is no longer dependent on optimism (equation 19, 26). The optimistic view of the plaintiff on the future (not necessarily his chance to prevail), which reduces the likelihood of settlement, is thus boosted the higher the interest rate (equation 26), the more distant the future (equation 27), the larger the confidence gap with the defendant.

3.1.4.   Positive plaintiff–defendant discount rate gap $(\rho_x < \rho_y \text{ or } d_x > d_y)$

Following equation 22, it is easy to see that a positive gap between the discount rates of the plaintiff and the defendant positively affects the likelihood to settle.

$$SR = 2C + (\rho_x - \rho_y)(C - 2\pi_x C - \pi_x V) \qquad (22)$$

While the defendant, who discounts future events at a lower rate, is confronted with higher total expected actualized costs of a trial due to the award of judicial interests, the plaintiff believes that he does not gain that much from such a distant award. As a consequence, the former's settlement offer will substantially increase while the latter is already content with a slightly higher amount.

$$\partial SR/\partial j > 0 \qquad (28)$$

$$\partial SR/\partial t > 0 \qquad (29)$$

Higher judicial interest rates raise the costs of the defendant comparatively more than the plaintiff's benefit from trial. It follows that the settlement range will increase (equation 28). The effect is felt even stronger, the larger the different valuation of the future by the litigants, which in turn is amplified by the passage of time (equation 29).

As a tentative conclusion, we state that when parties hold objective views on their chances to prevail, the award of judicial interests has a positive effect on the likelihood to settle if and only if the plaintiff–defendant internal discount rate gap is positive. Under these conditions, higher judicial interest rates tend to discourage the demand for trials. But do these results stand the test of optimism?

3.2. Optimism ($\pi > 1$)

As mentioned earlier, parties typically hold optimistic subjective views on their chances of winning in the trial. It follows that $\pi_x + \pi_y = \pi > 1$. Let us have another look at equation 21:

$$SR = 2C + (\rho_x + \rho_y)C - 2(\pi_x\rho_x + \pi_y\rho_y)C + (\rho_y - (\pi_x\rho_x + \pi_y\rho_y))V \qquad (21)$$

Again, we need to distinguish between four cases with different discount rates for the litigants.

3.2.1. Uniform discount rates with perfect compensation
$(\rho_x = \rho_y = \rho = 1$ or $j = d_x = d_y = d)$

Perfect compensation counteracts the depreciation of the stakes in the trial. The litigants are in a position as if the trial was held instantaneously. Although time diminishes the availability and quality of evidence and changes the relative positions of the parties, the defendant's gain is precisely the plaintiff's loss, hence the settlement range is unaffected. Following equation 21, we can easily re-establish equation 17 by imputing the assumptions of optimism and uniform discount rates.

$$SRZ = 2C + (1 - \pi)\rho(2C + V) \qquad (17)$$

When $\rho = 1$, it follows that (negative) impact on the likelihood to settle is fully and only determined by the degree of optimism (equation 30).

$$\partial SR/\partial \pi < 0 \qquad (30)$$

$$\partial SR/\partial t = 0 \qquad (31)$$

The outcome is self-evident, yet revealing. Normally, time mitigates the negative impact of optimism on the likelihood to settle (equation 16). But when the discount rates of the litigants are identical and equal to the judicial rate, time loses its influence on their behaviour (equation 31). What will happen when the litigants use the same discount rate, yet different from the court's?

3.2.2. Uniform discount rates with incomplete compensation
$(\rho_x = \rho_y = \rho < 1$ or $j < d_x = d_y = d)$

Following equation 17, it is clear that the settlement range is also determined by p which, in turn, depends on the gap between the judicial interest and the subjective discount rate. When there is incomplete compensation or partial depreciation, we can conclude that:

$$\partial SR/\partial \pi < 0 \qquad (30)$$

$$\partial SR/\partial t > 0 \qquad (32)$$

$$\partial SR/\partial j < 0 \qquad (33)$$

Assuming optimism, which remains a key determinant of the demand for trials (equation 30), the award of judicial interests does have a (negative) impact on the likelihood to settle even when litigants hold the same perspective on the future (equation 33). But the divergence between the parties over the future outcome of the trial ($\pi > 1$) becomes less important when the litigants care less about that future ($d > j$). And the more distant the future, the less their optimism matters in the settlement negotiations (equation 32). From an economic point of view, the judicial interest rate should stay well below the litigants' discount rate to counteract the negative effects of optimism on their eagerness to settle.

3.2.3. Uniform discount rates with overcompensation
$(\rho_x = \rho_y = \rho > 1$ or $j > d_x = d_y = d)$

With over-compensation or appreciation, the optimistic views on the chances to prevail are magnified into the present. Higher judicial interest payments (equation 34) and longer waiting periods (equation 35) thus worsen a deteriorated chance of settlement.

$$\partial SR/\partial \pi < 0 \qquad (30)$$

$$\partial SR/\partial j < 0 \qquad (34)$$

$$\partial SR/\partial t < 0 \qquad (35)$$

The policy recommendation stays the same: the judicial interest rate should equal the discount rate of the litigants. But is the gap between the interest rate and the discount rate still a relevant factor when the parties who have different views on their chances to prevail also hold different perspectives on the future?

3.2.4. Negative plaintiff–defendant discount rate gap
$(\rho_x > \rho_y \text{ or } d_x < d_y)$

Let us find out first what the effect of judicial interest payments is on the likelihood to settle when the plaintiff has a comparatively low subjective discount. We rewrite equation 21 as:

$$SR = 2C + ((1 - 2\pi_y)\rho_y + (1 - 2\pi_x)\rho_x)C + ((1 - \pi_y)\rho_y - \pi_x\rho_x)V \qquad (36)$$

From this, two conclusions can be drawn immediately. First, high judicial interest payments still have an increasingly negative impact on the settlement range. Second, it is the positive of negative difference between subjective discount rates of plaintiff and defendant and not the gap with respect to the judicial interest which determines the likelihood of settlement.

$$\partial SR/\partial j < 0 \qquad (37)$$

$$\partial SR/\partial t < 0 \qquad (38)$$

The results of this negative gap are completely similar to the case in which there was no optimism. The plaintiff proves to be a tougher negotiator in the settlement talks since he is more patient about the future. Time (equation 38), judicial interest payments (equation 37) and the gap with his opponent reduce the chances of settlement which have already become slim because parties are too optimistic about their chances of prevailing.

3.2.5. Positive plaintiff–defendant discount rate gap $(\rho_x < \rho_y \text{ or } d_x > d_y)$
When the plaintiff seems to live more in the present, his willingness to settle relatively increases since his NEB is less augmented by the award of judicial

interests. And the defendant, who discounts future costs and judicial interest payments at a comparatively low rate, is confronted with comparatively higher costs. The settlement range is thus bound to increase.

$$\partial SR/\partial j < 0 \tag{39}$$

$$\partial SR/\partial t > 0 \tag{40}$$

It should be noted that, unlike with the negative gap, there is one result (equation 39) that differs ceteris paribus from the no-optimism scenario. When $\pi = 1$, higher judicial interest rates raise the settlement offer by the defendant by more ($\rho_y > \rho_x$) than the higher minimum acceptable amount for the plaintiff. But when $1 - \pi_y < \pi_x$, higher interest rates are affecting the defendant less than the plaintiff since he has become more optimistic about the outcome of the trial. Consequently, higher judicial interest payments reduce the settlement range.

Thus, when parties are optimistic, the award of judicial interests has a negative effect on the likelihood to settle regardless of the plaintiff–defendant internal discount rate gap. Even when $\rho_x < \rho_y$ does a higher judicial interest rate stimulate the demand for trials. This contradicts our earlier conclusion when we assumed no optimism. The best thing to happen for the courts is that defendants take seriously into account the future verdict while plaintiffs want to end the conflict sooner rather than later and settle now. In other words, a positive plaintiff–defendant discount rate gap has a positive effect on the likelihood to settle. When the gap is zero, we should lower the judicial interest rate to let time play its mitigating role on optimism.

Table 6.1 clearly shows that the impact of court delay on trial demand is dependent on the judicial interest rate level (for suits) and the subjective discount rates of the litigants (for settlements). Time boosts the confidence of plaintiffs when they expect to be awarded high interest payments in every stage of the conflict (more suits, less settlements). But the judicial interest rate plays no role in this respect when litigants discount the future differently. Irrespective of judicial interest payments, time negatively affects the likelihood to settle when the plaintiff values future income more than the defendant.

4. THE NEED FOR UNIFORM JUDICIAL INTEREST RATES IN A FEDERALIST STATE

The question whether judicial interest rates should be determined at the federal level or at the state level is an issue which can be described in terms of Tiebout competition. Tiebout (1956) argued that competition between local authorities

Table 6.1   *Effect of time and the interest–discount rate gap on suits and settlements*

Suits	$\partial NEB/\partial t$	
1) $\rho_x < 1$	$-$	
2) $\rho_x = 1$	0	
3) $\rho_x > 1$	$+$	

Settlements	$\partial SR/\partial t$	
No/Optimism	$\pi = 1$	$\pi > 1$
4) $\rho_x = \rho_y = 1$	0	0
5) $\rho_x = \rho_y < 1$	0	$+$
6) $\rho_x = \rho_y > 1$	0	$-$
7) $\rho_x > \rho_y$	$-$	$-$
8) $\rho_x < \rho_y$	$+$	$+$

will lead to allocative efficiency when people with the same preferences cluster together in the same area. If, for example, citizens in one city prefer a public swimming pool and citizens in another town have a preference for public transportation, the first community will probably invest in a local swimming pool whereas the second will probably put their tax money into public transportation. If an individual living in the second town prefers a swimming pool, he could then move to the first city, which provides services that better suit his preferences. The crucial idea is that citizens can influence the provision of public goods either by voting or by moving.

The Tiebout model can also be applied to court procedures. Differentiation between court systems will lead to national judiciaries competing with each other, providing court services and procedures that correspond best to the preferences of litigants living in the federal state. The idea is the same: citizens will sue and go to trial in states that provide legal rules which correspond to their preferences, in particular their subjective discount rate. This could explain the variety and differences in both court delay and judicial interest payments in the national legal systems. Moreover, it shows that differences between the various court procedures and habits of different countries should not necessarily be judged as negative since discount rates may differ among citizens. In accordance with the subsidiarity principle, the courts presumably have the best information regarding the preferences of the litigants. Therefore, what are the (economic) arguments to put forward in favour of judicial interest-rate harmonization?

To answer that, we need to address two other questions first: why do economists prefer settlements over trials and what is the effect of judicial interest payments on the likelihood to settle. Litigation as such is costly for the parties and for society. While litigants (or their lawyers) are fighting their battles in court, resources normally spent on productive activity are now allocated to dispute resolution. As shown before, the benefit from settling is equal to the trial costs saved (2C). Moreover, a settlement reached by negotiation and mutual consent is superior to a decision taken by a third party, a judge or arbitrator, who stay rationally under-informed. Trials are useful when they create precedents. The optimal level of litigation is determined by the social benefits and costs of trials. The private and external benefits are the resolution of the dispute under the court's review and the deterrence of similar conflicts. The social costs consist of the legal expenses borne by the litigants and the tax money poured into the court system plus the costs of erroneous decisions. Following Olson (1973), we wish to point out that the performance of courts is hard to measure because the technical characteristics of collective goods such as verdicts make it difficult to assess their value. Although we could count for example, the number of verdicts produced per judge, the true value would not be known since there is no price system to reveal it and we do not know the citizens who benefited from the verdicts by learning to prevent similar conflicts. As a matter of fact, it would be inefficient to exclude non-payers from the information since the marginal cost of dissemination is practically zero. Consequently, there can be no general presumption about the relation between the actual and desirable levels of litigation. However, since the parties themselves hold all the information, a settlement is likely to produce a better outcome than a court decision. Moreover, it saves opportunity costs of litigation. It follows that the government and even the court system should motivate and teach people to solve their conflicts.

Is the use of judicial interest payments helpful in this respect? As Table 6.2 shows, the use of this technique to compensate litigants for waiting should be used with great caution. It bolsters the audacity of plaintiffs to sue. Under almost all circumstances this consequence will negatively affect the likelihood to settle. Only a plaintiff who is non-optimistic about the outcome of the trial and relatively myopic about future interest payments will be more easily inclined to settle.

The transnational character of this problem may be one reason to harmonize the judicial interest rates in the whole territory. High judicial interest rates in one state not only affect litigation behaviour within that jurisdiction. Mobility in the European trial market will bolster the ability to sue of plaintiffs from other states as well. It is clear that court-hopping in the European Union will lead to fewer settlements. There is indeed a risk of unintended destructive competition. National court systems already ridden with delay tend

Table 6.2 Effect of judicial interest rate on suits and settlements

Suits	$\partial NEB/\partial j$	
1) $\rho_x < 1$	+	
2) $\rho_x = 1$	/	
3) $\rho_x > 1$	+	

Settlements	$\partial SR/\partial j$	
No/Optimism	$\pi = 1$	$\pi > 1$
4) $\rho_x = \rho_y = 1$	/	/
5) $\rho_x = \rho_y < 1$	0	–
6) $\rho_x = \rho_y > 1$	0	–
7) $\rho_x > \rho_y$	–	–
8) $\rho_x < \rho_y$	+	–

to award high judicial interest payments to compensate for the depreciation of the stake awaited. This will not only attract but also induce more cases within the federalist state. Another argument in favour of harmonization is the creation of the European Monetary Union. The European Central Bank sets the reference interest rate for the whole Union, which, in turn, determines the return on state bonds. Since strict fiscal policies embedded in the Maastricht Treaty will prevent any member-state from defaulting on debt repayments, these returns will equalize and so will most citizens' discount rate. Monetary harmonization thus entails a plea for uniform judicial interest rates.

CONCLUDING REMARKS

Court delay is rightly interpreted as a problem of supply shortage. Yet, the solution will not come from padding the national court system with more judges and courts. The fact is that the demand for trials is not only determined by (subsidized) prices but also time. Since plaintiffs and defendants react in opposite ways to changes of the waiting period, a supply increase may eventually lead to longer waiting lists. Therefore, economic analysis as well as public policy should focus on the demand side.

In which ways can national policymakers reduce court delay? First of all, a conventional supply-side policy is effective when the subjective discount rate of the plaintiff is above the judicial interest rate or the internal rate of his opponent. To fulfil the first condition and deter opportunistic behaviour by potential plaintiffs, the court should use the instrument of compensatory interests with great caution, keeping it as low as possible. This will result in fewer suits. The second condition is easily met because it seems reasonable to assume that plaintiffs who, for instance, face a cash flow problem as a result of overdue or non-payments will have to borrow money at a rate above the average return earned by the late or non-paying defendants. So, a successful policy of supply-induced reduction of the legal process time requires incomplete compensation of plaintiffs.

As mentioned before, the court awards judicial interests to justly remedy the depreciation of the disputed good by time. Unfortunately, it also boosts the net expected benefit of trial, hence the ability of the plaintiff to credibly threaten his opponent and sue. The impact on the settlement process is devastating. From this perspective, the award of interest is not an efficient policy option. Assuming mobility of plaintiffs in the federalist court space, the spill-over effects of compensatory interest payments with respect to negotiation power are negative. To deter opportunistic use of the justice systems and stimulate settlements, national courts in a federalist state should apply the same and, preferably, low judicial interest rate. This is particularly meaningful in a monetary union. If, however, different interest rates are applied, the choice of jurisdiction will become a crucial element in pre-conflict contract negotiations. If there exists some choice of courts and judicial interest-rate harmonization cannot be achieved, then the federalist state is bound to be plunged into a situation of excessive litigation caused by the high compensatory interest payments in one national jurisdiction.

The fundamental reason for the excess demand for trials lies, of course, in the incomplete internalization of external costs, in particular the court's operating costs. Rationing trials by court fees is certainly an efficient policy, but may be difficult to implement for political reasons or for reasons of social justice. Several systems can guarantee, however, the access to justice for less wealthy citizens. The state may provide legal aid or *pro deo* lawyers. The indemnity system gives free access to the innocent, rich or poor. Under a contingency fee system, the lawyers agree to bear all costs, including court fees, in case they lose. And finally, people can insure themselves against legal expenses.

Optimism enforces the predominantly negative consequences of court delay and judicial interest payments. Therefore, any policy successful at making the subjective beliefs of litigants in their chances to prevail correspond with reality will lower the number of conflicts, suits and the social costs of trials after suit. Concrete measures to improve legal certainty are better training of judges, whose decisions are then seldom overruled or appealed and are not a source of conflict themselves, and the setting of good precedents.

The policies just mentioned offer a first-best remedy to inefficient court delay. However, it should be pointed out that delay can correct legal failures.

For example, strict liability is known to induce victims to take suboptimal levels of precaution (Cooter and Ulen, p. 274). While the court is highly likely to declare that the victim is in the right since the injurer is strictly liable, the former will realize that his rightful claim will materialize in the near future. The value of whatever compensation damages will diminish and the victim will take more care in order to prevent a less rewarding accident.

Given the collective nature of verdicts, states are best-suited to capture the external benefits from court decisions. When delay makes litigants turn to private dispute resolution agencies, the tax base is likely to diminish due to the replication of conflicts. Therefore, public policy should tackle delay. We offer three options: high court fees, better training of judges and, if that does not help, a low, equal judicial interest rate, which at least mitigates the depreciation of the claims without inducing excessive use of the court systems.

REFERENCES

Barzel, Y. (1974), 'A theory of waiting by rationing', *Journal of Law and Economics*, **17**(1), 73–94.

Cheung, S. (1974), 'A theory of price control', *Journal of Law and Economics*, **17**(1), 53–71.

Cooter, R. and T. Ulen (1996), *Law and Economics*, Addison-Wesley.

Fenn, P. and N. Rickman (1999), 'Delay and settlement in litigation', *Economic Journal*, **109**(457), 476–91.

Gravelle, H. (1990), 'Rationing trials by waiting: welfare implications', *International Review of Law and Economics*, **10**, 255–70.

Gravelle, H. (1995), 'Regulating the market for civil justice', in *Reform of Civil Procedure*, Oxford: Oxford University Press, 279–303.

Lindsay, C. and B. Feigenbaum (1984), 'Rationing by waiting lists', *American Economic Review*, **74**(3), 404–17.

Mühl, Manuela (2001), 'Economic analysis of settlement negotiation in a litigation process', *Economie Appliquée*, 3, 39–74.

Olson, Mancur (1973), 'Evaluating performance in the public sector', in M. Moss (ed.), *The Measurement of Economic and Social Performance*, National Bureau for Economic Research, New York: Columbia University Press, 355–409.

Samuelson, P. (1954), 'The pure theory of public expenditures', *Review of Economics and Statistics*, **36**, 387–89.

Shavell, S. (1982), 'Suit, settlement and trial: a theoretical analysis under alternative methods for the allocation of legal costs', *Journal of Legal Studies*, **11**(1), 55–81.

Spier, K. (1992), 'The dynamics of pre-trial negotiation', *Review of Economic Studies*, **59**(1), 93–108.

Tiebout, C.M. (1956), 'A pure theory of local expenditures', *Journal of Political Economy*, **64**(5), 416–24.

Vereeck, L. and M. Mühl (2000), 'An economic theory of court delay', *European Journal of Law and Economics*, **7**(3), 243–68.

7. European policymaking: An agency-theoretic analysis

Dieter Schmidtchen and Bernard Steunenberg

INTRODUCTION

In various European legal acts the Council has delegated power to the Commission to set common policy, conditional on specific procedural requirements. Those requirements are commonly known as 'comitology'. In this chapter we analyse whether and how far these implementation procedures help to overcome a dilemma of delegation,[171] which arises if (a) a principal and an agent have conflicting interests and (b) the principal, due to the structure of the principal–agent relationship, cannot perfectly control the agent (structure-induced agent discretion).

As is well known from the principal-agent literature (see Sappington 1991), conflicting interests and information asymmetry allow the agent to choose actions which are inconsistent with the preferences of the principal. However, as is often overlooked, conflicting interests and asymmetric information are sufficient but not necessary conditions for agent discretion. We also have room for agent discretion with perfect and complete information, if the structure of the principal-agent relationship allows the agent to deviate from policies preferred by the principal. This kind of discretion, that has been labelled by Steunenberg (1996) structure-induced discretion, can arise, for example, if the legislature has difficulties in deciding collectively on its actions (see also Cooter, 2000: 154–61). The legislative process can be hampered by majority rule cycles, which the agent may employ to its advantage (Hill 1985). Furthermore, new legislation can be blocked if political actors do not agree on any deviation from the current agent policy (see Ferejohn and Shipan 1990; Eskridge and Ferejohn, 1992). In these cases, it is

---

[171] According to Lupia and McCubbins a dilemma of delegation arises if a policymaking bureaucracy does not have common interests with its principals and possesses information about the delegation that their principals lack (see Lupia and McCubbins 1998: 214, 79). As for the latter we think of information about cause–effect relations, the details of existing policies and regulations, the pending decision agenda, and the distribution of benefits and costs of agency actions (see McCubbins, Noll, Weingast 1987: 247).

neither a lack of information nor the unwillingness of the legislature to control agent decisions, but rather the inability to reach legislative agreement that provides the agent with the opportunity to select a policy that is closer to its ideal point.

The 'political control' literature distinguishes two general ways of controlling an agent (see McCubbins, Noll, Weingast, 1987: 243): 'oversight', which consists of monitoring, researching and punishing bureaucratic behaviour and administrative procedures. Due to costs of monitoring, limits to sanctions and political costs of sanctions, monitoring and sanctions do not comprise a perfect solution to the problem of bureaucratic compliance (see McCubbins, Noll, Weingast, 1987: 246–53).[172] Administrative procedures 'affect the institutional environment in which agencies make decisions and thereby limit an agency's range of feasible policy actions'. As McCubbins, Noll, Weingast (1987) mention, 'the point of administrative procedures is *not* to preselect specific policy outcomes, but to create a decisionmaking environment that mirrors the political circumstances that gave rise to the establishment of the policy ... If these uses of administrative process are effective, the agency, without any need for input, guidance, or attention from political principals, is directed toward the decisions its principals would make on their own, even if the principals are unaware, ex ante, of what that outcome would be. By structuring the rules of the game for the agency, administrative procedures sequence agency activity, regulate its information collection and dissemination, limit its available choices, and define its strategic advantage.' (McCubbins, Noll, Weingast, 1987: 255.)[173]

Although oversight plays a role in shaping the relationship between Council and Commission, it is of minor importance compared to procedures. When the Council delegates power to the European Commission this is typically conditional on specific procedural requirements. These procedures are codified in the Council's so called 'comitology' decision.[174] In this comitology decision, the

---

[172] McCubbins, Noll, Weingast (1987: 244) mention hearings, investigations, budget reviews, legislative sanctions as means of standard political oversight. According to Lupia and McCubbins (1998: 81–82) the principal has three ways of obtaining information about her agent's actions: '*direct monitoring* of an agent's activities (the principal gathers information herself), attending to the *agent's self-report* of his activities, or attending to *third-party testimony* about the agent's actions.'

[173] There is a further advantage mentioned by McCubbins, Noll and Weingast: procedural controls 'enable political leaders to assure compliance without specifying, or even necessarily knowing, what substantive outcome is most in their interest.' (1987: 244).

[174] Decision of the Council of July 13, 1987 (*Official Journal of the European Union* 1987: L 197/33). On 28 June, 1999, the Council adopted a decision laying down the procedures for the exercise of 'implementing powers conferred on the Commission' (Council Decision 99/468/EC, O.J. 1999, L 184/23; Corrigendum in O.J. 1999, L269/45. Three declarations made on this decision in the Council minutes are set out in O.J. 1999 (203/1). The number of procedures has fallen from seven to four.

Council distinguished three types of procedures: the advisory committee procedure, the management committee procedure and the regulatory committee procedure. All these procedures have as a common element bodies of representatives or civil servants drawn from the member states. They consult, but also supervise, the Commission's execution of legal acts.

Although advisory committees, management committees and regulatory committees have become an integral part of the European institutional structure, there is surprisingly little research to be found from a rigorous rational choice perspective. The current comitology procedures have been analysed in Steunenberg, Koboldt and Schmidtchen (1996, 1997), using a rational choice approach and, more specifically, the tools of non-cooperative game theory. Institutional reforms regarding the involvement of the European Parliament are dealt with in Steunenberg and Schmidtchen (2000), Steunenberg, Koboldt and Schmidtchen (2000, 1997). However, all these contributions focus on the distribution of power in the European Union (see also Steunenberg, Schmidtchen and Koboldt, 1999). Although we strongly draw on the analytical insights derived in these earlier articles, the focus has changed from the power issue to the principal-agent problem.

The chapter is organized as follows.[175] In section 1 we present a simple model of structure-induced agent discretion. In section 2 we describe policymaking in the EU and point to ways in which the Council tries to restrict the discretion of the Commission in implementing European policies. In section 3 we analyse the current decision-making procedures, using a model in which the Commission may select a policy that is subject to review by a committee of representatives of the member states and the Council. Section 4 presents a measure of agent discretion. It adresses the ability of the Commission to set a policy according to its own preferences, given a specific procedure and a variety of possible preference constellations. Thus, the better the outcome of the policy-setting game from the perspective of the Commission, the worse is the workability of an implementation procedure in solving the dilemma of delegation.

1. STRUCTURE-INDUCED AGENT DISCRETION

The purpose of this section is to show how, in principle, institutional arrangements like committees matter with regard to decision-making by an agent. In

---

[175] The chapter is a slightly modified version of a paper entitled 'Comitology and the legislator's dilemma: on the architecture of decisionmaking in the European Union' published in *Yearbook for New Political Economy (Jahrbuch für Neue Politische Ökonomie)*, editors: Holler, M., H. Kliemt, D. Schmidtchen, M.E. Streit, vol. 21, Tübingen 2003.

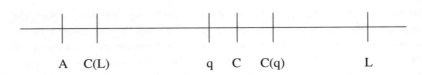

A   C(L)   q   C   C(q)   L

Figure 7.1   Gatekeeping procedure: simple majority

order to keep things as simple as possible we assume simple majority voting although it is not part of the comitology procedures. In section 4 dealing with the commission policies under the implementation procedures we introduce the more complicated case of qualified majority voting which characterizes the comitology procedures.

A legislature delegates policymaking authority to an agent and delegates supervision of the agent to a committee. The committee is assumed to have gate-keeping power: the only way for a policy proposal to come before the legislature is by the committee opening the gate to enable policy change. We distinguish two rules, according to what the legislature can do if the committee opens the gate: with a 'take-it-or-leave-it' rule the legislature may vote the agent proposal up or down; under the amendment rule the legislature may open the floor to amendments to the agent proposal.[176]

Let us first assume that the legislature as well as the committee decides under a simple majority rule. In this case the median's preferences determine the majority's preferences. In Figure 7.1 (it is taken from Ferejohn and Shipan, 1990: 7), assume that A is the ideal point of the agency, the median legislature member is at L, and the median member of the committee is located at C. C(L) stands for the point of indifference to the legislature median position. That is, median member of the Committee prefers a policy of L as much as the alternative policy C(L). Additionally, q represents the status quo and C(q) the committee's point of indifference to the status quo.

In an amendment-rule committee system the agency would not propose to implement any policy to the left of C(L) since the committee would open the gate and the legislature would amend to be equal to L. If the agency proposed a policy in the interval [C(L), L], the committee would not open the gate since the median committee member would (weakly) prefer such a policy to the outcome of legislature decision-making, i.e. L. Thus, the subgame perfect equilibrium is: the agency proposes $x = C(L)$ and the committee leaves the

---

[176] Note that these rules differ from the closed-rule and open-rule committee systems which are typical of the US Congress (see Shepsle, Bonchek 1997: 117). Whereas US committees have got monopoly proposal power in the EU context committees have only the exclusive right to open the gate.

gate closed. Note that if $C(L) < A$, the agency would choose $x = A$, a policy which prevails. This holds until $A \geq L$. If $A \geq L$ then $x = L$. As a general rule, the agency will choose $x = \max \{A, C(L)\}$ for $A < L$ (see Ferejohn and Shipan, 1970: 7).

The dilemma of delegation shows up in the difference $L - x = \max \{A, C(L)\}$. It exists as long as $C < L$. If $C = L$ the agency would choose a proposal $x = L$ and the committee would leave the gate closed. Note that the threat by the committee to open the gate if the agency does not propose a policy $x = C$ is an empty threat. It will never open the gate if $x \neq C$ since opening the gate would lead to L, making the committee worse off.

It is the sequential structure of decision-making which allows the agency to take an action that would not command a majority in the committee or the legislature. Three crucial features of this sequential policymaking under an amendment-rule committee system must be mentioned (see Ferejohn and Shipan, 1990: 7, 8, who analyse congressional influence on bureaucracy): 'First, at least in settings with complete information, in equilibrium the initial agency policy choice is never overturned.' Second, the equilibrium agency proposal depends on the legislature's and the committee's preferences. The legislature is influential in policymaking without taking action. The possibility of Council actions is what matters. Third, holding constant the position of the median member of the committee, the relationship between the preferences of the legislature median and the equilibrium policy choice of the agency will be negative. The further away from the agency's preferred position is L, the better the agency will do in equilibrium (see Ferejohn and Shipan, 1990:8).

In a take-it-or-leave-it-rule committee system the dilemma of delegation remains. If $x < q$, the committee would open the gate and the legislature would vote against the proposal leading to maintaining the status quo. If $C(q) \geq x \geq q$, the committee would open the gate and the policy x would be implemented. If $x > C(q)$, the committee is indifferent about opening the gate or leaving it closed, and the legislature would accept x; in the latter case, x would be implemented without involvement of the legislature. As is obvious, under this regime the committee median can only realize its ideal point if $x = C$. Since this ideal point is closer to L than $C(L)$, the dilemma of delegation is mitigated.

2. IMPLEMENTATION PROCEDURES

Based on the comitology decision, three main types of implementation procedures can be distinguished. In the *advisory committee procedure*, a committee of representatives gives its opinion on a draft measure of the Commission.

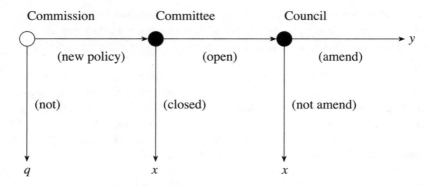

Figure 7.2   Gatekeeping procedure (management committee)

The Commission has to take into account this advice and is obliged to inform the committee about the way in which it has affected its final policy choice. This procedure will not be analysed further in this contribution since it does not grant any decision-making power to other players than the Commission.[177]

The second type is the *management committee procedure*.[178] In this procedure the committee of representatives gives an opinion on the Commission proposal, based on a qualified majority of its members. If the committee agrees with the Commission proposal or remains divided, the Commission proposal will be implemented. If the committee adopts a different view – which is called a 'negative' opinion – the Commission reports its proposal to the Council. The Council may only take a decision that deviates from the Commission proposal by a qualified majority. If the Council agrees with or does not respond to the proposal, the Commission is allowed to implement its proposal. The architecture and the outcomes of this procedure are presented in Figure 7.2.

The third procedure is the *regulatory committee procedure*. In this procedure, the Commission may only implement its proposal when the committee presents a *positive* opinion. This is the main difference from the management committee procedure. If the committee gives a *negative* opinion, or when the committee does not reach a decision, the Commission has to submit its proposal to the Council. A divided committee in this procedure means that the Commission proposal has to be submitted to the Council, which increases the involvement of the Council in the decision-making process. With

---

[177] In the recently adopted (1999) Council Decision the advisory procedure is defined in Article 3, which is identical to the procedure described in the 1987 comitology decision.

[178] In the recently adopted (1999) Council Decision this procedure is defined in Article 4. It remains largely unchanged.

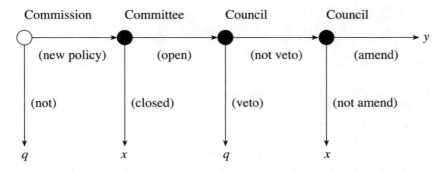

Figure 7.3   Gatekeeping procedure (regulatory committee)

regard to decision-making in the Council, two variants of this procedure can be distinguished. In both variants the Council may amend the Commission proposal by qualified majority. In variant (a), which will be called the *amendment procedure,* the Commission proposal will be adopted if the Council does not decide otherwise. A Council decision that deviates from the Commission proposal has to be based on a qualified majority. In variant (b) the Council may also veto the Commission proposal by simple majority. This variant of the regulatory committee procedure is known as the *contrefilet* procedure. This version will be called the *veto procedure.* The architecture and the outcomes of this procedure are shown in Figure 7.3.

The main difference between the two variants of the regulatory committee procedure, viz., the amendment and the veto procedure, is the voting procedure.[179] In the amendment procedure the Council can change the Commission proposal only if a qualified majority prefers a different point, including the initial *status quo.* If the Council fails to adopt a different view, the Commission proposal will be implemented. In the veto procedure, the Council is able to reject the Commission proposal by a simple majority in favour of the initial *status quo.* In that case, the Council has to make a comparison between the *status quo post* and the *status quo ante.* If the Council prefers the Commission proposal to the *status quo ante*, it will not use its veto power.

---

[179] Figure 7.3 is based on the old Comitology Decision from 1987. In the recently adopted (1999) Council Decision, the regulatory procedure is defined in Article 5. 'All in all, the new regulatory procedure comes fairly close to what existed under the 1987 Comitology Decision, although it leaves the Commission with more leeway,' (Lemaerts and Verhoeven, 2000, 676).

3. COMMISSION POLICIES UNDER THE IMPLEMENTATION PROCEDURES

Assumptions

To analyse different implementing procedures we use a simple game theoretical model that gives a stylized representation of the complex interactions in the actual decision-making process. In the model we distinguish three types of players, that is, the members of the Council of Ministers, the members of the committee of state representatives and the Commission, which will be regarded as a unitary actor. These players decide on a policy issue that can be represented with a single policy dimension. This dimension may, for example, represent regulations on telecommunications, different levels of integration of the internal market or consumer protection. Players are assumed to have single-peaked preferences, which have two important properties. First, each player prefers one policy to all other possible policies as the outcome of the decision-making process. This most preferred policy is represented with a player's *ideal point* on the policy dimension. Second, a player's preference for alternative policies depends on their distance from his or her ideal point. The farther away an alternative is from a player's ideal point, the less preferred this alternative is. In addition, we assume these preferences satisfy the single-crossing property, that is, preference for some alternative between two different players is determined by distance too.[180]

We assume that decisions are made sequentially. The sequence is based on the existing procedures that specify the order in which players are allowed to make a move. Players are assumed to have complete and perfect information. This assumption implies that the preferences of players, the structure of the game and the fact that players behave in a rational way are assumed to be common knowledge, while only one player is allowed to make a move at every stage of the game. The characterization of agent discretion in this chapter differs from the literature that explores bureaucratic discretion based on informational advantages (see Niskanen, 1971; Breton and Wintrobe, 1975; Miller and Moe, 1983) or uncertainty about agent preferences (Calvert, McCubbins and Weingast, 1989). In this chapter agent discretion is based on the structure of the principal-agent relationship. This is not to say that information asymmetry is not an important source of discretion. The point is that the agent has an additional opportunity to deviate from the policies preferred by the legislature. Since we are interested in analysing structure-induced discretion, policymaking will be analysed in an environment of complete and

[180] See Enelow and Hinich (1984: 8–13) for an introduction to the spatial theory of voting that is used.

perfect information.[181] Second, we assume that none of the players prefers its decision to be overturned. This preference can be viewed as imposing some cost on a proposal that is not the final outcome of the decision-making process. These costs are assumed to reduce the final payoff to a player. The Commission has an important 'first mover' advantage by making the initial policy proposal. This proposal has to be regarded as the new common policy, unless the Council is able to force the Commission to change its position by introducing a new bill. Commission discretion is approached as a set of potential policies that can be selected by the Commission without triggering an overturn by the Council. As the Commission is allowed to make the first move, it will select its best policy such that the Council cannot pass a bill that will change this choice. All implementation games that are considered in this chapter have a unique, subgame-perfect Nash equilibrium, which we take to define the outcome of the game. The equilibrium has two important properties: first, the agent selects a policy that will be accepted by the supervisor. The principal therefore does not introduce a new bill, so in equilibrium no action of the Council will be observed. Second, the public policy that will be implemented in equilibrium is not only a result of the preferences of the Commission, but it also reflects the constraints generated by the preferences of the supervisor and the Council. The Commission anticipates all future courses of action and chooses a policy that will not be reversed in a subsequent stage of the game.

Qualified Majority Voting

In the implementing procedures applied in the EU the committee of representatives and the Council have to decide by qualified majority. Under qualified majority rule each voter may cast a specific number of votes, and a special majority is required to adopt a proposal.[182] This voting rule may lead to some

---

[181] It is an open question whether these assumptions describe a worst-case scenario from the point of view of the principal. With complete and perfect information the agent as well as the supervisor will never commit an error. The agent maximizes its payoffs given the knowledge of the preferences of the other players and the institutional structure of decision-making. With incomplete information regarding the preferences of the principal and the supervisor the agent might be more cautious in approaching its maximum in order to avoid decisions which are overridden later on. How this affects the principal's payoff needs further analysis. In the spatial voting literature it is assumed that all points in the policy space can be implemented. As for the feasibility of a specific policy, the Commission has an informational advantage. The Commission can argue that the ideal point of the Council Median cannot be implemented, because there is no policy available to reach it. This represents a case of information-induced agent discretion. The Council knows that the policy is closer to the Commission's ideal point than to its median member but it may not be able to do much about it.

[182] See Article 205(2) EC, which specifies this rule for decision-making in the Council. From January 1995 until January 2003 this qualified majority rule implied that proposals need to be adopted with a 62/87 majority (71.3 per cent of the votes). Thus 26 votes in the Council were suffi-

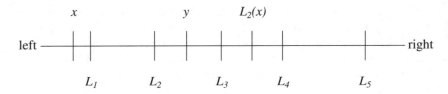

Figure 7.4   Qualified majority voting in a five-member Council: amendments

complications, which can be illustrated by a five-member Council, shown in Figure 7.4, in which, L_i denotes the ideal point of Council member i. Furthermore, $L_i(x)$ stands for this member's point of indifference to the Commission policy x. That is, Council member i prefers the current policy, x, as much as the alternative policy $L_i(x)$. Note that Council member i strictly prefers to the current policy all alternative policies that are found *between* the Commission policy, x, and its point of indifference, $L_i(x)$.

Now assume, for simplicity, that Council members have equivalent vote shares. Then, in a five-member Council, as illustrated in the figure, four members need to be in favour in order to adopt a new policy by a qualified majority of about 75 per cent of the votes. In that case, Council members 2 and 4 are pivotal, since they find the ideal points of four Council members to their right or left, including their own vote. These two players will be called *decisive qualified majority* members, since their support is necessary and sufficient to form a qualified majority in the Council.[183]

If the Commission policy, x, is found to the left of the ideal point of member 2, as in Figure 7.4, a qualified majority (i.e. members 2, 3, 4 and 5) strictly prefers an alternative proposal, y, to the current policy, x. Only member 1 prefers the Commission policy to the alternative, so it will vote against y. Consequently, if the Council is restricted to choice between x and y, it selects the alternative policy, y. However, under the current comitology procedures, the Council may amend the Commission proposal. All Council members are allowed to propose an alternative to the Commission policy, x.

---

cient to block a proposal. However, as a result of pressure from Spain and the United Kingdom, a compromise was reached at the European Council meeting held in Ioannina, Greece, in March 1994, to the effect that 23–25 opposing votes would ensure the continued discussion in the Council for a 'reasonable' period until a consensus was obtained. The Nice Treaty (ratified on 1 February, 2003) provides new rules (new voting weights, majority of member states, and 62 per cent of the population).

[183] For simplicity, in this chapter we assume a five-member Council, and later on, a five-member committee of national representatives. However, this (limited) number of Council or committee members does not affect our results, since decisive qualified majority members can be defined for any number of members.

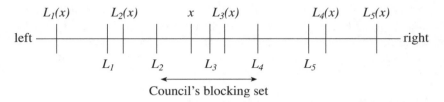

*Figure 7.5   Qualified majority voting in a five-member Council:
no amendments*

Using a well-ordered agenda,[184] the Council will then decide on a new policy that is equivalent to member 2's ideal point, L_2.[185]

A different situation occurs when the Commission policy is found between member 2 and member 4 as illustrated in Figure 7.5. Now the Commission policy, x, divides the members of the Council. Members 1 and 2 prefer a policy change to the left, while members 3, 4 and 5 prefer a change to the right. However, neither of them is able to propose a new policy that is supported by four members. In other words, no qualified majority can be formed against the Commission proposal. Consequently, the Council is not able to adopt a new policy, and the Commission can implement its proposal.

This result indicates that when the Commission selects a policy between the ideal points of the decisive qualified majority members 2 and 4, the Council is not able to amend it to another point. These proposals form what we call the 'blocking' set of Council decision-making, since the Council cannot form a qualified majority against such a proposal. Commission proposals that are located in this interval are invulnerable to amendments.

The committee of representatives which, like the Council, also decides by qualified majority, acts as a *gatekeeper* in most comitology procedures.[186] It decides whether the Council has to be involved in the decision-making process. If the committee 'opens' its gates, the Council may amend the initial proposal. If, however, the committee keeps its gates 'closed' and decides to accept the Commission proposal, the Council cannot impose its preference on the Commission policy. In other words, the committee can only choose

[184] We assume that the Council uses a well-ordered agenda in the following sense: first, all proposed amendments are collected and ordered according to their deviation from the initial proposal; second, each amendment is compared with the initial proposal in a binary vote starting with the amendment that deviates most from the initial proposal.

[185] A similar conclusion can be derived for a current policy to the right of member 4 in Figure 7.4. The Council will then select an alternative policy that is equivalent to the ideal point of member 4, L_4.

[186] See Ferejohn and Shipan (1990: 6–8), Steunenberg (1996: 321–23) and Steunenberg (1992, 1994) for analyses of the role of gatekeepers in policymaking processes in which an agent may set a policy that will be implemented unless other players are able to agree on another alternative.

between the initial proposal, *x*, by keeping its gates closed, and the amended proposal, *y*, which it can expect to result from opening its gates. As for the Council, proposals may exist that divide the committee of representatives, that is, a qualified majority of committee members will prefer neither the initial proposal, *x*, nor the amended policy, *y*.

Modelling the Implementation Procedures

The implementation procedures can be modelled as sequential games in which the Commission moves first (see Steunenberg, Koboldt and Schmidtchen, 1996). In these games, the Commission proposes a draft measure or new policy, which has to be considered by a committee of national representatives in the second stage. This committee considers the Commission proposal, and it may decide by qualified majority whether or not to support the Commission. When it disagrees with the Commission, or, depending on the procedure involved, when it cannot form an opinion on the proposal, the committee has to submit the proposal to the Council. The Council, in the last stage of the game, may decide to reject the proposal by simple majority (veto version of the regulatory committee procedure), or propose amendments to the proposal by qualified majority (management committee procedure and the amendment version of the regulatory committee procedure).

Knowing the responses of the other players, the Commission selects its best policy such that it does not trigger Council involvement. In order to demonstrate the *differences* in outcomes between the different implementing procedures we use a specific preference configuration, which is presented in Figure 7.6. Other preferences that differ from this configuration are possible, of course, but may lead to equilibrium outcomes that are less diverse between

regime:

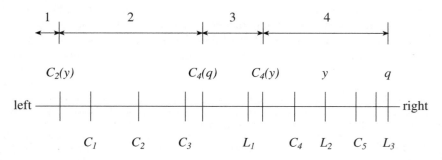

Figure 7.6　Implementing procedures: different regimes for Commission preferences

these procedures.[187] Most committee members are assumed to have more progressive preferences than their ministers in the Council, while the preference of the Commission is varied along the segment of the policy dimension that is found to the left of the median Council member, L_3.[188] The *status quo ante*, which plays a role in the veto version of the regulatory committee procedure, will be denoted as q. This policy, which is the initial policy before the Commission has made its proposal, is assumed to be located between L_2 and L_3.

Based on points that are critical for the outcome under some procedure, we distinguish four different intervals or regimes for Commission preferences in the figure. Regime 1, for example, includes Commission preferences to the left of committee member 2's indifference point to y. Then, under the management committee procedure, the optimal policy to the Commission is $C_2(y)$, which leads to an indecisive committee. Keeping its gates closed, the Commission can implement its proposal. For the amendment and the veto version of the regulatory committee procedure, these optimal proposals are $C_4(y)$ and $C_4(q)$, respectively. A qualified majority of committee members will only support these policies, which are (weakly) preferred to the policy the Council will select in the last stage of the game.[189] The equilibrium policies for the four different regimes are presented in Table 7.1, where A denotes an outcome that is equivalent to the ideal point of the Commission.

Two important observations can be based on these results. First, the Commission is the least restricted in selecting a new Community policy under the management committee procedure. It may successfully select any new policy between $C_2(y)$ and L_3 in Figure 7.6 without any interference from the Council. In other words, having a preference for a policy that is found in regime 2, 3 or 4, the Commission is able to implement a new policy that is equivalent to its own ideal point. Under the regulatory committee procedure, this set of feasible policies is reduced to points between $C_4(y)$ and L_3 for the amendment version (i.e. regime 4), or $C_4(q)$ and L_3 for the veto version (i.e. regimes 3 and 4). The reason for this is that under the management committee procedure an indecisive committee may keep its gates closed, while under the regulatory committee procedure it is induced to submit the Commission proposal to the Council. Only when a qualified majority of committee

---

[187] See Steunenberg, Koboldt and Schmidtchen (1996) for more general results, which do not depend on a specific configuration of player preferences.

[188] This restriction does not affect our conclusions. The interested reader can easily derive the results for the symmetric case of Commission preferences to the right of the median Council member.

[189] Note that when the Commission proposes a policy that is found in the Council's blocking set, that is, the set of policies between L_2 and L_3 in Figure 7.6, the Council will not act and therefore accepts the Commission proposal. Knowing this, the committee will not open its gates and present a 'positive' opinion on the Commission policy.

Table 7.1   Comparative analysis: outcomes for the implementing procedures

	regime 1	regime 2	regime 3	regime 4
1. management committee procedure	$C_2(y)$	A	A	A
2. regulatory committee procedure: amendment	$C_4(y)$	$C_4(y)$	$C_4(y)$	A
3. regulatory committee procedure: veto	$C_4(q)$	$C_4(q)$	A	A

Note: Key to the table: A is the ideal point of the Commission; y is the Council proposal, which is equivalent to the ideal point of Council member 2 in Figure 7.6; q is the *status quo ante*; $C_2(y)$ is the indifference point to y for committee member 2; $C_4(..)$ is the indifference point to y or q for committee member 4. The results presented in this table are based on the propositions presented in Steunenberg, Koboldt and Schmidtchen (1996).

members prefers the Commission proposal to the Council alternative, is it able to present a 'positive' opinion, which allows the Commission to implement its policy.

Second, both versions of the regulatory committee procedure lead to different results.[190] The veto version allows the Commission to successfully propose a new policy that is equivalent to its own ideal point under regimes 3 and 4, while the amendment version restricts this ability of the Commission to regime 4 only. In other words, and using the preference configuration in Figure 7.6, the additional veto power of the Council under the *contrefilet* procedure increases the set of proposals that is open to the Commission.[191] This is a result of the policy the Council will select in the last stage of the game. In the figure, a majority of Council members prefers the *status quo ante*, q, to the alternative Council policy, y. So, under the veto version, the Council will not amend but will consider vetoing the Commission proposal, when it is allowed to make its move. Knowing this, the committee will present a 'positive' opinion on those Commission proposals that are (weakly) preferred to the *status quo ante*. This allows the Commission to select any initial policy up to committee member 4's point of indifference, $C_4(q)$. For the amendment version, where no veto is available, the Council will either select y or 'accept' the Commission proposal.

---

[190] This is not always the case. The amendment and the veto version of the regulatory committee procedure do not differ if the *status quo ante*, q, is found to the left of the ideal point of Council member 2. Then, the Council will not use its veto power, since a qualified majority (and thus also a simple majority) of its members prefers the amended policy, y, to the *status quo ante*, q.

[191] Note that the opposite is true for a configuration where committee member 4 has an ideal point to the right of Council member 2 such that $C_4(q)$ is found to the right of L_2.

4. MEASURING AGENT DISCRETION

The discretion of the Commission in the implementation game to set new policies that coincide with its own preferences is affected by the rules of the decision-making game as well as by the preferences of the other players. The discretion of the Commission can be associated with how close the outcomes of a given procedure come to the Commission's ideal point, given different constellations of preferences. Clearly, a player is worse off the further away the outcome of the implementation game is from its ideal point. Since implementation procedures are used for a multitude of decisions about topics on which player preferences may vary, we need to take account of these different configurations in order to show how the implementation procedures influence agent-discretion of the Commission. In this analysis, in which player preferences will be varied, we consider the mean distance between the outcomes and the ideal point of the Commission as a proxy for the Commission's discretion.

We also calculate the mean distance between the outcomes and the ideal point of the Council. This mean distance is considered to be a proxy for the legislator's dilemma. The smaller this distance, the less severe is the legislator's dilemma. Since the European Parliament is also legislator, we additionally calculate a mean distance for the Parliament based on the ideal point of the median member of the Parliament.

In order to calculate the mean distance between the outcomes and the ideal points of the players under different procedures we make the following simplifying assumptions. First, we assume that the ideal points of the players and the *status quo ante* are distributed at equal distances along the policy dimension, and the minimum distance between two possible ideal points is the same for all configurations. This minimum distance is denoted as . Second, the ideal points of all decisive players (i.e. the median and decisive Council member, the Commission, the decisive members of the committee of representatives, and the median representative in Parliament) may, but need not, differ from each other and may, but need not, differ from the *status quo ante*. Finally, we concentrate on configurations in which the ideal point of the Commission and the *status quo ante* are found to the left of the median Council member, L_3. We have used this kind of preference in the various figures in the chapter. Moreover, without this restriction, the number of possible configurations would increase, while the mean distance remains the same. The outcomes that will be found for preferences to the right of the median Council member just mirror the outcomes for preferences to the left of this player. We assume that the preference configurations to which we restrict our analysis are equiprobable.

Given these simplifying assumptions, the number of feasible preference constellations (including a possible *status quo ante* point) is finite. This number depends on the length of the interval over which the ideal points are

Table 7.2   Mean distance between equilibrium policies and the ideal points of the Commission, the median representatives in Parliament and Council

Mean distance for	Commission	Council	Median member of Parliament
procedure:			
1. management committee procedure	0.29	2.46	2.58
2. regulatory committee procedure: amendment	0.71	2.17	2.36
3. regulatory committee procedure: veto	1.01	1.87	2.23

distributed. In our computations, we use an interval of length 7 , which implies that the number of possible values an ideal point may take is 8. The mean or expected distances between outcomes and the ideal points of the Commission, the Council and the median member of Parliament are summarized in Table 7.2.

The indices in the table show how the Commission, the Council and the Parliament are affected by the implementing procedures.[192] Focusing on the Commission first, the three comitology procedures appear to convey a different amount of discretion to the Commission. The mean distance between the outcomes of the implementation games and the preferred policy of the Commission is smallest in the management committee procedure and largest in the regulatory committee veto procedure. Based on expected distances, the Commission prefers the management committee procedure to the regulatory committee procedure, and the amendment version of the latter procedure to the veto version. The favourable effect of the veto version for the Commission, which we observed in Section 3, depends on the specific preference configuration depicted in Figure 7.6. On average, the veto version of the regulatory committee procedure leads to a larger distance between the equilibrium policy and the Commission's ideal point, which indicates that this procedure reduces Commission discretion the most.

The difference in Commission discretion between the management procedure and the amendment version of the regulatory committee procedure results from the fact that both procedures differ with respect to the consequences of an undecided committee. Whereas, in the management committee procedure, a qualified majority is required to open the gates, in the regulatory committee

---

[192] We want to stress that neither the absolute nor the relative change in the respective figures should be generalized, because the figures are highly sensitive to the assumption about the probability of different preference constellations. Thus we want to consider only implications drawn from the *direction* of change.

procedure the committee must be able to form a qualified majority to keep the gates closed. The difference in Commission discretion between the veto version and the amendment version of the regulatory committee procedure results from the fact that the commission is restricted in the veto version by the possibility that the Council may veto the Commission proposal in favour of the *status quo ante*.

As the figures for the Council show, the Council is confronted with a legislator's dilemma. This dilemma is less serious in the veto version of the regulatory procedure – but it exists – and is largest in the management procedure. Given these results, the Council's preference over different procedures can be written as: (management committee) > (regulatory committee: amendment) > (regulatory committee: veto). However, it would be a mistake to conclude that the Council will always choose the regulatory committee. This procedure involves higher opportunity costs than the others, and one would expect this procedure to be chosen in very sensitive policy areas.

The Commission's Annual Report of Activities (European Commission, 1995) describes the activities of about 400 different committees that prepared more than 4000 opinions covering almost all areas in the Union's budget. The activities of these committees cost about 18 million ECU, or on average 42 400 ECU per committee. The largest proportion of the committees specified in this report are advisory committees. They comprise about 42 per cent of the total number of committees; 17 per cent of the committees are management committees, and 20 per cent are regulatory committees. Mixed cases exist too (European Parliament, 1995: 9). In another report the Commission indicates that in about 30 cases the Commission has had to follow a version of the regulatory committee procedure in which the Council can block its decision. However, this rarely occurs. Over the last three years there have been only six cases where the Commission decision was referred back to the Council, and no cases are known in which no decision was taken (European Commission, 1995: 22).

While the European Parliament currently plays an important role in the European legislative process, it is not yet formally involved in the decision-making process on the implementation of measures. It is only the Council which has the exclusive power to intervene at the implementation stage. However there is an agreement that the Parliament shall receive agendas for committee meetings, draft measures submitted to the committees and the results of voting; it shall also be kept informed wherever the Commission transmits to the Council measures or proposals for measures to be taken (see *Official Journal* 1998, C 279/5).

Even if Parliament is not involved in the game, it is better off under the regulatory committee procedures, among which the veto version is better for the Parliament. This is based on the condition that both the Commission and Parliament have more progressive preferences concerning European integration than the Council; that is, both are found to the left of the median Council member.[193] Under this condition, we expect the Parliament to rank the three comitology procedures opposite to the Commission. It prefers the veto version of the regulatory committee procedure to the amendment version, and the amendment version to the management committee procedure. The figures show that the legislator's dilemma is more serious for the European Parliament in comparison to the Council. That is the reason why the Parliament has always been interested in gaining a foothold in the implementation process.[194]

From the analysis of the implementation procedures we can derive the following general results:

- A procedure requiring a qualified majority in the committee to open the gates restricts agent discretion to a lesser degree than a rule requiring a qualified majority to keep the gates closed.
- Adding a new outcome option in the form of the *status quo ante* restricts the agent more than the possibility of an amendment to the Commission proposal (= *status quo post*).
- Combining the amendment and veto version of the regulatory procedure by introducing an additional player, for example the European Parliament, reduces agent discretion the most (see Steunenberg and Schmidtchen, 2000).

What has not been shown in the chapter is the following.

- If a committee can decide by simple majority whether or not a Commission proposal has to be considered by the Council before it can be implemented, Commission discretion is less than in the management procedure and has the same level as in the regulatory amendment procedure.

Why should the Council delegate policymaking authority to the Commission, or confer monitoring authority on a committee, if it risks ending up with a policy not in accordance with its ideal position? The reason for delegating policymaking authority is to achieve efficiency gains that otherwise would not be available; the Council simply does not have the competence and the time to take the correct policy-decision. The same argument holds for the delegation of monitoring power. The difference $L - x$ measures the agency

---

[193] See also Garrett (1992) and Tsebelis (1994: 132), who assume that the Commission and most members of Parliament are more pro integration than Council members on a policy dimension that presents positions towards European integration.

[194] See Steunenberg and Schmidtchen 2000, where alternative procedures with parliamentary involvement are analysed.

costs (= costs of delegation) which have to be balanced against the benefits of delegation.

A last question remains to be answered: Why does the Council permit the committee median, C, to be different from L? There are several possible explanations for committee outliers (see also Ferejohn and Shipan, 1990: 9). First, it is not the Council delegating some of its members monitoring power. Rather, each government decides independently about whom to send off into a committee. Second, a state belonging to a minority in the Council might attempt to implement its favoured policy by influencing the median position in the committee. Third, a principal might delegate power in order to solve a self-commitment problem. Fourth, the committee is captured by the agency. The latter (and its clients) work to shift committee preferences over policy 'in a manner sympathetic to the agency' (Ferejohn and Shipan, 1990: 9). Fifth, the Council may find perfect compliance to be excessively costly. Imperfect compliance of a committee is another cost of delegation to be balanced against the benefits derived from saving the costs of monitoring and sanctions.

CONCLUSION

Political theory holds that policy decisions in a representative democracy are responsive to the interests of citizens. A lot of institutional safeguards such as elections create incentive structures for elected representatives to respond to the interests and preferences of the citizenship. But policymaking requires delegation of authority to unelected bureaucrats. How can elected political officials assure that bureaucracies do what political officials want them to do in order to retain and secure office?

We have analysed several policymaking procedures, which are commonly known as 'comitology'. Our main findings are that the three comitology procedures differ as to their contribution to overcome the dilemma of delegation. The advisory committee procedure does not restrict the Commission in the slightest way. Both the management and the regulatory procedure impose some restrictions on the Commission, with the regulatory procedure being most restrictive.

We used a three-tier description of the architecture of decision-making in the European Union. In fact the European architecture is much more complex. The European Parliament and the Council can be either principals or agents. Both serve as agents as far as the people are concerned; both are principals with respect to the European Commission. Thus, we have actually a higher-order vertical structure, forming a network of overlapping or nested principal/agent relationships (Tirole, 1986: 181). Also, horizontal elements can be superimposed on the vertical structure (see Tirole 1986). For example, the

Commission can be monitored by several supervisors. There may also be repercussions from the implementation stage to the legislative stage of decision-making, which we neglected, as well as correlation between the preferences of the different players. For example, if most members of Parliament and the Commission have similar preferences, Parliament may benefit from those procedures which restrict the Commission least. In selecting a policy that is close to its ideal point, the Commission will also set a policy that is in line with the preferences of Parliament.

Our chapter analyses the principal–agent relationship in a constitutional law and economics context (see Schmidtchen and Cooter 1997), which requires a focus on procedures (institutions) as a means of inducing agent compliance. We did not analyse methods of monitoring and punishing the Commission. In fact, we have in Europe a mix of both measures. Whether it is an optimal mix remains to be analysed.

REFERENCES

Breton, A. and R. Wintrobe (1975), 'The equilibrium size of a budget-maximizing bureau: a note on Niskanen's Theory of Bureaucracy', *Journal of Political Economy*, **83**, 195–207.

Calvert, R.L., M.D. McCubbins and B.R. Weingast (1989), 'A theory of political control and agency discretion', *American Journal of Political Science*, **33**, 588–611.

Cooter, R. (2000), *The Strategic Constitution*, Princeton, NJ: Princeton University Press.

Enelow, J. and M. Hinich (1984), *The Spatial Theory of Voting: An Introduction*, Cambridge: Cambridge University Press.

Eskridge, W.N. and J. Ferejohn (1992), 'Making the deal stick: enforcing the original constitutional structure of lawmaking in the modern regulatory state', *Journal of Law, Economics, and Organization*, **8**, 165–89.

European Commission (1995), *Report on the Operation of the Treaty on European Union*, 10 May (Sec (95) 731), Brussels.

European Parliament (1995), *Report on the Commission's Response to Parliament's Request for Information on the 1994 Activities of Executive Committees*, Committee on Budgets, 25 July (A4-0189/95).

Ferejohn, J. and C. Shipan (1990), 'Congressional influence on bureaucracy', *Journal of Law, Economics, and Organization*, **6**, special issue: 1–20.

Garrett, G. (1992), International cooperation and institutional choice: the European Community's internal market', *International Organization*, **46**, 533–60.

Hill, J.S. (1985), 'Why so much stability? The impact of agency determined stability', *Public Choice*, **46**, 275–87.

Lenaerts, K. and A. Verhoeven (2000), 'Towards a legal framework for executive rule-making in the EU? The contribution of the new comitology decision', *Common Market Law Review*, **37**, 645–86.

Lupia, A. and M. McCubbins (1998), *The Democratic Dilemma*, Cambridge: Cambridge University Press.

McCubbins, M.D., R.G. Noll and B.R. Weingast (1987), 'Administrative procedures as instruments of political control', *Journal of Law, Economics, and Organization*, **3**, 243–77.
Miller, G. and T. Moe (1983), 'Bureaucrats, legislators, and the size of government', *American Political Science Review*, **77**, 297–322.
Niskanen, W.A. (1971), *Bureaucracy and Representative Government*, Chicago: Aldine-Atherton.
Official Journal (1987), L 197/33.
Official Journal (1998), **279**(5).
Official Journal (1999), C 203/1.
Sappington, D. (1991), 'Incentives in principal–agent relationships', *Journal of Economic Perspectives*, **5**(2), spring: 45–66.
Schmidtchen, D. and R. Cooter (1997), *Constitutional Law and Economics of the European Union*, Cheltenham, UK: Edward Elgar.
Schmidtchen, D. and B. Steunenberg (2003): 'Comitology and the legislator's dilemma: on the architecture of decisionmaking in the European Union', in *Jahrbuch für Neue Politische Ökonomie (Yearbook for New Political Economy)*, M. Holler, H. Kliemt, D. Schmidtchen and M.E. Streit (eds), **21**, Tübingen: Mohr Siebeck.
Shepsle, K. and M. Bonchek (1997), *Analyzing Politics: Rationality, Behavior, and Institutions*, New York: Norton.
Steunenberg, B. (1992), 'Congress, bureaucracy, and regulatory policymaking', *Journal of Law, Economics, and Organization*, **8**, 673–94.
Steunenberg, B. (1994), 'Regulatory policymaking in a parliamentary setting', in Ph. Herder-Dorneich, K.E. Schenk and D. Schmidtchen (eds), *Yearbook of New Political Economy*, **13**, 36–57, Tübingen: Mohr Siebeck.
Steunenberg, B. (1996), 'Agent discretion, regulatory policymaking, and different institutional arrangements', *Public Choice*, **86**, 309–39.
Steunenberg, B. and D. Schmidtchen (2000), 'European policymaking with parliamentary involvement', in O. Heffen, W. Kickert and J. Thomassen (eds), *Governance in Modern Society. Effects, Change and Formation of Government Institutions*, Dordrecht: Kluwer Academic Publishers, 15–33.
Steunenberg, B., Chr. Koboldt and D. Schmidtchen (1997), 'Policy making, comitology and the balance of power in the European Union', *International Review of Law and Economics*, **16**, 329–44.
Steunenberg, B., Chr. Koboldt and D. Schmidtchen (1997), 'Comitology and the balance of power in the European Union: a game theoretic approach', in D. Schmidtchen and R. Cooter (eds), *Constitutional Law and Economics of the European Union*, Cheltenham, UK and Lyme, US: Edward Elgar, 37–66.
Steunenberg, B., Chr. Koboldt and D. Schmidtchen (2000), 'Beyond comitology: European policymaking with parliamentary involvement', in P. Moser, G. Schneider and G. Kirchgässner (eds), *Decision Rules in the European Union. A Rational Choice Perspective*, Macmillan Press, 72–98.
Steunenberg, B., D. Schmidtchen and Chr. Koboldt (1999), 'Strategic power in the European Union. Evaluating the distribution of power in policy games', *Journal of Theoretical Politics* **11**(3), 339–66.
Tirole, J. (1986), 'Hierarchies and bureaucracies: on the role of collusion in organizations', *The Journal of Law, Economics, and Organization*, **2**(2), 181–214.
Tsebelis, G. (1994), 'The power of the European Parliament as a conditional agenda setter', *American Political Science Review*, **88**, 128–42.

8. Accounting for centralization in the European Union: Niskanen, Monnet or Thatcher?[*]

Pierre Salmon

INTRODUCTION

Competition among governments, internationally (among national governments) or in the setting of federations (among subcentral governments), is seen in a much more favourable light today than even only one or two decades ago (see Breton, 1996). This applies to the law-making and regulatory activities of governments as it does to the policy areas that involve public finance. In the setting of a single governmental system, inasmuch as intergovernmental competition is deemed beneficial, it provides an additional and powerful argument in favour of decentralization (see Salmon, 1987). In the case of the European Union (EU), this suggests that centralization, at least in some areas, by hampering beneficial competition, may go too far. In fact, a number of economists argue or feel that it does. This chapter is not primarily concerned with the normative, or quasi-normative, issue of whether the EU governmental system is too centralized. Its focus, rather, is on the question of the mechanisms that may account for the present state or trend of centralization (of course, an answer to the second question may affect one's opinion about the normative issue).

What are these mechanisms? Centralization in the EU is often ascribed (not only by the famed English tabloids) to the existence, inherent in the present arrangements, of a bureaucratic bias. Such a claim reflects a conception of bureaucracies that stress their tendency to expand – which evokes the name of William Niskanen. This first view of EU affairs is on the whole pessimistic and thus particularly likely to be voiced by the 'Eurosceptics'.

On the other side of the debate, the 'Europhiles' will more willingly explain

* I am grateful for the interesting comments made on earlier drafts by participants in the 2001 Meetings of the European Public Choice Society, participants in the Second Corsica Workshop in Law and Economics, and Alain Wolfelsperger.

centralization as the embodiment of the European project itself. More precisely, they will relate it to the roundabout and progressive recipe devised, in the 1950s, by the founders of the European project – the so-called 'Euro-strategists' – to construct Europe. It is often found convenient to summarize this particular form of the integration process as the 'Monnet method', from the name of perhaps the most illustrious of these 'Euro-strategists', Jean Monnet.[195]

European construction, and with it centralization, was stalling in the 1970s but it resumed and accelerated in the second half of the 1980s. With some variation in time, this renewed strength endured in the 1990s. Ironically perhaps, the impressive steps accomplished over that period in the direction of European construction can be associated with the name of Margaret Thatcher. Inspired, on her part at least, by a liberal or neo-liberal doctrine, the Single Act of 1987 – which included the Single Market project and, to implement it, the extension of qualified majority voting – allowed considerable centralization of decision-making at the 'Brussels' level. It is also often held to be ultimately responsible for further centralizing schemes such as the European Monetary Union and the Stability Pact.

We thus have three stories potentially able to account for centralization in the EU. I discuss them respectively in sections 1, 2, and 3. Each story will need a preliminary clarification of some important points. They (the stories) should not be considered as rival explanations but as building blocks in a more general account. I will not undertake to provide such an account but, in the concluding section, I will defend the idea of an explanatory hierarchy – with the European project placed at the top as the driving force and both the bureaucratic bias and the market completion project serving as its instruments.

Other sets of factors of centralization than the three retained here will be left out, in part for convenience but also because I am not convinced of their importance. One obvious omission is the influence of interest groups. Some authors see this factor as essential. Other authors disagree. Neither the typically emphasized fact that the Commission has succeeded in inducing many groups to set up offices in Brussels nor the empirical evidence that some groups do exert a strong influence on decision-making at this level imply that the influence of lobbying is not stronger still in the member states and then does not often work against centralization. Only very detailed case studies could allow us to decide whether, in each particular policy area or on each issue, interest groups, acting at various levels, play or have played an important part in the centralization or

---

[195] The distinction made in the text simplifies the array of opinions on centralization and the European project itself. In particular there are many 'Europhiles' who agree with the claim that there is a bureaucratic bias, deplore that bias, and ascribe it to recourse to a wrong-headed strategy for constructing Europe. They favour a more direct, democratic and federalist way to achieve this goal. This position is certainly consistent. Whether it is also realistic is another matter.

absence thereof that we observe. Because this chapter is mainly concerned with the general level and trend of centralization, rather than with its comparative importance or strength across areas or issues, case studies of that kind, even if they could be undertaken, would not be very relevant.

Another omission is the normative rationale for centralization (and decentralization) as suggested by the theory of fiscal federalism, broadly defined.[196] The explanatory power of that theory with regard to the existing state of affairs in the EU is not as impressive as many economists would wish it to be (see, for example, Persson *et al.*, 1997; Oates, 2001). Typically, policy areas that should be entrusted to the highest tier of the governmental system according to the theory of fiscal federalism (defence, income redistribution etc.) have not been assigned, to a significant degree, to the Brussels level. At the same time, Brussels is doing many things that should have stayed well inside the exclusive domain of competence of the member states (or jurisdictions below) according to the same theory. In other words, one must admit that, on the whole, present arrangements do not obey the prescriptions of the theory. This does not necessarily make the theory irrelevant from a normative point of view but it certainly undermines its capacity to explain. 'Undermine' is not 'eliminate' though. Some residual explanatory relevance of the theory must be assumed – albeit under a dynamics or path-dependency perspective – in any account of the 'engrenage' strategy advocated by Monnet and others to push integration. In other words, the considerations that the theory of fiscal federalism stresses may be a poor guide to predict, in a static framework, the overall distribution of competences in the EU, but the said considerations may play a significant role when the object of attention is a decision to amend the existing state of affairs in the form of some new, incremental, transfer of competences.

1.   CENTRALIZATION AS A BUREAUCRATIC PHENOMENON

Bureaucratic expansionism is associated with the name of Niskanen.[197] However, can Niskanen be at all relevant in the EU context? Doubts about this have been expressed. But one may wonder whether these doubts do not often derive from a mistaken perception of Niskanen's message. Thus it is important

---

[196] Including the form it takes when applied to particular issues pertaining more specifically to law and economics (see, for example, Faure, 2000; Van den Bergh, 2000).

[197] Niskanen's model is developed in terms of statics and thus cannot formally predict the growth of any variable. In the following discussion, however, I will assume that it can be used, informally, to account not only for a variable being too large but also if need be for the excessive growth of that variable.

for our purpose to clarify several points about that author's approach. We must also take into account the presumption that if bureaucratic mechanisms à la Niskaken operate at the level of 'Brussels', they also operate at the level of the member states. How is the process at work on the two levels to be interpreted so that it is internally consistent?

Doubts about the Relevance of Niskanen's Model in the EU Setting

Can Niskanen's model of bureaucracy have anything to say about centralization in the European Union? Independently of its well-known general short-comings (Wintrobe, 1997), is not the model clearly irrelevant in this particular setting? Widespread opinions on this matter are well represented in a recent exchange of views between Patrick Dunleavy (1997) and Gebbard Kirchgässner (1997). Dunleavy notes that the budget-maximizing hypothesis which he considers as the main characteristic of the Niskanen model is hardly consonant with the fact that 95 per cent of the budget of the EU institutions, already extremely small compared to public expenditures in the member countries, is passed on to other actors. Thus he writes (p. 198): 'If budget maximization was indeed the dominant bureaucratic motivation then EU officials should pursue direct implementation strategies so as to create large budget agencies with many personnel. Instead EU officials remain a tiny fraction of the overall numbers of member state personnel.'

Kirchgässner responds as follows: 'It is correct that – at least prima facie – these facts are hardly compatible with the Niskanen model. However, this model is not the only public choice model of bureaucratic behaviour. It is just a special, extreme case of a more general model where the size of the budget as well as bureaucratic slack are arguments in the bureaucrats' utility functions. It is not a fair way to take a special case of a more general model to attack the model altogether, especially as there is also ample prima facie evidence that there is bureaucratic slack in the Brussels bureaucracy. One has to look only at the income differences between public officials of the same level in Brussels and in Paris, London or Bonn, respectively. Qualifying this indictment of Niskanen's model, Kirchgässner adds: 'if . . . the core budget is a fixed share of the total budget, a budget-maximizing bureaucrat will try to maximize his total budget.'

I think that both formulations – Dunleavy's and Kirchgässner's – of Niskanen's main message are, in a different way, somewhat unfaithful to it. I attempt to identify that message in the next sub-section. Before turning to that, however, I must mention an obstacle to the use of the model which is completely different from the problem just considered. To discuss centralization, is it really satisfactory, as suggested by Dunleavy (1997, p. 197), to restrict the potential scope of the Niskanen model to 'the personnel of the EU central institutions, especially the bureaucracy of the European Commission'?

Whether it is interpreted as referring to a state of affairs at one point in time or to a process (or change in the state of affairs) over a period of time, the idea of centralization requires that those institutions, budgets, powers or activities that pertain to the 'centre' be considered not in isolation but together with those that are subcentral. Thus one cannot limit oneself to the question of how Niskanen's model applies to the bureaux in Brussels. The mechanisms that Niskanen's model purports to capture are meant to be operative in bureaucracies at all levels. Thus one must also check the compatibility of one's analysis with what one can surmise of the working of similar mechanisms at the level of the bureaux of the member states, and then one must relate any claimed centralizing tendency to differences in the specific strength or effects of the mechanisms at the two levels. As Dunleavy notes himself (in a slightly different context), it is difficult for a rational choice approach to assume that rational actors do not try to keep their powers and scope of action.

In fact, on a priori grounds, because the bureaucracies of the member states are so entrenched and powerful, what a public choice bureaucratic approach would be best-suited to do is to explain why there is not more integration – that is, here, more centralization. And in fact, this is exactly an argument that Europhiles and European federalists have often had recourse to. Especially in the 1970s, a widespread claim among supporters of European integration was that the process was stalling because of the hostility and resistance of the all-powerful bureaucracies of the member states.

Some of the main problems, or potential problems, having being noted, one can turn to a positive account of how one could, in spite of them, defend the application of a model of bureaucracy à la Niskanen to the elucidation of centralization in the EU. I will divide that attempted account into a first part devoted to clarifying some points about Niskanen's approach that seem particularly relevant when the characteristics of the bureaucracy in Brussels are considered, and a second part concerned with the relationship between this bureaucracy and the public administrations of the member states.

A Clarification of some Aspects of Niskanen's Approach[198]

First, contrary to a widespread formulation, the originality of Niskanen does not lie in the claim that bureaux 'seek' to get budgets as large as possible.[199]

---

[198] By 'Niskanen's approach', I mean here the approach underlying his book of 1971, not the revised views that he formulates in retrospect, in particular in the 'Reassessment' published in 1994.

[199] Nor, for that matter, in the unoriginal explanation given by Niskanen for this motivation. Thus I do not concur in the assessment expressed in Blais and Dion (1991, p. 359) that 'the great appeal of the Niskanen model lies . . . in its capacity to account for the well-established propensity of bureaucrats to seek larger budgets'.

We all know from personal experience that most bureaux we are familiar with do try to get budgets as large as possible – even though we also know of cases and circumstances in which bureaux do not pursue that objective (see, for example, Dunleavy, 1991). What is far more original in Niskanen's view, and also much more controversial, is the purported demonstration that bureaux 'succeed' in getting budgets that are larger than they would if voters or their representatives had at their disposal all the informational means to decide. Niskanen's point is bureaucrats not merely desiring excessive budgets but obtaining them.

Second, is this (that is, success in getting a larger than optimal budget) not only a better interpretation of one feature of Niskanen's theory but also the most important prediction that the theory makes? In some contexts, certainly. But if it were also the most important prediction in the context of the issues discussed in this chapter, this would justify the opinion discussed above that Niskanen's model does not apply to these issues. As noted, the budgets or, more generally, the resources that are available to EU institutions are, given the impact these institutions have on everybody's life, extremely limited. Thus increases in these budgets, or in the numbers of officials they support, or excesses in the remuneration of these officials compared to officials of similar rank in the member countries, are variables that, *per se*, do not amount to much. Inasmuch as there is a serious problem of centralization, they do not measure up to it. Centralization in the EU is first of all about competences and regulatory powers.[200]

Third, in this context, it is important to remember that, in Niskanen's model, the way a bureau may get a large budget is by supplying too much. This is sometimes overlooked because, in that model, oversupply is a means to an end, and in the original setting considered by Niskanen, as in many other important contexts, the result or prediction that appears as deserving the most attention is not this excess in production but oversize budgets or public spending. But this need not be so in all settings. In the context of the EU, it is certainly the other way around. Outside public choice economics and a few milieux here and there, EU budgets create no real anxiety. They remain too modest for that. If the budget-maximizing behaviour of EU bureaucrats is relevant, it draws this relevance from the possibility that it causes overprovision. It is the flow of regulations and directives produced by Brussels, or the launching of new programmes that cost little in budgetary terms but imply a considerable centralization of powers, that constitute the main subject of preoccupation.

Ultimately, for a policy-oriented analysis focused on the EU, we could do without the assumption of budget-maximizing motivations and start directly

---

[200] For some recent figures, see Pollack (2000).

from the assumption of an expansionary drive among the bureaucrats of the Commission or the judges of the European Court of Justice. If they produce too much of whatever they produce, seek ways to increase further their reach and undertake, almost continuously, new activities, the ultimate motives of these bureaucrats or judges may be to get larger budgets, as suggested by the Niskanen approach, but their behaviour could have completely different causes – for instance, simply, *hubris*. For the purpose of getting an overall picture of European integration it hardly matters.

Fourth, Niskanen's model can also predict slack.[201] But I submit that this is a much less interesting prediction of that model, in general and particularly in the EU context, than predicting oversupply – except when slack is viewed as a deviation of policymaking from what would follow from the policy prefer- ences of principals, but this is not what Niskanen really had in mind and it raises issues, to be in part discussed below, that his model cannot really deal with. Like oversize budgets, slack in the more usual sense of production above minimal cost cannot be a source of serious concern, even if it could be estab- lished that there is more slack in the Brussels institutions than in the ministries of the member countries. Furthermore, it is not clear that variables such as higher salaries are indicators of slack, as suggested for instance by Kirchgässner, in the citation above, or by Roland Vaubel (1994, 1995). These high salaries, like perks and other apparent 'takings', may well be efficiency- enhancing. They may for instance reflect concerns about selection and incen- tives along the lines of the theory of efficiency wages, or about incentives and trust along the lines of Breton and Wintrobe's theory of bureaucracy (1982). It could also be the means by which bureaucrats in Brussels are deprived of their Niskanenian instincts to seek higher budgets (the argument being that they are so well-paid that they can expect nothing from increased responsibilities).

Books and articles purporting to be based on direct observation of behav- iour, from former insiders or from outsiders familiar with the bureaux in Brussels, are perhaps a less bad way to form an opinion about whether these bureaux have a problem of slack. They suggest that the degree of work inten- sity in the Commission and the other EU institutions varies a lot in time and across departments and policy areas. Intensity of work also seems to be highly dependent on the exact phases of integration and personalities of the commis- sioners in office. Thus, a reading of Ross (1995) does not convey, to say the least, the impression that the administration of the Commission under Jacques Delors operated in such a way as to enjoy 'a quiet life'.

---

[201] When, in the citation above, Kirchgässner refers to a 'more general model', it is clear that he has in mind Migué and Bélanger (1974). But it must be recalled that the original Niskanen model (1971) also predicts slack in some circumstances. In that model, production is no longer realized at minimum cost when the constraint which is binding is not cost but demand (that is, the necessity for the marginal benefit of the political principal to remain positive).

Centralization and the Hypothesis of Niskanen Mechanisms Operating at all Levels

To make centralization of powers in Brussels compatible with the Niskanen mechanisms operating also at the level of the member states, there are at least three possibilities. First, one may want to draw inspiration from a point suggested by Dunleavy (1997) and argue that there is a specialization of tasks between the two levels of bureaucracy. The reasoning could be as follows. In the policy areas in which it is active, the bureaucracy in Brussels concentrates on the thinking or shaping, so to speak, and the bureaucracies of the member states on the implementing – and spending. If, *pace* Dunleavy, we assume Niskanenian behaviour and outcomes at all levels, we may observe that, within each of these jobs or activities, Niskanen's mechanisms may operate unimpaired, implying, in the policy areas considered, an oversupply of thinking or shaping in Brussels and an oversupply of implementing (and spending) in the member states.

This may sound somewhat strange – the second part of the proposition perhaps even more than the first. In fact, there are several problems raised by that line of thinking, at least if it is considered alone. One problem is the distribution of competences between the member states and Brussels. In a policy area conquered in part by Brussels, why should member state bureaucrats previously entitled both to think (and shape) and to implement (and spend) agree to be confined to the latter task, even if that task is also amenable to a Niskanenian process of expansion in production? Conversely, this time at the Brussels level, even if such a process is also available within the task of thinking and shaping, why would there be no tendency of bureaux at this level to enter the job of implementation and spending – a question raised by Dunleavy, as we saw? One could attempt to answer these queries by the means of a distinction, within the personnel situated at the two levels, between those bureaucrats who are the most competent and ambitious and the rest. Only the former would insist on thinking and shaping, and they would be able to do so by moving either to Brussels or to policy areas in which thinking and shaping remain largely a national activity. This line would not be very Niskanenian, however. Thus we might prefer an answer to both questions which is based on the following characteristic of Niskanen's model: the model applies to a qualitatively given policy task or programme set by the politicians. The decision that a task should be performed and a programme to that end started remains exogenous.

Although the distribution of tasks is thus assumed to be out of reach of the bureaucracy, this does not imply that it is impossible, within the limits of this first possible argument, to imagine an effect of Niskanenian mechanisms on centralization. Although both kinds of bureaux may press for higher budgets and aim at expanding their production, the thinking and shaping kind may achieve more in that respect than the implementing and spending kind. Such an effect is made plausible by the fact that expansionism is probably easier when production consists of regulations, decisions, sub-programmes etc. than when it takes the form of spending resources for the purpose of implementing what others have decided. It is for instance easier to double the number of rules organizing the surveillance of something than to double the number of inspectors who will ensure that these rules are implemented. If this is so, in spite of Niskanenian behaviour at all levels including the ones on which implementation is the main activity, centralization may well be accompanied by a problem of insufficient implementation (I think here of implementation on the ground, so to speak, rather than implementation in the sense of enactment of EU directives by the national legislatures).

I turn to the second possibility. To introduce it, we may start from a mechanism whose importance is stressed by Vaubel (1994, 1995), even though, by disregarding interest groups, I interpret it differently to the way he does. Both globalization and market integration within the EU endanger some of the activities and/or financial resources of the member state bureaucracies. They may consequently be favourable to increased powers at the level of Brussels if this may, in the form of harmonization, co-ordination or pre-emption by the EU level, help them safeguard at least in part these activities and resources. If we follow that line, the fact that the budget of the EU remains small is irrelevant. What counts is that the total budget available to the bureaucracy in the whole of the EU (the bulk of it being in the member state bureaucracies) is larger than it would be without centralization. Niskanen's model can then be claimed to apply more convincingly to the aggregate bureaucracy of Europe, member-state bureaux included, than to the bureaucracy of the EU proper. And its significance is not to be assessed in terms of budget size or budgetary growth but in terms of budget maintenance in the face of trends that work to downsize it.

As noted by Vaubel, all member countries are not in the same position with regard to the effects of globalization and market integration. The countries in which the bureaucracy may feel the most endangered in its activities are those in which these activities are the most extended, typically the richest countries. Thus we may expect the bureaucracies of these countries to be the ones who are the most favourable to increased centralization.

There are some possible objections to this line of argument. One potential objection is, again, that bureaux are not assumed in the Niskanen model to decide transfers of competences or tasks to a higher level. However, we can remain faithful to the spirit if not the letter of Niskanen's model by arguing as follows. Bureau X in a member state A does not really want to do something else. What it wants is being enabled to go on in its activities and safeguard its budget, thanks to coordination or harmonization at the EU level in particular. To convince politicians of A that this must be done, it may, for instance, make them believe that without such coordination the level of activity concerned would be downsized to a level unacceptable to these politicians. As a consequence the politicians in A will favour coordination or harmonization at the EU level.

Another objection is that there is no evidence that globalization or market integration necessarily have, in the absence of coordination, a significant downsizing effect on administrations. Here we can invoke both the observation that small open economies have typically a larger public sector than have large, less open economies, and the evidence, provided in particular by a country such as Switzerland (Kirchgässner and Pommerehne, 1996), that market integration within a country does not erode as much as one would think the capacity of subcentral governmental units to act. This objection sets a limit to the magnitude of what a bureaucracy may fear, or obtain on the basis of such fear, from its political principals, but it does not preclude some occurrence of the mechanism of the kind described.

The third possibility announced above starts from the existence, anterior to but favoured by the institution of 'comitology' (see Steunenberg *et al.*, 1997), in a broad sense, of specialized networks, each including bureaux at the Brussels level and bureaux or departments at the level of the member states. Bureaux concerned with the issue or policy area X in each country gain some additional strength vis-à-vis politicians or voters, or ministries of finance, in the same country from being members of transnational networks specialized in X and coordinated by a department of the Commission (or a bureau subordinated to the Council of Ministers or the European Parliament), that is, also in charge of X in 'Brussels'. The Niskanen mechanism in that case applies to the relationship between the set of bureaux included in the specialized network and the set of its principals in the member countries.

To conclude this section, we may, indeed, accept that there is some scope for bureaucratic expansionism à la Niskanen in the EU arrangements. The question though is whether this expansionism is imposed on other actors – in particular the governments of member states and, behind them, the voters who support them – or remains ultimately under their control.

2. CENTRALIZING TO IMPLEMENT THE EUROPEAN PROJECT

Before analysing the integration strategy which may be responsible for centralization, some attention must be given to the highly ambiguous and complex way decision-making in general takes place in the EU.

Decision-Making in the EU

The EU system of decision-making is amenable to very different interpretations, depending on the theoretical perspective one adopts or the aspect of the system one wants to emphasize. My purpose is not to give a complete account of that system, about which there is an abundant and growing literature, but to stress those characteristics that may have a direct bearing on our discussion of centralization. The aspect of present arrangements that I will treat as the most important in this context is the fact that a large part of decision-making in the EU involves or brings together several issues and takes place under a perspective of repeated interaction. In my opinion, this undermines the relevance of the otherwise extremely interesting theoretical analyses that assume a single issue or dimension and/or a one-shot game or interaction.

A possible approach to the nature of the EU starts from the idea, defended in particular by Bruce Ackerman (1997), of a continuum between international treaties and federal constitutions, and, correlatively, between international organizations and federations. In the course of time, an arrangement based on an international treaty, possibly embodied in an international organization, can progressively transform itself into a genuine federation, and the original treaty explicitly or implicitly be given the status of a constitution (the possibility and even existence of transformations in the reverse direction, that is, a process of internationalization of a federation, must also be acknowledged). In the opinion of Ackerman, this transformation was central to the evolution of the United States at its beginnings, and it is currently at work in Western Europe. Along the continuum, the European Community/Union has moved a long way towards a constitutionalization of the founding treaties and a federalization of its decision-making mechanisms.

This is true mostly with regard to the capacity to legislate or regulate. Over a long period of time, almost inconspicuously, the main mechanism developing that capacity was a judicial one, centred on the decisions of the European Court of Justice. Together with the (non-constitutional) courts of the member countries, the ECJ succeeded in getting two things accepted: first, an interpretation of the Treaty of Rome that implied, in the vast policy areas that it directly or indirectly covered, the supremacy of European law over national law; second, the 'direct effect' of a large subset of European law on legal proceedings in the member countries. As noted by legal scholars (e.g. Weatherhill, 1995), a hierarchy of laws typical of federal systems ensued.[202]

---

[202] The function of the ECJ as planned in the treaties was modest but the Court managed to interpret it in a way that in some areas made it a real constitutional court and thus placed it above its creators. (For an interesting parallel with the evolution that took place in the United Kingdom and the United States, see Josselin and Marciano, 2000).

Since the Single Act of 1987, the role of the ECJ has been less central – the reason being that the rule-making capacity of the other EU institutions has been greatly enhanced by the enlarged scope for qualified majority voting in the Council of Ministers provided by the Act. Overall, however, this has allowed European law to affect even more profoundly than before the legal landscape in each of the member countries. Finally, new rules concerning fiscal discipline have been imposed on the member country governments themselves in the Treaty of Maastricht and in the Stability Pact which followed in the wake of the European Monetary Union. New developments are currently contemplated.

The European institutions, however, are still far from constituting a federal level of government. Among the characteristics by which they differ from it, one is the very limited amount of financial and human resources they can rely on. However, nothing prevents a federation from being very decentralized. Thus, more importantly, what differentiates the EU institutions from constituting the higher tier of a federal system is their fundamental lack of independence with regard to the member states whenever these states agree among themselves. As a consequence, an essential characteristic of federalism is lacking: the ownership of constitutional rights by the two levels of government (see Breton *et al.*, 1998). Although probably neither sufficient nor indispensable for vertical competition to take place (see Salmon, 2000), the existence of entrenched rights that cannot be suppressed by one level alone is certainly favourable to the development of such competition. In the case of the EU, there is a powerful systemic obstacle to vertical competition between the EU level and the member states, and one can observe that such competition is, in fact, more or less absent. I return to that essential characteristic below.

Another way to approach the on-going constitutional or quasi-constitutional debate about the EU is based on the distinction between the 'supranational' and the 'intergovernmental' dimensions of present arrangements – these two terms being defined indifferently with regard to the way decisions are made as well as to the nature of the various institutions. For the time being, it is really of the essence of the EU that it combines supranationality and intergovernmentalism at the heart of its decision-making capacity. A crucial element of supranationality is clearly the European Court of Justice, and more generally the hierarchy of laws referred to above. Another very important element now is the European Central Bank. Less neatly or decisively, the European Parliament, the Commission (with its bureaucracy), and the use of majority voting in the Council of Ministers also belong to the supranational side of the present arrangements. On the other side, expressions of intergovernmentalism are notably the requirement of unanimity voting (in the Council of Ministers in particular) in important policy areas, and the strategic role of the European Council (the regular 'summit' among the heads of government and the president of the Commission that was started in an informal way in the 1970s and became institutionalized in the recent treaties).

As a consequence of supranationality, there are many things that can legally be imposed on any country against its will, but as a consequence of intergovernmentalism, there are also many decisions that any country can veto if it wishes. This does not mean, as is often believed, that there is a precise dividing line between two sets of issues, depending on whether they are decidable or not by means of majority voting. In a set-up in which the same decision-making institution operates in many issue areas, even if unrestricted majority voting is available, there will always be a strong incentive among decision-makers to bargain and engage in trading positions over issues (Cooter, 2000).[203] The fact that, for some types of decisions, majority voting is unavailable and unanimity required can only strengthen that incentive. The consequence, in the EU context, is that the representatives of countries will often accept measures that they do not like and – because these measures are subject to a 'unanimity requirement' – could oppose. Conversely, a qualified majority, even when it is entitled to do so, will typically avoid imposing on a country a solution that its representatives intensely disapprove of. This does not imply that the extension of the domain of qualified majority voting has no consequences. When the representative of a country is opposed to a proposal and gets a majority not to impose its adoption even though it could, a cost is incurred, a debt is taken up which will have to be repaid in the form of a concession in another area or on another occasion (a form of capital is spent). Majority voting sometimes exerts its power in a straightforward way. On other occasions, decision-making will require complicated bargaining and the reliance on the leadership of some member countries.[204] One can also note, as does Peter Ludlow (2000), that supranationality has gone quite far in some areas because it seemed clear that intergovernmentalism was not so completely put aside that it would be unavailable if really needed.

With regard to the issue of centralization, the most important characteristics to keep in mind are the availability of intergovernmental decision-making when it is really needed and the pervasiveness of a repeat business perspective. The combination of these two characteristics means that the 'lowest common denominator' syndrome so often assumed to plague intergovernmentalism is far from being generally at work, as confirmed in fact by

---

[203] Issues can be expected to be linked more clearly at the, so to say, 'constitutional' level of decision-making, especially when the heads of the governments meet, than in more mundane or technical settings, when the Council of Ministers is composed of the heads of some specialized department (agriculture etc.).

[204] For an analysis of leadership in federations and in the context of integration, addressing also the question of whether the recently unified Germany was likely to play this role, see Salmon (1992).

observation: many policies exist that are not wanted *per se* by a majority of member states but are accepted as parts of logrolling compromises. The said combination also means that, at the same time as each country is offered a safeguard with regard to its most basic interests, a majority, frustrated by the rule of unanimity of a collective decision to which its members give a high priority, will often be able to overcome that obstacle by means of exchanges and side-payments. Sometimes, the intensity of interests and preferences is symmetrical, and relative power will settle the matter, or the status quo will prevail and there will be talk of a deadlock. Often, though, that deadlock will only be apparent, and the apparent impotence of intergovernmental decision-making will reflect or hide half-hearted demands or insincere priorities.

How does all this fit into our general argument? Because of the availability of intergovernmental decision-making when needed, and of the setting of repeat business in which member state governments interact, nothing important can happen in the EU that runs against the will of a sufficiently large number of member states (not necessarily against the pre-exchange preferences of these states, though). This applies to centralization as to other issues. Thus, contrary to what may be the case of genuine federations – in which, in spite of constitutional protection, de facto centralization can be forced on junior governments[205] – centralization in the context of the European Union is to be ascribed first of all to a desire for centralization among most of the governments of the subcentral units, that is, in the present case, of the member countries.

There is a well-known and apparently persuasive theory of bureaucratic drift based on the existence of a multiprincipal set-up. To block the drift, a unanimous decision of the principals is required. But, up to some size of the drift, unanimity is precluded by some principals drawing increased utility from it. I am not sure that even in the original American context to which the theory was applied, this drift mechanism is not likely to be strongly constrained by the repeat business perspective under which the principals (in this case, the two houses and the president) interact. In the case of the European Union, anyhow, the foregoing arguments suggest that, if need be, there will be no insuperable obstacles to the formation of an agreement among member states to prevent any unwanted occurrence of bureaucratic drift or creeping expansion of competences.[206]

If, contrary to what tends to be suggested by public choice theory of the traditional variety, the member state governments, rather than the European

---

[205] For instance in the case of fiscal powers in Australia and Canada (see Winer, 2000).

[206] This does not mean that the Commission, or possibly another EU institution, like the European Central Bank, cannot in turn become part of the exchange mechanism and thus obtain voluntary acquiescence to something it desires, a centralizing step, for instance.

bureaucracy in Brussels or elsewhere, are largely responsible for the centralization observed in the EU, how is this to be explained? This brings us to a second blind spot in the vision of centralization suggested by public choice: its neglect of the existence of a European project.

The 'Ever Closer Union' Goal and Strategy

The main reason why (as mentioned) the governments of the member states as a whole cannot engage in vertical competition with the Brussels level is a simple one: *they have pledged to build up that level*. In other words, there is a European integration project, to which all member states subscribed when they became members, and centralization is the process seen as the only one available for the realization of that project. This brings us to the so-called Monnet method, whose interpretation deserves some care. When nowadays authors refer to the Monnet method they often have in mind an implementation of the European project whose democratic credentials are somewhat suspect. From the standpoint of historical accuracy, they can claim some basis for thinking in this way because it seems clear that Monnet himself believed in doing things for the people by dealing with the elites. This trait is often ascribed to the European project as a whole, deemed to be a kind of conspiracy among elites. However, the Monnet method can be understood more aptly as not having been exclusively his own but as a strategy that he contrived or adopted together with the other 'co-fathers' of the European project such as Paul-Henri Spaak, Robert Schuman, Konrad Adenauer or Alcide de Gasperi. Contrary to Monnet, all of them were democratic politicians, who gave a high priority to obtaining the support of voters (see Milward, 1992, pp. 336–37). Thus I will not follow that part of the literature that gives the main role in European integration to agreements among elites.

If elites, as decisive actors, are out, what is the content of the Monnet method? As noted among others by George Ross (1995, p. 20): 'Europe's strategists – Jean Monnet, Robert Schuman, Konrad Adenauer, Paul-Henri Spaak – were astute in their modesty. Transnational unity of purpose, they reasoned, could best be created by concentrating on specific areas. Once Europe had begun to cooperate in these areas, interdependence of policy logics would promote 'spill-overs' into others. Great proclamations of federalist principles were to be avoided.' But Ross sees Jacques Delors's method (in his capacity as President of the Commission) as a hybrid version of the Monnet method. Because I identify the latter with the one adopted not only by Monnet but also by Schuman etc., I prefer to consider 'Delorism' simply as another instance of it. According to Ross, 'Delorism' was like the Monnet method in seeking to use policy linkages strategically and in placing a premium 'on locating new programs which promised linkages to more far-reaching areas', but differed from it in promoting 'public dramatization of what was at stake' and 'at critical junctures' emphasizing 'the high political importance of direct confrontation with central problems' (Ross, 1995, p. 230). I do not see any difference here from the attitude of Schuman and the others.

To understand the rationale for that strategy, two questions arise. First, why the goal of ever-closer union in general? With many other authors, I have suggested in a previous essay that this goal is to be explained by the desire to create ties among nations that had been engaged in ruinous wars several times over the last century. Thus the underlying original concern was something like peace (an opinion also elaborated recently by Brennan and Hamlin, 2000a). However, this first concern may be completed by at least two others. In a world of already huge and self-assertive nation-states, such as the United States, China, India, or Russia, with a number of other nation-states soon attempting to compete with the former for major roles on the world scene, it may be somewhat hazardous to rely too much, as do a subset of the Eurosceptics (see, for example, Vaubel, 1995), on the optimistic view that nation-states are becoming obsolete, that only individuals, as citizens of the world, count, and that relatively undemanding international arrangements will ensure peace, justice and the rule of law. If the future is held to be highly uncertain, it may be a good idea to build up a union, such as the EU, among small or medium-sized countries which already share many interests. There is also a more economic consideration. From an economic perspective, it seems clear that the European project has also been based on the vague idea that the provision of a large market ruled by a single overarching state-like institution has been, somehow, largely responsible for the strength, prosperity or resilience of the American economy, and that an arrangement of the same kind is thus also to be sought in Europe.

The second question is, why the roundabout, somewhat conspiratorial, strategy used to generate that ever-closer union? In the same essay (Salmon, 1995), I have argued that, many people, in each member country, were senti-mentally attached to their country and, as a consequence, did not like to think too much about the end or diminished intensity of such attachment and its replacement by an attachment to another entity.[207] Thus many people, who tacitly acquiesce to the European project, may not like to think about its ulti-mate destination and, if faced with the need to approve expressly a drastic and irreversible change that would take place to implement the project in the short run, may feel too guilty about its consequence on their attachments to provide that approbation. For that or similar reasons, no straightforward path to a European federation that would provide for sufficiently strong links among its

---

[207] For an exploration in general terms and under a perspective of rationality of the mechanism of 'not thinking about something' or 'thinking about something else', see Salmon (2001).

various national constituencies seemed likely to be really available until recently. Now, however, many people claim that the time has come for a formal agreement on an EU constitution, or even a federal constitution. Has the long-standing rationale for not doing so suddenly disappeared?

Before attempting to answer that question, let me note an essential characteristic of the strategy to construct Europe that is implied by the 'Monnet method', and thus in a sense justified by the foregoing discussion. Because they support the ever-closer union objective, the need to build up bit by bit the EU level is always present in the back of the mind of the Commission in Brussels, and behind the Commission, of majorities or influential minorities (of citizens, elites, opinion etc.) in a majority of the member countries of the EU. Those who support this project will tend to welcome occasions to transfer new responsibilities to the Brussels level. For that purpose they will be prone to conclude alliances with various other constituencies, pursuing completely different objectives. Thus, depending on the circumstances, they will ally with groups and politicians mainly concerned with continuing redistribution in favour of farmers, with constituencies anxious to save the welfare state, with large firms concerned with reducing transaction costs, with regional actors thirsty for subsidies, or with the supporters of competitive markets who demand that national public services monopolies be dismantled.[208] The famous *engrenage* or spillover strategy associated with the 'Monnet method' should be interpreted in a way that gives a sufficient role to the foregoing mechanism. When a problem arises, often as a result of previous transfers of competence, whether the solution which involves a new transfer of competence in favour of Brussels is the best one is not discussed only on its own merit. In many cases, the discussion is somewhat biased in favour of the 'integration-friendly' solution. This is of course a powerful factor of centralization.

It must thus be conceded, I think, that the 'Monnet method' often leads to transfers of competence that are not really necessary or even advisable from any perspective unconcerned with European construction per se, or for those Europhiles who think that only the pure, straightforward, rationalist path to that goal should be followed. Even from a perspective that does include both a concern for European construction and the acceptance as inevitable of the roundabout character of the strategy leading to it, centralization may be judged to go too far in some cases. The ensuing concerns have led to the introduction in the Treaty of Maastricht of a 'subsidiarity clause' (see Inman and Rubinfeld,

---

[208] There is also an active opposition to that project, although it must be stressed first that the expression 'ever-closer union' is included in the official documents agreed on by all the governments, and, second, that the politicians and other individuals who oppose increased supranationality often justify their position by the claim that it is too early for it, that public opinion is not ready, that there is no European identity yet etc. - which shows that they do not contest at least openly this direction in the absolute.

1998; Seabright, 1998; Breton *et al.*, 1998). Most importantly, they currently underlie the motivation of many supporters of a European constitution. As argued in particular by economists, a clearly federal constitution might do a lot to prevent some harmful consequences of the centralization process inherent in its current, indirect, substitute (see, for example, Vaubel, 1995; Breton, 1996; Alesina, 1999). An obvious obstacle to such a momentous step is the well-known divergence of conceptions about European integration in general that remains as strong as ever among the different countries. But, more fundamentally, I wonder whether the time has really come to stop keeping in the dark the final aims or destination of European integration, as well as the significance of its major steps forward, even in the countries that are the most favourable to it. Given the rationale for pursuing the strategy, and the pro-European bias noted above, one may also wonder whether the call for a constitution, even if motivated by a desire to avoid creeping centralization, will not in the end be used to justify additional centralization. In a sense, a reinterpretation or capture of that kind is what happened to the neo-liberal foundation of the 'single market' initiative, as we will see now.

3. CENTRALIZING TO COMPLETE MARKET INTEGRATION

The Fact[209]

Political decentralization implies that as much autonomy and decision-making capacity as possible be left to subcentral governments. In particular a major reason to favour decentralization is the hope that junior governments will experiment and innovate, that is, try to make new services available to citizens or to implement new or more efficient ways to deliver the existing ones – what has been called 'laboratory federalism' (Oates, 1999).[210] However, a government that departs from what other governments are doing almost always fragments the economic space. As a side-effect of this difference from others, which reflects its innovativeness, it creates a non-tariff and non-border barrier to trade – implying additional transaction costs for private-sector activities that straddle jurisdictions and rents for those that do not – and/or a distortion of

[209] In this subsection, I borrow most developments from Salmon (2002). For a more elaborate analysis of several of the points mentioned here, see also Breton and Salmon (2001).

[210] More generally, competition among junior governments can take the form of performance or yardstick competition, with voters comparing what they get from their junior government to what their fellow voters in other subcentral jurisdictions get from their own governments (see Salmon, 1987). Whether mobility complements or undermines this mechanism is discussed, in the context of the EU, in Salmon (2002).

competition. In particular, 'domestic' regulations have side-effects that frag-
ment some markets and can thus be considered as barriers to trade, whereas
subsidies, 'state aids' to domestic activities, and in particular to firms, distort
competition and jeopardize the prospect of maintaining a 'level playing field'
among competing firms.

In most existing federations, a concern with leaving sufficient autonomy to
subcentral governments inspires substantial self-restraint in the endeavour to
eliminate non-border barriers to trade and violations of the 'level playing
field' principle. The observation of what obtains in federations such as the
United States, Canada or Switzerland shows that fairly unified internal
markets are quite compatible with states, provinces and cantons remaining free
to implement policies that, as side-effects, do generate non-border barriers to
trade among them. In similar fashion, both the normative principle that
competition must be enforced for the benefit of consumers rather than for the
convenience of competitors (Mueller, 2000), and, again, the observation of
practice in existing federations, are powerful reasons to tolerate subcentral
government subsidies to private firms – whether for stabilizing local employment or for other possibly legitimate purposes.[211]

The European Community/Union has adopted an increasingly ambitious
agenda of elimination of all barriers to trade and distortions of competition.
This has included, as a major target, side-effects of domestic policies, as is
clear from the emphasis on the elimination of 'non-border' barriers to trade,
and, as another target, state subsidies to firms, as is manifest from the adoption of 'fair competition' and a 'level playing field' as legal criteria for correc-
tive action. It is hardly disputable that, in one way or another, the eradication
of all barriers to trade and distortions of competition is bound to seriously limit
the autonomy of national and subnational governments. But it can conceivably
do so in two ways. One may summarize the difference between the two as
coming down to the question of whether the decision-making capacity lost by
national and subnational governments goes above all to the private sector or
whether it mainly goes to collective decision-making in Brussels – in other
words, whether the main tendency is deregulation or regulation centralization.
Ironically, the more ambitious the content given to the objectives of free trade
and level playing field, the more centralization will tend to prevail over deregulation.

Over a long period of time, things seemed bound to move in the first direction. This phase was dominated by the judicial interpretation of the disposi-
tions and legal rank of the Treaty of Rome. The principle of freedom of trade
and movement that the European Court of Justice instituted was given a
constitutional status comparable to that of the Commerce Clause in the United

---

[211] See also Besley and Seabright (1999).

States Constitution (Majone, 1996). At the same time, the capacity to regulate at the European level was hampered by the rule of unanimous decision-making – at least so long as the stakes were not too high (we saw previously that this voting rule does not necessarily inhibit decisions when some governments desire with sufficient intensity that they be made). In this context, everything depended on the activism of the courts – or of the part the European Commission that plays a role akin to that of the courts. With sufficient activism on their part, many activities of national and subnational governments could be prohibited or curtailed.

This process of 'negative integration', or 'integration by law' (see also Weiler, 1999), thus seemed to give some plausibility to the prospect of a European Union resembling the US economy of the 19th century in the two characteristics that made it successful according to Barry Weingast's 'market-preserving federalism' (1993): 'the authority to regulate markets . . . not vested with the highest political government in the hierarchy', and 'the lower governments . . . prevented from using their regulatory authority to erect trade barriers against the goods and services from other political units'. No centralization at the level of Brussels seemed to be implied. However, with even more judicial activism, taking the form of an interpretation of trade barriers inclusive of all the side-effects on interjurisdictional trade of the activities of national and subnational governments, Weingast's two requirements would have implied a downsizing of government in general that was, given what is expected from it in modern societies, clearly unrealistic in the European context.[212]

In any case, a completely different perspective was introduced by the Single Act of 1987 and the 1992 project. One of its two main ingredients was a renewed emphasis on the achievement of a perfect internal market, implying the eradication of all barriers to trade and competition distortions.[213] But the other ingredient was, thanks to greater allowance of majority voting in the Council of Ministers, a much-enhanced capacity to make laws or regulate at the level of the EU. The combined effect of these two ingredients has

---

[212] For a well-argued criticism of Weingast's 'market-preserving federalism' and some striking examples of re-centralization under Ronald Reagan, see Rodden and Rose-Ackerman (1997).

[213] The 'mutual recognition' principle, as spelled out notably by the European Court of Justice in its famous *Cassis de Dijon* ruling (1979), is also part of the 'new approach' adopted in the Single Act. It says that, although the production of a good remains regulated by the government of the jurisdiction where this production takes place, the good can be freely exported to another jurisdiction whatever the regulation applicable to its production in that other jurisdiction. This clearly eliminates one barrier to the free trade of goods. The economic space remains, however, fragmented in the sense that imposed modes of production of the good are different across jurisdictions and this may distort the choice between producing in one jurisdiction or in several. It may for instance protect a local firm from a firm from another jurisdiction opening up in its own jurisdiction. It may also distort the trade of intermediate goods. Thus if the objective is a completely unique market, mutual recognition will have to be superseded by full harmonization.

been an extensive process of harmonization or standardization of regulation. Member-state and subnational governments have been deprived of much of their autonomy in some areas, but the main regulatory capacity has been firmly relocated at the centre – not quite the division of responsibilities prescribed by Weingast as a condition for 'market-preserving federalism'.

Interpretation

The Single Act was approved by Margaret Thatcher and her government. Given, on the one hand, her well-known aversion to the transfer of new powers to the level of Brussels or, more generally, of any form of centralization in the EU context, and, on the other hand, the considerable increase in centralization which has been the outcome of the Single Act, the obvious question is why she, together with many other Eurosceptics, supported the project. This question is increasingly raised. Several complementary answers can be provided. I will single out four.

A first answer is that the approval of the project was part of a deal, along the lines of the interpretation of decision-making in the EU analysed in Section 3. Delors and his new Commission wanted to accomplish a major step in the direction of European integration. Delors rapidly discovered that the only possible step consisted in combining the completion of the internal market, as an objective, and qualified majority voting, as an instrument (or, perhaps rather, in his mind, the other way round). Other political leaders wanted both to accomplish a major step forward and to revitalize the economy of their country, which was losing ground compared not to the other European economies (equally subject to 'Eurosclerosis'), but to outside competitors such as the United States or Japan. The Single Market programme seemed a way to achieve that. Thatcher wanted both a free-market Europe and 'her money back'.

Secondly, the intrinsic effects of the Single Act in terms of centralization were perhaps not clearly anticipated by some of the actors. It is probable that many thought that deregulation rather than re-regulation at the centre would ensue.[214] They underestimated the need or pressure for regulation in our modern societies.

Mistakes exist but recourse to them for explanatory purposes should be parsimonious. Thus, it seems more interesting to stress, as a third reason, the existence of an unheeded divide among supporters of free markets and of

---

[214] As recalled by Moravcsik (1991), 'in March 1984, British Foreign Minister Geoffrey Howe called for the removal of "all and I mean all, economic barriers" ' (p. 57), whereas the general feeling was that 'Britain had nothing to fear from qualified majority voting on the internal market program' (p. 61).

political decentralization. Some supporters of these two goals argue that they are compatible even in their most extremist versions.[215] Getting rid of 'all' non-border and involuntary barriers to trade and transferring most political powers to subcentral governments are compatible in their view because government in general should do as little as possible. Thus, in their case, our earlier reference to laboratory federalism à la Oates is largely irrelevant. Their position is fully consistent, however, only if they also give up the need for competition policy (including policies about public monopolies, public procurement, state aids etc.). Otherwise they would have to acknowledge the necessity of an essential source of centralization.[216] I suggest that a larger number of self-proclaimed adversaries of political centralization among supporters of a strong interpretation of free markets give in fact the priority to the second objective and are de facto quite ready to sacrifice the first. In Britain, to implement her policy preferences, in particular regarding markets, Thatcher herself did not hesitate to centralize many competences that belonged to junior governments. The same happened in the United States under the Reagan administration (see Rodden and Rose-Ackerman, 1997). Conversely, the most convinced supporters of political decentralization also strongly believe, in general, in the importance of fully active, competitive, government.

A fourth explanation is that the Europhiles or Euro-strategists, especially among the officials of the Commission or the judges of the ECJ, exploited the ambiguity of the position of Thatcher and others and decided to interpret the elimination of all barriers and distortions in a maximalist way. The programme offered them a wonderful instrument to labour for centralization. As noted, the principle of subsidiarity introduced in the Treaty of Maastricht did reflect a new concern with the protection of some decision-making capacity at the national and subnational levels of government. But, it is not clear that the contradiction between extensive interpretations of subsidiarity and subcentral government autonomy on the one hand, and a somewhat extremist single-market and fair-competition agenda on the other hand is as yet fully perceived. Centralization is still imputed exclusively to the bureaucrats in Brussels, not in the least to the partisans of unfettered markets in London and elsewhere.[217]

---

[215] They are of course fully compatible in their moderate versions, as illustrated for instance by countries such as the United States or Switzerland.

[216] A very active competition policy at the level of the Union is inevitably a powerful factor of centralization, even justifying, again according to an opinion expressed this time in retrospect by Geoffrey Howe (now Lord Howe of Aberavon), 'a fully-fledged, supranational, quasi-federal and enforceable legal system' (Howe of Aberavon, 1999, p. 4).

[217] In an article entitled 'Barriers real and imagined', *The Economist* (9 December 2001, p. 112) displays some awareness of the problem but tries to avoid what should be for it a real dilemma by denying the existence of barriers to trade as side-effects of useful domestic policies.

CONCLUSION: A HIERARCHY OF CAUSES WITH THE MONNET METHOD AT THE TOP

Centralization in the EU takes the form of increased competences and responsibilities at the level of Brussels, with in particular a much enhanced, if not dominant, role relating to that level in the provision of rules. To account for this phenomenon, I have explored the possibility of an expansionary bias within the bureaucracy along the lines suggested by Niskanen. To use Niskanen's approach in that particular context, it has been necessary to specify some points about the interpretation of the approach and, also, to take into account the fact that the reasoning may apply to the bureaux of the member states as well as to those belonging to the EU institutions. I have then turned to a discussion of decision-making in the EU with the view of assessing the extent to which any of its characteristics, in particular centralization, can develop without the acquiescence or agency of a majority of the member-state governments. This extent is probably very limited because two major traits of decision-making in Brussels are that it allows connecting different issues and that it operates under a perspective of repeat business.

The natural question to raise then is whether centralization as a process is not first of all simply a way to implement, in the manner suggested by Jean Monnet, the 'ever closer union' that was – and, to a degree, still is – the underlying rationale for the European construction project. I have sympathy for that interpretation, whose plausibility, however, required the clarification of a number of points about the Monnet method. Actually, its acceptance by economists – especially economists working in public choice or in law and economics – who adopt a narrow view of rational behaviour is not that natural or straightforward. That the construction or integration of Europe can be a genuine goal in itself, and moreover that many voters may prefer it to be roundabout and somewhat conspiratorial, is difficult to accept for economists working in that tradition. However, I think that, when the act and content of voting are concerned, our methodological allegiance, as a research strategy, to the assumption of rational behaviour cannot be based on too narrow an interpretation of that assumption without becoming counter-productive. In political matters, we must interpret rationality in such a way that it allows a richer array of motivations than we need, perhaps, to concede in other settings (see Brennan and Hamlin, 2000b).

Finally, I have argued that a third set of causes of centralization can be found in the objectives of 'completing the single market' and of setting a 'level playing field' that were adopted, with the backing of Margaret Thatcher, in the Single Act. A policy which pursues the objectives of eliminating all kinds of fragmentation of the common market and of distortion of competition among firms implies, under modern conditions, a massive transfer of responsibilities in the area of regulation and policymaking from the level of the member states to that of the Union. Why did Thatcher engage in a policy which was bound to increase centralization in that way? Among the possible reasons considered for that surprising behaviour, probably the most promising for future research (as well as the less idiosyncratic or contingent) points to the limits of what is often taken as a natural congruence between the objective of free, unregulated markets and that of political decentralization. An illustration of these limits is the political centralization that took place in the United States and in Britain under the liberal policies of Reagan and Thatcher.

As suggested several times in this chapter, I see the objective of 'ever closer union' together with the 'Monnet method' as constituting the main factor of centralization in the EU. This does not mean that the other two sets of factors that I have discussed do not also play a role. But this role is not only dependent on the continuing impulsion provided by the first factor but can also be seen as contrived or manufactured in its service. The observation by Thatcher (1993, p. 558) that the European Commission has 'always had a yen for centralized power' is correct but, to go deeper, it must be fully acknowledged that the rationale for that is a central component of the European project. As noted by Ross (1995): 'The European Commission . . . was meant constitutionally to be an institution whose explicit task it was to work for change – generating greater Europeanization' (p. 6), or 'the founding fathers wanted to establish [the Commission] as an activist motor at the center of the Community whose most important job would be to expand the EC's mandate over time' (p. 23). Other EU institutions are also genetically biased in favour of centralizing, that is, integrating solutions. Thus we can agree both with Fritz Scharpf (1999, p. 69) that the European Parliament has a 'general bias for more integration of any kind', and with Vaubel (1994, p.153) that, in the long run, the European Court of Justice is more likely to represent 'in Euro-speak, "an engine of integration" than a "bulwark" against centralization'.

With regard to acquiescence to the Single Market project, this time on the part of social democrats who should not be particularly concerned with freeing markets, Vaubel (1994, p. 175) is also right to detect their motivation in that sentence of the Delors Report of 1989: 'The completion of the internal market will result in a marked easing of the overall burden of regulation, but for the Community institutions it will mean a substantial addition to their executive and policing functions'. A statement of fact, but also an expression of the basic logic.

REFERENCES

Ackerman, B. (1997), 'The rise of world constitutionalism', *Virginia Law Review*, **83**, 771–97.

Alesina, A. (1999), 'Is Europe going too far?', *Carnegie-Rochester Conference Series on Public Policy*, **51**, 1–42.

Besley, T. and P. Seabright (1999), ' The effects and policy implications of state aids to industry: an economic analysis', *Economic Policy*, **28** (April), 13–53.

Blais, A. and S. Dion (1991), 'Conclusion: are bureaucrats budget maximizers?', in Blais and Dion (eds), *The Budget-Maximizing Bureaucrat: Appraisals and Evidence*, Pittsburgh, PA: University of Pittsburgh Press, 355–61.

Brennan, G. and A. Hamlin (2000a), 'Nationalism and federalism: the political constitution of peace', in G. Galeotti, P. Salmon and R. Wintrobe (eds), *Competition and Structure: The Political Economy of Collective Decision-Making: Essays in Honor of Albert Breton*, Cambridge and New York: Cambridge University Press, 259–83.

Brennan, G. and A. Hamlin (2000b), *Democratic Devices and Desires*, Cambridge and New York: Cambridge University Press.

Breton, A. (1996), *Competitive Governments: An Economic Theory of Politics and Public Finance*, Cambridge and New York: Cambridge University Press.

Breton, A. and P. Salmon (2001), 'External effects of domestic regulations: comparing internal and international barriers to trade', *International Review of Law and Economics*, **21**(2) June, 135–55.

Breton, A. and R. Wintrobe (1982), *The Logic of Bureaucratic Conduct*, Cambridge and New York: Cambridge University Press.

Breton, A., A. Cassone, and A. Fraschini (1998), 'Decentralization and subsidiarity: toward a theoretical reconciliation', *University of Pennsylvania Journal of International Economic Law*, **19**(1) spring, 21–51.

Cooter, R. D. (2000), *The Strategic Constitution*, Princeton, NJ: Princeton University Press.

Dunleavy, P. (1991), *Democracy, Bureaucracy and Public Choice: Economic Explanations in Political Science*, Hampstead: Harvester Wheatsheaf.

Dunleavy, P. (1997), 'Explaining the centralization of the European Union: a public choice analysis', *Aussenwirtschaft*, **52**(1–2), 183–212.

Faure, M.G. (2000). 'Product liability and product safety in Europe: harmonization or differentiation?', *Kyklos*, **53**(4), 467–508.

Howe of Abevaron, Lord (1999), 'Europe: single market or political union?', *IEA Economic Affairs*, December, pp. 4–9.

Inman, R.P. and D.L. Rubinfeld (1998), 'Subsidiarity and the European Union', in P. Newman (ed.), *The New Palgrave Dictionary of Economics and the Law*, vol. 3, London and Stockton, NY: Macmillan, 544–51.

Josselin, J.-M. and A. Marciano (2000), 'Displacing your principal: two historical case studies of some interest for the constitutional future of Europe', *European Journal of Law and Economics* **10**(3), 217–33.

Kirchgässner, G. (1997), 'Supply and demand factors of centralization: comment to Patrick Dunleavy', *Aussenwirtschaft*, **52**(1–2), 213–220.

Kirchgässner, G. and W.W. Pommerehne (1996), 'Tax harmonization and tax competition in the European Union: lessons from Switzerland', *Journal of Public Economics*, **60**(3) June, 351–71.

Ludlow, P. (2000), 'A debate that makes no sense', *The Financial Times*, 20 October.

Majone, G. (1996), *Regulating Europe*, London and New York: Routledge.

Migué, J.-L. and G. Bélanger (1974), 'Towards a general theory of managerial discretion', *Public Choice*, **17**, spring, 27–43.

Milward, A.S. (1992), *The European Rescue of the Nation-State*, Berkeley, CA: University of California Press.

Moravcsik, A. (1991), 'Negotiating the Single European Act: national interests and conventional statecraft in the European Community', *International Organization*, **45**(1), 651–88, reprinted as 'Negotiating the Single European Act', in R.O. Keohane and S. Hoffman (eds), *The New European Community: Decisionmaking and Institutional Change*, Boulder, CO: Westview Press, 1991, 41–84.

Mueller, D.C. (2000), 'Public subsidies for private firms in a federalist democracy', in G. Galeotti, P. Salmon and R. Wintrobe (eds), *Competition and Structure: The Political Economy of Collective Decision-Making: Essays in Honor of Albert Breton*, Cambridge and New York: Cambridge University Press, 339–63.

Niskanen, W.A. Jr. (1971), *Bureaucracy and Representative Government*, Chicago: Aldine-Atherton.

Niskanen, W.A. Jr. (1994), 'A reassessment', in *Bureaucracy and Public Economics*, Cheltenham, UK: Edward Elgar, 269–83.

Oates, W.E. (1999), 'An essay on fiscal federalism', *Journal of Economic Literature*, **37**(3) September, 1120–49.

Oates, W.E. (2001), 'Fiscal competition and European Union: contrasting perspectives', *Regional Science and Urban Economics*, **31**, 133–45.

Persson, T., G. Roland and G. Tabellini (1997), 'The theory of fiscal federalism: what does it mean for Europe?', in H. Siebert (ed.), *Quo Vadis Europe?*, Tübingen: J.C.B. Mohr, 23–41.

Pollack, M.A. (2000), 'The end of creeping competence? EU policy-making since Maastricht', *Journal of Common Market Studies*, **38**(3) September, 519–38.

Rodden, J. and D. Rose-Ackerman (1997), 'Does federalism preserve markets?', *Virginia Law Review*, **83**(7) October, 1521–72.

Ross, G. (1995), *Jacques Delors and European Integration*, Cambridge: Polity Press.

Salmon, P. (1987), 'Decentralisation as an incentive scheme', *Oxford Review of Economic Policy*, **3**(2) summer, 24–43.

Salmon, P. (1992), 'Leadership and integration', in G. Bertin and A. Raynauld (eds), *L'intégration économique en Europe et en Amérique du Nord (Economic integration in Europe and North America)*, Paris: Clément Juglar, 367–85.

Salmon, P. (1995), 'Nations conspiring against themselves: an interpretation of European integration', in A. Breton, G. Galeotti, P. Salmon and R. Wintrobe (eds), *Nationalism and Rationality*, Cambridge and New York: Cambridge University Press, 290–311.

Salmon, P. (2000), 'Vertical competition in a unitary state', in G. Galeotti, P. Salmon and R. Wintrobe (eds), *Competition and Structure: The Political Economy of Collective Decision-Making: Essays in Honor of Albert Breton*, Cambridge and New York: Cambridge University Press, 239–56.

Salmon, P. (2001), 'Thinking about something else: a rationality-compatible mechanism with macroscopic consequences', *Kyklos*, **54**(2/3), 453–64.

Salmon, P. (2002), 'Decentralization and supranationality: the case of the European Union', in E. Ahmed and V Tanzi (eds), *Managing Fiscal Decentralization*, London and New York: Routledge, pp. 99–121.

Scharpf, F.W. (1999), *Governing in Europe: Effective and Democratic?*, Oxford and New York: Oxford University Press.

Seabright, P. (1998), 'Centralized and decentralized regulation in the European Union', in P. Newman (ed.), *The New Palgrave Dictionary of Economics and the Law*, vol. 1, London and Stockton, NY: Macmillan, 214–19.

Steunenberg, B., C. Koboldt and D. Schmidtchen (1997), 'Comitology and the balance of power in the European Union: a game-theoretic approach', in D. Schmidtchen and R. Cooter (eds), *Constitutional Law and Economics of the European Union*, Cheltenham, UK and Lyme, US: Edward Elgar, 37–66.

Thatcher, M. (1993), *The Downing Street Years*, New York: HarperCollins.

Van den Bergh, R. (2000), 'Towards an institutional legal framework for regulatory competition in Europe', *Kyklos*, **53**(4), 435–66.

Vaubel, R. (1994), 'The political economy of centralization and the European Community', *Public Choice*, **81**(1–2) October, 151–90.

Vaubel, R. (1995), *The Centralization of Western Europe: The Common Market, Political Integration, and Democracy*, Hobart Paper 127, London: The Institute of Economic Affairs.

Weatherill, S. (1995), *Law and Integration in the European Union*, Oxford and New York: Oxford University Press.

Weiler, J.H.H. (1999), *The Constitution of Europe*, Cambridge and New York: Cambridge University Press.

Weingast, B.R. (1993), 'Constitutions as governance structures: the political foundations of secure markets', *Journal of Institutional and Theoretical Economics*, **149**(1), 286–311.

Winer, S.L. (2000), 'On the reassignment of fiscal powers in a federal state', in G. Galeotti, P. Salmon and R. Wintrobe (eds), *Competition and Structure: The Political Economy of Collective Decision-Making: Essays in Honor of Albert Breton*, Cambridge and New York: Cambridge University Press, 150–73.

Wintrobe, R. (1997), 'Modern bureaucratic theory', in D.C. Mueller (ed.), *Perspectives on Public Choice: A Handbook*, Cambridge and New York: Cambridge University Press, 429–54.

9. From fiscal competition to juridical competition. Lessons from the French experience

Didier Danet

INTRODUCTION

The growing opening of markets and economies has given rise to a fiscal competition which is usually considered as potentially damaging (Marini, 1998, OCDE, 1998; Owens, 1999). The drawback is well-known: many reports, books or papers describe harmful practices and suggest solutions in order to avoid the consequences of 'fiscal wars'.[218]

Competition between legal systems has its origins in the same tendencies. Fiscal competition and legal competition are moreover related to each other: countries which try to divert investments, registered offices etc. usually reduce taxes concerning corporates, salaried staff, accounting etc. Its impact is also of great importance even if it is more complicated and less visible. There is less literature analysing legal competition in France, and the literature that exists tends to underestimate the fact that legal competition exists in France or assumes that there is no competition.

The first purpose of this chapter relates to the definition and typology of juridical competition (section 1) With regard to this typology, the chapter aims to describe the extent and the intensity of the competition which does exist in the French legal system (section 2). Then, as far as private rules can widely compete with public rules in this system, the chapter tries to explain why private rules, usually considered more suitable and less expensive, do not fully supplant public rules (section 3).

1.   A TYPOLOGY OF COMPETITION

According to such a distinguished scholar as Pascal Salin, competition between legal rules is a specific application of the self-regulation principle

---

[218] On the contrary, some scholars consider that economic consequences of competition between fiscal systems necessarily benefit those who are generally considered as the main victims of the 'fiscal war' (Salin et Guillaumat, 2001)

which can clear up all kinds of problems that human societies may face (Salin, 1995) As far as competition is a universal regulatory mechanism, it ought to apply to the production of rules as well as the production of goods or services.

Regarding common law and statute law, Salin vigourously condemns the latter in which the creation of rules is under the monopoly of the Parliament. Because of this monopoly, statute law is unable to engender legal provisions in accordance with public interest: according to the usual theory, the monopolistic supplier of rules is not prompted to act towards general interest; he is unable to collect scattered information; he is mainly motivated by pressure for wealth transfers etc. Contrary to this, the common law system relies on competition since the judge can set out a new specific rule for a new specific set of facts. The system is 'open' and, as circumstances require, new rules may be created or imported for new facts. Whereas Parliament is the unique source of law in civil law countries, numerous courts exist to dispense the common law. Consequently, the statute law is frozen into rigid principles and cannot evolve in accordance with economic and social needs. Common law rules can be changed from time to time and realities of modern life can be addressed in a more timely fashion (Priest, 1977; Rubin; 1977, Tetley, 1999).

In an ideal competitive system, numerous suppliers of law offer various rules and procedures, economic agents can freely choose the rules they are bound by and the judge they appeal to if a litigation occurs. Before reaching this paradise of competition, French law ought to pass through many stages. According to Salin, three levels of competition may be distinguished.

Competition by Location of Activities or Assets

Competition between legal systems exists if economic agents are entitled to re-allocate their activities and/or assets from one country to another one in accordance with specific advantages that they can benefit from. This kind of competition is well-known, for instance, among extremist shopkeepers' unions. These unions recommend their members to register their office in certain islands in order to evade French social legislation and taxes. A similar problem arises with the growth of e-business. In a recent report to Parliament, the French MP Christian Paul estimates that suppliers who sell products in France may locate their computers abroad in order to avoid constraints resulting from consumer protection, price regulation etc. This kind of competition relies on the same mechanisms as fiscal optimization (Paul, 2000).

Competition by Exportation of National Rules

At this second level of competition, economic agents take advantage of foreign rules whose legal scope has been extended beyond their national boundaries. As regards European law, prohibition of quantitative limitations leads to a situation of this kind. In the famous 'Cassis de Dijon' case German national law was prohibiting drinks with a high alcohol proof in order to prevent addiction of consumers. In accordance with this law, the German administration rejected the request of an importing firm which wanted to sell a liquor consistent with French standards. The European court considers that, even if German law applies to all beverages, it amounts to a quantitative restriction. 'L'effet pratique de prescriptions de ce genre consiste principalement à assurer un avantage aux boissons spiritueuses à forte teneur alcoolique, en éloignant du marché national les produits d'autres États membres ne répondant pas à cette spécification . . .' (CJCE, 1979) [The practical effect of prescriptions of this kind consists mainly in granting an advantage to spirits with a high alcohol content, by removing from the national market products from other member states which do not meet this specification. *Editor's translation*]. The development of this jurisprudence is quite impressive. It concerns such fields as the nature of goods (Italian vinegar (CJCE, 1980), Dutch bread (CJCE, 1981), German Beer (CJCE, 1987; Funck-Brentano, 1987), packaging (margarine (CJCE, 1982)), retailing system (French auctioneers (Com., 1992) Swedish alcohol retailers (CJCE, 1997)) etc. It obviously enforces competition between national rules in the sense that a standard which is available in one country of the European Union is available in any country of the Union so that economic agents may choose the legal framework they are working with.

Competition by the Free Supply of Legal Rules

In comparison with the 'dreadful' monopoly of Parliament, competition by exportation of national rules is a remarkable improvement. But, a free competition system would only exist under two conditions. The first one is the free supply of public or private rules. In this ideal configuration, individuals or institutions of any kind can create material or procedural rules and offer help to agents who have to prepare contracts, resolve disputes etc. The second condition lies in the freedom of choice between numerous rules and procedures: private or public, national or foreign, for example.

This third level of competition comes near to the 'spontaneous private legal ordering' which is described and promoted by such authors as Friedman (1979) or Milgrom, North and Weingast (1990). Founded on costs–benefits analysis and threat of ostracism, private rules result from the co-existence of many groups which interact with each other. This co-existence creates incentives for each group to produce rules whose relevance may attract numerous members. In doing so, a mutual insurance emerges to prevent free-riding (Parisi, 1999).

This ternary classification seems to ignore what Anthony Ogus calls 'self-regulation', i.e. 'deliberate delegation of the state's law-making powers to an agency, the membership of which wholly or mainly comprises representatives of the firms or individuals whose activities are being regulated' (Ogus, 1999). According to Ogus, this delegation is threatened with the market power of the self-regulation agency which may let itself be tempted to promote the interest of the regulatees instead of that of the public. But, this drift of the principal-agent relationship is avoidable if state lawmaking power is devolved to several agencies which compete in providing rules. Under certain conditions (consumer information, absence of externality, heterogeneity of regulated industry) competition between self-regulation agencies prevents cartelization and induces suppliers to provide rules that meet consumers' preferences. Regarding the three levels of classification, self-regulation may be assimilated to the competition by exportation of national rules. As Ogus writes: 'Thus envisaged, competitive self-regulation is, in essence, no different from competition between national public regulatory regimes. If there is mutual recognition of national standards and freedom of trade[219], consumers can choose between the different quality standards imposed by the national systems in accordance with their own preferences.' (Ogus, 1999, p. 595)

According to Pascal Salin, the French legal system is short of the third level of competition. To a certain degree, individuals can re-allocate their resources and/or assets to reduce the tax burden. They also benefit from the prohibition of quantitative restrictions in Europe. But, on the one hand, nobody is authorized to compete with Parliament in supplying rules and, on the other hand, agents cannot choose the rules which govern individuals' interactions.

Getting an insight into French law clearly invalidates this conclusion. Quite an open competition exists on the supply side and on the demand side as well. The fact is all the more interesting that, in the domains where competition exists, private rules or procedures do not completely replace the rules or procedures coming from the public sector.

2.   THE SUPPLY OF RULES: PARLIAMENT'S MONOPOLY OR SUPPLIERS' COMPETITION?

For most of those who support the common law model, the continental system suffers from the monopoly held by Parliament in the provision of legal rules. No supplier can enter the 'legal market' and offer rules that could be more

---

[219] Which is precisely the meaning of the 'Cassis de Dijon' jurisprudence.

useful or convenient than legal ones; no agent is allowed to choose the rules which govern his behaviour.[220]

Regarding the French experience in civil and commercial law, both these conclusions are false. They betray a simplistic analysis and a fancy view of statute law which, in fact, allows to a large extent the entry of suppliers and the competition of rules and institutions. This competition is expanding in both creation and implementation of legal rules.

Competition in the Creation of Rules

Let us first consider the creation of rules (*'droit matériel'*). In commercial as well as civil law, Parliament's monopoly is often nothing more than a fantasy. Entry of suppliers is scheduled, defined and guaranteed by the combination of two basic articles of the Code Civil. The first one (art.1134) stipulates: 'Les conventions légalement formées tiennent lieu de loi à ceux qui les ont faites.'[221] From this article the fact ensues that two people who want to contract together can become their own legislator and create specific rules (*'consensualisme'*). Nevertheless, the right to create private rules is not unlimited. In virtue of Article 6 of the Code: 'On ne peut déroger, par des conventions particulières, aux lois qui intéressent l'ordre public et les bonnes mœurs.'[222] The combination of these articles divides the entire field of non administrative law into two parts: the special field in which legal order must prevail and the rest of human behaviour and relationship. The entire civil and commercial law is not under the exclusive control of Parliament. Apart from restricted areas where public order is at stake, private rules can compete with parliamentary will.

Restricted competition in public order areas
Article 6 does not define what is and what is not a matter of public order.

During the 19th century, the doctrine supported a very individualistic point of view. According to most legal scholars, freedom of contract can only be restricted by express legislative will. Until Parliament makes a law in which public order is mentioned, judges cannot cancel a contractual private rule. From this perspective legislative area is an exception and competition between public and private order is the rule.

---

[220] 'Dire qu'il y a monopole c'est à dire qu'il n'y a pas liberté d'entrée sur le marché. C'est bien le cas dans les systèmes juridiques modernes puisque personne ne peut venir concurrencer le Parlement en prétendant produire de meilleures lois et que personne ne peut choisir les règles de Droit sous lesquelles il vit et entre en rapport avec autrui.' Salin, 1995, p.117.

[221] As far as contracts abide by general rules (ability of contractors, licit cause and object of the contract etc.) contracts bind their authors as strongly as laws can do.

[222] Private rules cannot depart from public order or morals.

In 1929, the Supreme Court departs from this opinion. 'La cause est illicite quand elle est contraire à l'ordre public, sans qu'il soit nécessaire qu'elle soit prohibée par la loi; par suite, la nullité du contrat litigieux pouvait être prononcée sans qu'il eût été passé en violation de l'article 166§3 de la loi du 30 novembre 1892' (Civ., 1929). With regard to this decision, 'public order' is considered a changing concept and, because the legislator cannot anticipate all events which may occur, courts have to adapt the boundaries of 'public order' to social needs.[223] If the contractual stipulation undermines basic social rules (even if these social rules are implicit) courts have to cancel it.

In the wake of this decision, a growing number of topics have been falling into the exclusive realm of Parliament. Consequently, as far as these topics are concerned, the principle is that individual will cannot compete with legislative rules ('imperative laws'). For instance, a contract in which a man commits himself not to get married is null and void (Paris, 1963). An agreement between an employer and his employee cannot elude social security duties (Ass.Plén., 1976). In these fields, public order prevails and private rules cannot compete even if both contractors are in agreement.

One may nevertheless argue that the monopolistic power of Parliament is far from being absolute. Even if the growing 'blacklist' of areas invaded is well-known (Social security, car insurance, consumer protection etc.), the entire field of civil and commercial law is not considered as being a matter of 'public order'. In many cases, courts have to estimate whether the law is imperative or not. They do not systematically enlarge the area of public order (Civ., 1991). Therefore, they also have to balance imperative rules which clash with each other. For instance, the activity called 'dwarf tossing' gives rise to the clash of two principles which both come under public order: on the one hand, human dignity (to make use of someone as a kind of dead weight may be considered as a rough and degrading treatment); on the other hand, (the dwarf person does not act under duress and receives pay for services). If the human dignity argument is accepted, the activity has to be stopped; on the contrary, it may continue if the employment law argument prevails. The choice exceeds Parliament's power; the arbitration is a matter for the courts. In the special case of 'dwarf tossing', the protection of human dignity takes precedence and the activity has to be stopped (Conseil d'Etat, 1995).

Even in the area of public order, it cannot be said that Parliament holds a monopolistic power in the creation of rules. This power is limited by

---

[223] Sur la nullité des clauses contractuelles contraires au cours forcé de la monnaie: Civ. 11 février 1873, DO-Delattre c/Scouteten, DP 1873, 1, 177, note Boistel; Civ. 12 janv. 1988, de Brancovan c/ Mme de Schultess, Rev.Trim.Dr.Civil 1988, p. 740, note Mestre; sur la validation des clauses contractuelles d'échelle mobile au regard des mêmes exigences: Civ. 27 juin 1957, Dalloz, 1957, p. 649, note Ripert.

intervention of the courts which can, to a certain degree, modulate the field and the hierarchy of public order.

Competition of rules' suppliers outside public order areas

If public order is not at issue, many private individuals or institutions can compete in supplying rules:

Parliament: Most legislative rules are not imperative and individuals can depart from them ('interpretative law'). For instance, codified selling rules stipulate that buyers must pay cash down (C.Civ. art.1650). Nevertheless, the Code makes provision for alternative solutions: 'S'il n'a rien été réglé à cet égard lors de la vente, l'acheteur doit payer au lieu et dans le temps où doit se faire la délivrance.' (C.Civ. art.1651) Prosperity of bankers mainly relies on everyday violations of codified solution and breaches of the alleged monopoly power of Parliament. But, even if these rules are optional, they do exist and they apply if contractors have no explicit preference for another solution. Article 1651 may be considered as a pure application of transaction costs' theory: if contractors have not enough time nor competence to organize their relationship (who has to pay, when and how), they can refer to the legislative scheme which is assumed to be as simple and complete as possible and honestly balanced. The cost of the negotiation and, consequently, the total cost of the contract is lowered by comparison with a 'made-to-measure' private scheme.

Private institutions: many private institutions compete with Parliament in supplying rules such as unions or professional orders (architects, doctors etc.). For instance, a private institution (AFNOR) is creating standards which are founded on negotiation and mutual agreement of experts, consumers, company unions etc. Many of these standards are nothing more than interpretative laws but some of them (NF standards) are quasi-imperative rules (Danet, 2001).

Individuals: if Parliament is composed of hundreds of people who produce legal rules during parliamentary sessions, the fabric of society is composed of millions of people who create private rules every day. A minority of these rules are created consciously. Contractors do not agree with the provisions of law which are relevant to their transaction. They shape their own juridical scheme (in so far as public order is not at issue). For instance, on the occasion of a corporation's transfer, the buyer is usually paying by instalments and he is demanding special warranty regarding assets and liabilities. Lawyers are requested to write specific clauses which create a private rule (Danet, 1992). Most of the time, these private rules are created with full knowledge by only one person, for instance banks, car makers, supermarkets. The other contractor usually agrees unknowingly to this private rule: he accepts the transaction but he does not even know that legislative provisions have been amended ('contrats d'adhésion'). As regards the process of the creation of rules, Parliament's monopoly is in competition once again.

The French experience clearly demonstrates that the creation of rules is not the exclusive domain of Parliament. All in all, the combination of articles 6 and 1134 strongly favours private supply of rules even if freedom of entry is not absolute.

Competition in Implementation of Rules

Not only do individuals or institutions compete with Parliament in the creation of rules but they also play a leading part as regards the implementation of rules.

Most ordinary disputes are resolved by public judges. But, all the same, many claimants prefer to choose their judge in accordance with article 2059 of the Code Civil: 'Toutes personnes peuvent compromettre sur les droits dont elles ont la libre disposition'. In this respect, individual wills can depart from the jurisdiction of public courts and lay a request before a court of arbitration.

Contrary to a tenacious and common opinion, arbitration is not only relevant in international litigations. It is a frequent method of the resolution of disputes in commercial, inheritance or real estate areas, for example.

Competition between the two types of courts is favoured by two legal principles. First, the matters in which arbitration cannot compete with public courts are limited to public order questions. 'On ne peut compromettre . . . dans les matières qui intéressent l'ordre public.' (C.Civ. art.2060) This sentence is narrowly interpreted by the courts. Claimants can rely on an arbitrator in disputes which concern public order as long as legal rules are not violated. For instance, a contract breaches a public order provision. The claim necessarily comes within the monopolistic jurisdiction of public courts and the contract is cancelled. A new dispute arises with regard to the consequences of the cancellation: restoration of deposits, damages etc. Even if the two disputes are tightly linked to one another, the second one may be settled by an arbitrator (Orléans, 1966). The legislative provision is not interpreted in a literal sense, which enlarges the jurisdiction of arbitration courts. In the same sense, judges consider that arbitrators do not exceed their powers as long as public order provisions are not directly violated (Paris, 1956).

The second argument is related to the compromise clause. The Code Civil prohibits this kind of clause in which contractors commit themselves to appeal to an arbitrator in case of conflict ('La clause compromissoire est nulle s'il n'est disposé autrement par la loi' C.Civ. art.2061). As far as private individuals are concerned, they cannot choose their judge before the dispute arises. But those most directly affected, public or commercial agents, are allowed to use the compromise clause (C.Civ. art.2060 *in fine*, C.Com. art.631).

Thus, competition between public and arbitration courts prevails in many juridical disputes and economic agents can often choose their judge.

3.   TOWARDS EVICTION OF PUBLIC RULES?

Unlike Salin's opinion, the French legal system is not under Parliament's thumb. Competition between public and private rules does exist regarding creation as well as implementation. It might even be said that this competition has been growing dramatically for many reasons: international exchanges and multinational companies are smashing national rules to pieces; new technologies make drafting and distribution of rules easier; pressure of individualistic doctrine leads to the enlargement of private initiative.

The Example of the SAS (Société par Actions Simplifiée)

French company law is a good example of this tendency. Since the beginning of the 19th century, the constant obsession of Parliament has been to protect savers against swindlers who can collect large sums of money through the intervention of joint-stock companies. As a consequence, the control of managers has been strengthened to such an extent that the regime of joint-stock companies is unanimously perceived as fastidious and formalistic (Merle, 2000, Bulle, 1998) As far as competition between rules is concerned, this regime is considered to be a very good example of unreasonable constraint which can easily compete with foreign public rules (for instance, localization of registered offices in the Netherlands). Conscious of the risk, Parliament has completely reversed this traditional tendency with the creation of the 'société par actions simplifiée' (simplified joint-stock company). Under this legal regime, managers can freely design relationships with associates, rules governing decisions, stipulations of entry etc. (Paillusseau, 1999). The only important restriction (SAS is not authorized to publicly collect savings) is not absolutely insuperable because a joint-stock company can be an associate (or even the only associate) of an SAS. When this juridical tool was created, many scholars thought that the joint-stock company was definitely old-fashioned. In fact, even if the SAS is successful (Rép. Min., 2000), one has not observed massive change in the structure of the existing companies and most of the new firms are classical joint-stock companies (Champaud et Danet, 1999). This is a surprising result: a legal institution is unanimously considered as finicky and constraining. Parliament encourages competition with the creation of a 'light' legal regime, but the constraining regime is far from being supplanted.

A similar result may be pointed out regarding the respective role of public and private courts. Public courts are often accused of prohibitive defaults.

They are slow in dispensation of justice because of formalistic and expensive procedures. Moreover, public judges are not always specialized in the cases they have to deal with and legal or private rules may be distorted. As regards these criticisms, arbitration should systematically oust public justice when competition is possible. Yet, judgements from public courts are in the majority.

Why Private Order does not Rule Out Public Order?

How is it possible to explain such 'irrational' behaviour? A preliminary explanation lies in the exaggeration of the so-called advantages of private rules (Guyon, 1992, no. 792, Weill, 1973). For instance, unless public courts are especially congested and the litigation is simple, arbitrators cannot make a decision at short notice. Arbitrators are often busy; they have to study the case and to work together; an expert may be required etc. In the same way, the low cost of arbitration is most often a fantasy. On the one hand, lawyers, experts and varied advisers are as essential as they are if the authority concerned is a public court. On the other hand, parties must pay arbitration fees which usually are rather expensive. In fact, the only true advantage of arbitration lies in discretion. Judgements which are made by public courts are always attainable by everyone whereas arbitration is a private affair. Competitors, financial or commercial partners, tax authorities etc. ignore the litigation and the solution as well. Yet, in so far as discretion is not a requirement, the advantages of arbitration are not so important that public judgement should be ruled out.

A second explanation lies in the high transaction costs that characterize private order. For instance, if the shares of a corporation are sold, the public order is quite in favour of the seller who only indemnifies the buyer from non-existence of the shares (C.Civ. 1693).[224] This minimum guarantee is dangerous because assets and debts are not related to the existence of the firm (Notté, 1985; exception: Champaud et Danet, 1996). If the firm has to pay a back tax (Champaud et Danet, 1992) or if it has to reimburse customers (Champaud et Danet, 1996b), the seller is not liable for damages. Buyers' advisers recommend placing a debt and assets guarantee clause into the contract. But these clauses are often unclear and they engender numerous litigations (for instance, Champaud et Danet, 2001). In many cases, the total transaction cost (drafting of contract, lawsuit etc.) is so large that the best solution consists of using a legal regime paired with an economic and financial analysis of the firm.

---

[224] 'Celui qui vend une créance ou autre droit incorporel doit en garantir l'existence au temps du transport quoiqu'il soit fait sans garantie.'

A third explanation relates to the nature of legal competition itself. In the special case of fiscal competition, the objective of the firm is obvious: relaxation of the tax burden. In comparison, legal competition is different by nature, not only by degree. The objective does not lie in cost savings but in managing multiple legal tools in order to promote and protect a number of different interests of the firm. As far as business law is concerned, legal competition hinges on three main subjects: internal organization of the firm (allocation of patrimonial assets and design of power and control), external organization of the firm's relationship (alliances, mergers, holdings etc.), management of constraints which rest on the firm (regulation of investments, working law etc.) (Champaud, 1995). The firm is both creditor and debtor of its environment: the legal system imposes it duties but provides it with protection. In countries where duties are low, protection is generally limited: the firm is on its own. High duties may be acceptable if the firm's assets and interests benefit from a high degree of protection. For instance, French law is rather suspicious with regard to competition. On the one hand, this mistrust lies heavy on the firm because production, sale, credit etc. are closely regulated. On the other hand, firms are protected against rash assaults from their competitors: comparative advertising is severely limited, unfair competition is penalized, commercial property is firmly protected etc. The firm suffers or profits from, as the case may be, this mistrust of competition.

CONCLUSION

As regards the competition of juridical systems, three conclusions may be deduced from the French experience. Contrary to widespread opinion, the French legal system is not characterized by the existence of a monopolist parliament. It does not ignore competition between public and private rules which may exist in many fields of material and procedural law. These private rules may originate in professional practices, individual or collective will, foreign rules etc.

In the fields where competition exists, private rules and public rules co-exist. In spite of the so called advantages of private rules, they do not systematically supplant public rules. *Prima facie*, the main reason may lie in insecurity and transaction costs which are inherent in the adoption of a 'do-it-yourself' order.

More basically, it appears that juridical competition cannot be interpreted in terms of constraints' minimization. The legal system also provides tools which enhance the legitimate interests of the firm. Small constraints are usually linked to weak protection; therefore juridical minimalism is necessarily the best policy either for the firms or for the governments.

REFERENCES

Ass.Plén., 18 June 1976, Dalloz, 1977, p.173, note Jeammaud (les règles de la Sécurité Sociale sont d'ordre public et ne peuvent être écartées par un accord entre l'employeur et le salarié).

Bulle J-F. (1998), 'Les assemblées sur papier', *Droit des sociétés*, juin, p. 7.

Civ., 4 December 1929, Croizé c/Veaux, Sirey, 1931, 1, 49, note Esmein.

C.E, 27 October 1995, Ville d'Aix-en-Provence, Dalloz, 1996, p. 177, note Lebreton (interdiction de la pratique du 'lancer de nains').

Champaud C. and D. Danet (1992), 'Cession de parts sociales', *Revue Trimestrielle de Droit Commercial*, **45**(3), 622.

Champaud C. and D. Danet (1996), 'Cession de parts sociales', *Revue Trimestrielle de Droit Commercial*, **49**(2), 286.

Champaud C. and D. Danet (1996b), 'Cession de parts sociales', *Revue Trimestrielle de Droit Commercial*, **49**(4), 680.

Champaud C. and D. Danet (1999), 'Formes de sociétés', *Revue Trimestrielle de Droit Commercial*, **52**(4), 872.

Champaud C. and D. Danet (2001), 'Garantie de passif', *Revue Trimestrielle de Droit Commercial*, **54**(1), 137.

Civ. 5 November 1991, Bull.Civ., I, no. 297, (Les règles déontologiques qui fixent les devoirs des membres de la profession ne sont assorties que de sanctions disciplinaires et ne relèvent pas de l'ordre public. Leur violation n'entraîne pas à elle seule la nullité du contrat).

CJCE, 20 February 1979, aff. 120/78, Rec. CJCE, p. 649 (Cassis de Dijon).

CJCE, 26 June 1980, aff. 788/79, Gilli, Rec. CJCE, p. 2071 (Vinaigre italien).

CJCE, 19 February 1981, aff. 130/80, Kelderman, Rec. CJCE, p. 527 (Pain hollandais).

CJCE, 10 November 1982, aff. 261/81, Gaz. Pal. 1983, 1, jur., p. 93, note Fourgoux J.-C. (forme des paquets de margarine).

CJCE, 12 March 1987, aff. 178/84, D. 1987, som., p. 394, obs. Cartou (Pureté de la bière).

Com., 28 January 1992, RTD com. 1992, p. 850 (Commissaires priseurs français).

CJCE, 23 October 1997, aff. C-189/95, Franzen (distribution d'alcool en Suède).

Danet, D. (1992), Cession de droits sociaux: information préalable ou garantie des vices?', *Revue Trimestrielle de Droit Commercial*, **45**(2), 315–49.

Danet, D. (2001), 'Entre droit spontané et droit légiféré: la production de droit par la normalisation', *Economie Publique*, **7**(1), 83–101.

Friedman, D. (1979), 'Private creation and enforcement of law: a historical case', *Journal of Legal Studies*, **8**, 399–415.

Funck-Brentano L. (1987), 'Du cassis de Dijon à la bière ou de la difficulté de créer un espace sans frontière', *JCP* éd. E, I, no. 16237.

Guyon Y. (1982), 'Droit des affaires', *Economica*, 2nd édition, no. 792 et sts.

Marini (1998), 'La concurrence fiscale en Europe: une contribution au débat, *Rapport d'information*, Sénat, no. 483 (98–99) www.senat.fr/rap/r98–483/r98–48312.html.

Merle P. (2000), *Droit commercial, Sociétés commerciales*, 7th edn, Dalloz Précis.

Milgrom Paul R., Douglas C. North and Barry R. Weingast (1990), 'The role of institutions in the revival of trade; the medieval merchant law private judges and the Champagne Fair', *Economics and Politics*, **2**, 1–23.

Notté G. (1985), 'Les clauses dites de "garantie de passif" dans les cessions de droit sociaux', *JCP*, 1, 3193.

OECD (1998), 'Concurrence fiscale dommageable: un problème mondial', www.oecd.org/publications/observer/daf/fa/tax_comp/taxcomp.htm

Ogus A. (1999), 'Self-regulation', in Baudovin Bouckaert and Gerrit de Geest *Encyclopedia of Law and Economics*, vol. V, *The Economics of Crime and Litigation*, Cheltenham, UK: Edward Elgar.

Orléans, 15 February 1966, Dalloz 1966, p. 340, note Robert.

Owens J. (1999), 'Combattre les pratiques fiscale dommageables, *L'observateur de l'OCDE*, no. 219, January, www.oecd.org/publications/observer/215/f-owens.htm.

Paillusseau J. (1999), *La nouvelle SAS. Le big-bang du droit des sociétés*, Dalloz, Chr., 333.

Paris, 15 June 1956, Dalloz, 1957, p. 587, note Robert.

Paris, 30 April 1963, Dalloz, 1963, p. 428, note Rouast (nullité de la clause de non convol).

Parisi, Franceso (1999), 'Spontaneous emergence of law: customary law', in Baudouin Bouckaert and Gerrit de Geest (eds), *Encyclopedia of Law and Economics*, vol. V *The Economics of Crime and Litigation*, Cheltenham, UK: Edward Elgar.

Paul C. (2000), 'Du droit et des libertés sur internet', Assemblée Nationale, Rapport au Premier ministre, 29 June.

Priest G-L. (1977), 'The common law process and the selection of efficient rules', *Journal of Legal Studies*, **6**, 65–82.

Rép.Min., 2000, JO Débats Sénat, 8 June.

Rubin P.-H. (1977), 'Why is the common law efficient?', *Journal of Legal Studies*, **6**, 51–63.

Salin P. (1995), *La concurrence*, PUF, Que-Sais-Je?

Salin P. and F. Guillaumat (2001), 'Tous les gens honnêtes gagnent à la concurrence fiscale entre Etats', Séminaire Jean-Baptiste Say, Université Paris IX Dauphine.

Tetley W. (1999), 'Mixed jurisdictions: common law vs civil law (codified and uncodified)', www.unidroit.org/english/publications/review/articles/1999–3.htm.

Weill A. (1973), *Droit civil, Introduction générale*, Dalloz, 3rd edn, no. 151 et sts.

Index